JAPAN
IN
SINGAPORE

JAPAN IN SINGAPORE

Cultural Occurrences and Cultural Flows

Edited by

Eyal Ben-Ari

and

John Clammer

CURZON

First Published in 2000
by Curzon Press
Richmond, Surrey

Editorial Matter © 2000 Eyal Ben-Ari and John Clammer

Typeset in Sabon by LaserScript Ltd, Mitcham, Surrey
Printed and bound in Great Britain by
Biddles Ltd, Guildford and King's Lynn

British Library Cataloguing in Publication Data
A catalogue record of this book is available from the British Library

Library of Congress Cataloguing in Publication Data
A catalogue record for this book has been requested

ISBN 0–7007–1245–3

Contents

Acknowledgements

Many people's input has gone into shaping this book in its present form. In particular we would like to record our gratitude to our respective departments at the time this project was conceived – the Department of Japanese at the National University of Singapore (Ben-Ari) and the Department of Comparative Culture at Sophia University (Clammer) and for our students there who contributed in many ways. Likewise we would like to thank the Department of Sociology and Anthropology at the Hebrew University of Jerusalem whose hospitality made possible a visit to Israel by Clammer during the editing process and to the Nissan Institute of Japanese Studies at the University of Oxford and its Director for secretarial and logistic support. We would also like to thank Lise Skov and Brian Moeran for comments on an earlier draft of the book which enabled us to sharpen many of the arguments and generally to improve the text.

Chapter 1

Japan in Southeast Asia: An Introductory Essay

John Clammer and Eyal Ben-Ari

This volume is about the presence – the impact, effect or influence – of Japan in Southeast Asia, and more specifically, on the city state of Singapore, the primary and in many was paradigmatic case of the contemporary Japanese presence in the region. In Singapore the largest Japanese expatriate community is to be found, very visible socially, culturally, in business and in leisure – not surprising, perhaps, given the concentrated impact that such a large group can have on a small and almost entirely urban society, one furthermore still struggling with the problems of its own identity and its relationship to the geopolitical sphere of which it is an integral part. But before focusing on Singapore, that society needs itself to be situated in the context of Southeast Asia and an exploration made of the broad forces of change which have shaped and are shaping the region as a whole.

Southeast Asia – broadly defined as the ASEAN nations, Indochina and Burma – along with an emerging south China, is booming economically and is fast developing into what is beginning to be termed the 'Pacific Century'. The presence of Japan is felt in a diverse set of areas such as production and service facilities, financial and banking institutions, tourism and travel, departmental stores and supermarkets, restaurants and nightclubs, foods and clothing, comics and movies, and more intangible tastes, as in fashion and architecture. But is there an 'order' or 'orders' underlying these presences? How are these 'orders' arranged and how are they changing? How are they related both to local and transnational social, political and economic circumstances? And how are we to theorize these emergent 'orders' and their changes? This volume seeks to answer these kinds of questions, specifically in relation to Singapore, and through the Singapore case study, to the rest of a region which, despite its cultural diversity, has begun to experience very widely the issues of urbanization, rapid industrialization and the management of cultural identities in plural societies that Singapore has already faced within its own small geographical boundaries.

We justify our focus on our two entities – and we do not assume the unitary nature either of Japan or Southeast Asia – on the basis of two interrelated reasons, one empirical, one theoretical. Our contention is first that both area merit special attention because of their sheer economic (industrial and financial) importance. Secondly, we justify our focus for theoretical reasons. Asking about these two areas steers our social analyses of the present world from too strong a focus on 'things Western'. We can instead ask about the intercultural patterns of influence between non-Western areas and about the now emergent and much debated notions of Asian-ness which are beginning to appear throughout the region in new guises and of which a primary source is Singapore and to some extent its immediate neighbour Malaysia, not least through the mechanisms of the former's Senior Minister Lee Kuan Yew and the latter's Prime Minister Mahatir Mohamad, who has even penned a book on the subject, revealingly with one of Japan's most prominent nationalists (Mahatir and Ishihara 1994). While much has been written about the contemporary circumstances in which Japan and the West (i.e. America and Europe) are 'present' in each other's societies and cultures, we know relatively little about the mutual influences and effects between Japan and Southeast Asia. For example, scholarly studies of Japan and Western societies have been published with regard to such issues as mutual perceptions (Iriye 1975) or literary portrayals and power relationships (Miyoshi 1991). But little comparable work has been done on relationships between non-Western nations. Are for example Thai perceptions of modernization (Yoshihara 1989) different from American ones? Or to take another example, Vishwanathan (1992: 291), speaking about India's civilizational legacy, suggests that

> Japan does not present itself as 'an opposite, different or exotic nation' when viewed directly by Indians. At times, even the explanations of Western scholars about Japanese

thought patterns and practices, which seem strikingly unique to them, seem to bring Japan closer to Indians rather than further distancing them from each other.

It is to raising these questions in relation to the mutual influences of Japan and Southeast Asia that this volume is devoted, by way of a detailed exploration of the single 'case' of Singapore, the smallest nation in the region certainly, but precisely the one in which Japanese influence has been most keenly experienced.

In this introduction we provide a map, a tentative sketch, of the main issues involved in examining the broader picture, the context: the presence of Japan in Southeast Asia generally, and of the articles presented in this volume. We realize that inventories are always a problem. They change and must be continually amended. Nevertheless what we offer here is a preliminary catalogue of the problems and issues that we have identified, and we offer this introduction as a programmatic or polemical essay aimed at prodding us to rethink the current notions of Japan, Southeast Asia and of the nature of international flows of influence, peoples, materials and ideas of which Singapore lies at the geographical, economic and social epicentre.

History: The Ebbs and Flows of Cultural Influence

Southeast Asia has, throughout its recorded history and probably beyond, been a nexus of cultural influences. In particular four great forces have worked historically to transform the cultural landscape of the region and even in some sense to 'construct' it as a geographical and cultural entity. These forces have been the influence of Indian, Chinese, Islamic and Western civilizations. The history of much of Asia (including South and East Asia) has been the result of the ebbs and flows of cultural influence. Even as India changed the face of China through the influence of Buddhism, so China formed the civilization of Vietnam through the profound effects of its written language and political models. Cambodia and Java derive much of their high culture from Hinduism and the Philippines its dominant religion and much of its language from the Spanish. A stroll through any major city of contemporary Southeast Asia confirms this impression: the profusion of faces, races, cuisines, architectures and fashions indicates that many forces have been at work to shape the present.

3

Each of these influences however has produced its own patterns which today overlay each other in complex ways. Indian civilization had its most direct effect not only on its immediate neighbour Burma, but also on what are now Thailand and Cambodia, and on much of Indonesia, especially southern Sumatra, Java and Bali. Indian influence has been profound in all these places, transforming religion and through religion ideas of architecture, social stratification and statecraft. To this day the court rituals of Thailand and the temple rituals of Bali are Hindu in inspiration and the Javanese love of hierarchy and its minute gradations derives in part from the influence of the caste system. During the heyday of Western colonialism, especially in its later more economically intensive forms (late nineteenth century until the Pacific war) large numbers of Indians moved, often permanently, to Southeast Asia as labourers, policemen, members of the colonial armies and as railway workers. To this day the Malaysian plantation industry is largely dependent upon Indian (mainly Tamil) labour, often by now second, third or even fourth generation descendants of the original settlers (Vella 1968).

Chinese influence has been felt in other ways. Certainly through the huge influx of Chinese labour throughout the colonial period, bringing with it languages (mainly the southern Chinese dialects) Mahayana Buddhism, forms of architecture which still dominate many of the trading towns of Southeast Asia. But also through ideas of political culture, bureaucratic organization and literature, ideas felt most directly in Vietnam and reflected for example in the architecture and culture of the old Vietnamese imperial court city of Hue and in the fact that Vietnamese was, until the invention of the current Romanized script by a French missionary in the nineteenth century, written in Chinese characters. Islam, the great fourth force spread from the Arabian peninsula and the Gulf via India to Southeast Asia from the fourteenth and fifteenth centuries on, creating a religious culture which, like Hinduism, extends far beyond any narrow conception of spirituality to encompass concepts of political organization, social and gender arrangements, dress, food, and world view, and which now forms the basis of much of the politics and everyday life of Southeast Asians from southern Thailand throughout Malaysia and the southern Philippines to the far eastern reaches of Indonesia (Geertz 1968).

Western colonialism, the late – comer in this play of forces, has had no less far-reaching effects, having brought with it Western ideas of political organization, institutions political, educational and social which form much of the civic culture of, especially, urban Southeast Asia (schools, universities, hospitals, bureaucracies, transportation networks), religion (specifically Christianity in its many guises), massive influxes of foreign labour and global trading networks. Today all these forces continue to intersect and to influence each other. Malaysian politics today is largely the result of British colonial policy; Muslims and Christians fight each other in the southern Philippines, probably unaware that the former received their religion from the Persian Gulf via India and the latter from Spanish and (in the case of Protestants) from American missionaries. The Vietnamese intellectual reading in French, the Malaysian one in English, the former a Catholic, the latter a Muslim educated in the United States, are both products of this endless process of mixing, reformulation and renegotiation which is the very stuff of Southeast Asian history and sociology.

This thumb-nail sketch indicates two things. The first is that Japanese cultural influence, a late-comer in this chronology, is entering an already crowded field. Its effect on the sophisticated Singapore consumer and the Thai villager, the Malaysian Muslim already committed to a deeply rooted religious faith bound up with his very identity and ethnicity and his Chinese neighbour who is vaguely 'Buddhist', but who practises no particular religion, is very differential, and the variety of these effects is part of the texture of the essays that follow and of the volume as a whole. Here again Singapore appears as a paradigmatic case because of its multi-ethnic character, its profusion of religions, lifestyles, cuisines, architectures and languages, a veritable microcosm influenced by all the major forces we have just enumerated, deeply by the West in colonial times and today open to the influence both of its regional members and by the operation of the world system as a whole. The reasons behind the original foundation of Singapore as a city state – location, proximity to sources of raw materials and at the centre of trading networks quite literally at the intersection of East and West and North and South – still apply even if in the new forms of economic and technological globalization (Singapore's status as a regional and international aviation centre being a prime example of this).

The second is that Japanese influence (like American influence) is part of a very long term and pervasive set of cultural and civilizational forces and is part of a much wider ebb and flow of historical actors. In this bigger context it may be that this current presence is just a passing phenomenon which in a few years will lack the persistence and urgency that we now feel. Perhaps – to put this point in terms of the post-war era – the 'Japanese stage' is just a passing phase in between the great presences of China and America. Or maybe, like the lasting influence of Indian civilization in the area, it will be internalized and will long remain a lingering element in Southeast Asia.

Unlike the southern Chinese, the Japanese have not proved to be great travellers, and even less so great settlers abroad, with the notable exceptions of those who went to the Americas – to Hawaii in particular in the north and to Brazil in particular in the south. Nevertheless there has been Japanese contact with Southeast Asia for a very long time, beginning with very modest trade contacts in the distant past and expanding in the more recent past (pre-war specifically) to include the movement of Japanese farmers to the region to undertake pioneer agriculture, of professionals (dentists in particular), businessmen large and small, students, scholars, priests of Buddhist sects, artists and engineers (Iwasaki 1983). Increasing Japanese political involvement in Southeast Asia, culminating in the concept of the Great East Asian Co-Prosperity Sphere and Japan's entry into, or rather precipitation of, the Pacific war, was actually motivated by mixed interests including economic expansionism, the pressures of rising militarism at home and objection to Western colonial presence in Asia. As Morris-Suzuki aptly puts it

> Increasingly, a generalized interest in the resource wealth and economic potential of the region was transformed into both covert and overt opposition to western colonial rule in Southeast Asia, and into demands for a more aggressive Japanese government stance toward the colonial regimes (Morris-Suzuki 1984: 153).

Japanese opposition to Western colonialism however took the form of Japanese colonialism. The short-lived Japanese colonial empire, which extended from the invasion of China via the occupation of Korea and Taiwan to the *Nanshin*, the 'Southward Advance' of 1941–42, which led to the seizure of the Philippines, Malaya, Singapore and Indonesia and which eventually reached as far south as the heights overlooking Port Moresby in what is now Papua New Guinea, has left its own legacy. It is still not uncommon to meet Southeast Asians who were youths or young adults during the years of the Japanese occupation who can still speak Japanese, and not a few will point to the infrastructural improvements (in roads, railways and education) made by the Japanese in those areas longest occupied, as well as refer the questioner to the crucial role that the Japanese played in fuelling local anti-colonial movements, movements that eventuated in the Non-Aligned Movement and its famous summit in the Indonesian city of Bandung.

Between 1945 and the 1960s, Japan was concentrating too much on economic reconstruction at home to be concerned with major involvement in Southeast Asia, an involvement in any case still psychologically constrained by memories on both sides of the harshness of Japanese colonial rule. But by the late 1960s the large-scale movement of Japanese business interests outside Japan began in earnest and a shift towards major investment in Southeast Asia began in the early 1970s. During this period Japanese companies began to enter Southeast Asia, first through Singapore, later through other parts of ASEAN and latterly through parts of Indochina. At its beginning this movement comprised mostly production and servicing facilities, but in the last decade or so it has increasingly come to include banking, securities and other financial services. Concurrently, while the first moves into the area were carried out by the large firms, in recent years small and medium-sized companies have increasingly come in their wake. While increasing amounts of Japanese direct investment and aid are now going to Thailand, Singapore still stands at the forefront of Japan's move into Southeast and South Asia. A plethora of Japanese production facilities, headquarters, and sales and financial centres are now located in this small country and by some estimates as much as one quarter of Singapore's GDP is generated by Japanese companies (Cronin 1992; Chong and Yeo 1990). The attention given to Singapore in this book reflects its strategic and historical role in these economic transformations in Southeast Asia.

Economics of course implies sociology, and the economic impact of Japan has been mirrored in social and cultural changes which have accompanied it. Changes in work habits, diet, entertainment, management practices are but a few of these transformations. Others are signalled by the movement of humans between Japan and Southeast Asia, with large Japanese expatriate communities springing up all over the region, together with shops, schools and community organizations, with a massive flow of tourists in both directions and with increasing numbers of Southeast Asians seeking jobs and education in Japan, a country which is slowly but surely displacing the United States as the perceived land of opportunity. Japan has the reputation of being an isolated and insular society. In fact it is now the major force in transforming culture and social attitudes throughout large tracts of Southeast Asia (and beyond), and it is on this dimension of the presence of Japan that the essays in this volume concentrate.

The Political Economy of the Japanese Presence

With the expansion of Japan's post-war economy, Southeast Asia has become of vital importance as a rapidly growing market increasing quickly in consumer sophistication, as a source of raw materials (for example tropical timber) and, following the appreciation of the yen, a major site for off-shore manufacturing. In many discussions of Japan's relationship with Southeast Asia it has been this economic dimension that has tended to predominate (e.g. Dobson 1993). While to discuss only economics is to overlook the many other levels of relationship, economics is an important starting point because of the many sociological and cultural consequences that flow from it.

It is widely said in Southeast Asia that what Japan failed to conquer by force of arms during the war has been successfully and peacefully conquered by Japanese corporations since. While the older ex-colonial powers (France, Britain and Holland) continue to play a major investment role, and while the US and the European Union have also developed very major presences in the region, Japanese investment either in direct form or through joint-ventures has expanded at the fastest rate. With the high yen as an incentive, more and more Japanese manufacturing companies have relocated plants 'off-shore' in Southeast Asia where labour is plentiful, much cheaper than in Japan, and often well educated, where communications are good, tax laws favourable and anti-pollution legislation is often weak.

In the international division of labour Southeast Asia, and Singapore in particular, has thus come to take on a major role for transnational companies, especially as a base for manufacturing of products for local sale, for sale in third countries, or for export back to the investing country. Similarly the region has become an important market for Japanese products, especially as the new middle classes expand and their ability to consume increases with rising incomes (Robison and Goodman 1996), and Singapore, with its high GNP and high levels of income, is at the forefront of this trend. And as suggested, it is also a supplier of primary commodities essential to Japan's own industrialization – timber, minerals, oil and natural gas being amongst some of the most important. The industrialization of Japan owes a great deal to the skills, labour, raw materials and markets of Southeast Asia, and reciprocally governments in the region have attempted actively to attract Japanese investment as a means of promoting the industrialization of their own economies. This has promoted debate within the region on the extent of real transfer of technology to Southeast Asia or of the retention of profits within the area, and of the problematic consequences of a pattern of industrialization that has created in many countries a large, but semi-skilled proletariat out of what were originally skilled farmers.

Economic might brings with it many secondary effects. An important example of this is the perception of Japan as a political model. In an Asia that still suffers from problems of authoritarianism and militarization, Japan is the best example of a society that has successfully made the transition from militarist authoritarianism to democracy. While some of the aspects of this democracy are worrying (such as the role of money politics), other aspects, such as the creation of a highly professional bureaucracy staffed with some of the best-educated people in the country, are often cited as models for other developing countries. This model is appealing not only to governments, but also to oppositionists, since Japan has proved that it is possible to have both democracy *and* development, contradicting the often-stated belief of some local leaders that you cannot have both.

Closely related to the issue of domestic politics is that of regional stability. The Association of Southeast Asian Nations (ASEAN) is not a security grouping and with the withdrawal of the military forces of the former colonial powers it was the US that became the guarantor of security in the region. However the end of the Cold War, the final withdrawal of the US forces from their bases in the Philippines, the increasing international reach of the Chinese armed forces, conflicts over seabed resources in the South China Sea and the continuing instability in the Korean peninsula, have not created conditions where peace and stability can necessarily be guaranteed. While a rearmed Japan (and despite its low profile, Japan has one of the largest armed forces in the world) is still seen as dangerous by Southeast Asian nations with memories of the war (or at least, such sentiments are expressed in political rhetoric), it is also the case that Japan is being looked to as a promoter of stability through encouraging trade, as the major force for containing China and North Korea by diplomatic and economic means and as a creator of peace by building democracy and development throughout the region through investment and aid.

The other economics-related issue that has provoked most debate within Southeast Asia has been that of ecology. One of the attractions of locating manufacturing in Southeast Asia has been that pollution controls are often weaker. The manufacture and transport of hazardous materials is easier to accomplish and laws regulating atmospheric and noise pollution are less stringently applied in situations where local governments are eager to attract foreign investment in order to bolster their own legitimacy through the promotion of economic growth. The massive export of primary and in some cases irreplacable commodities has also had major ecological effects. Most conspicuously Japan's huge appetite for timber is the direct cause of much of the deforestation of Malaysia, Burma and parts of Indonesia, a pattern that is likely to be repeated with the opening up to economic exploitation of Vietnam and other parts of Indochina.

The Japanese economic presence, some of the social effects of which are examined by the individual essays in the volume as they pertain to Singapore, has in summary come in three forms. The first of these is direct investment, with Japan now having risen to the status of the largest investor in the region with a by now enormous presence in manufacturing, transportation, financial services, tourism, retailing and entertainment. The second is through technology transfer and managerial know-how (Koike and Aoki 1987). While it is often claimed that the Japanese do not transfer state-of-the-art technology to Southeast Asia, it is nevertheless the case that an enormous amount of technology is transferred (the creation of automobile manufacturing in Malaysia being one such example) which has transformed the face of local industry, and through it consumption patterns, agricultural practices and a host of knock-on effects. The area that has probably received the most positive evaluation has been Japanese management practices, and the wide dissemination of literature on the subject indicates its profound impact. Japanese management techniques and company organizational structure are widely studied, and taught in regional universities and management schools, for their insights into recruitment practices, in-house training, promotion and motivation (Matsumoto 1991). Behind the perceived advantages of Japanese management itself are seen to be other qualities of Japanese society, especially the educational system which is seen as delivering a high level of literacy and numeracy and as contributing to the formation of a disciplined and able workforce. Southeast Asians quickly learnt indeed that management practices do not exist in a cultural vacuum, but are effective only when they are rooted in specific sociological conditions (the issue addressed by Tom Stanley in his paper in this volume). Much of the motivation for the study of Japanese language, culture, society and history in Southeast Asia has come precisely from this desire to understand the trajectory of Japanese modernization and to discover the conditions which made it possible, and it is now estimated that Japanese is the most popular foreign language (other than the old colonial languages) now learnt throughout the region, and certainly in Singapore. As Stanley demonstrates, the Japanese model has had great influence on the thinking of Singaporean policy makers, both in terms of management practices and of the values that are assumed to be the basis of Japan's success. But he also shows how, while Japanese labour practices and policies – quality control circles, methods of improving company loyalty, house unions and mechanisms for controlling conflict – are very attractive to local economic planners and investors, an image of 'Japan' is also used to legitimate controls and policies already in place. While Japan appeals as a distinctively Asian model, the cultural differences between Singapore and Japan must give pause when considering its genuine usefulness or applicability. In the pursuit of 'Confucianism' in contemporary Singapore for example, those with short historical memories will have forgotten that a not dissimilar policy in pre-war Japan led not to economic prosperity, but to authoritarianism and militarism.

The third element of the Japanese economic presence is through development aid. In dollar terms, Japan is now the biggest aid donor in the world, and a high percentage of that aid goes to Southeast Asia. As with most aid programmes, it has received its fair share of criticism especially due to the fact that a high percentage of Japanese aid is in the forms of loans rather than grants and because of its close ties to Japanese business interests. In addition to the usual criticisms of aid – that it promotes dependency, creates ecological problems and so forth – many critics see Japanese aid as frequently ineffective in promoting real development while favouring Japanese corporations which almost always win the contracts in construction and infrastructure projects into which most Japanese aid is poured (rather that is than into social development projects). Whatever the virtue of these criticisms – and there is substantial evidence to suggest that they are correct – Japanese aid has had profound effects on local economies and on local societies through the consequences of such activities as road and bridge building which have transformed patterns of social and spatial interaction (Ensign 1992, Soderberg 1993). Examples of this can be seen in Singapore, both in Japanese aid given to promote technical training for young Singaporeans and in the heavy Japanese involvement in infrastuctural projects, of which the most conspicuous is the MRT or subway system.

The forces of globalization, of international security and the interlocking nature of the world economy and trading system are slowly forcing Japan to come to terms with its diplomatic and security role in Southeast Asia (Scolinos 1988, Juwana 1993). The perception both within Japan and on the part of the wider world that Japan is a society without a foreign policy except a form of aggressive mercantilism is encouraging debate within Japan about the responsibilities attendant upon economic might and of the consequences (social, political and economic) of massive intervention through aid in the nations of Southeast Asia. Japanese participation in the Cambodian peace-keeping force and the huge domestic debate that even this modest contribution occasioned is a sign of this shift. Japanese economic and political relationships with Southeast Asia do at this moment stand at something of a crossroads, with the proponents of a more equal and genuinely pro-development role contending with both the forces of political inertia at home and of naked mercantilism abroad. Many lessons have still not been learnt, and the existence of little known post-war developments such as the creation of exploitative banana plantations set up in the Philippines specifically to supply the Japanese market (Tanaka 1984) still indicate the nature of the concrete problems that exist between Japan and Southeast Asia today.

Leisure and Consumption

Linked also to economics and ecology in many ways is the subject of tourism. Japanese are already amongst the world's great tourists, a tendency strengthened by the rising power of the yen. Southeast Asia has become a very popular tourist destination, a trend exemplified by Singapore: cheap by Japanese standards with a tropical climate, attractive hotels and resorts, good shopping, sufficient exoticism and perceived as for the most part safe and friendly. Even though the bursting of the Japanese 'bubble economy' and the weakening of the yen has brought about an attenuation of both the numbers and the purchasing power of Japanese tourists in Southeast Asia (and Singapore was already becoming a fairly expensive destination before the Asian economic and currency crisis of 1997–8), they nevertheless continue to have a major economic impact in the region. Tourism, despite its recent (and possibly temporary) relative decline has brought large numbers of Japanese into (at least superficial) contact with Southeast Asians and has had, like most forms of mass tourism, mixed effects on local cultures and societies. At its best it has helped promote cross-cultural understanding, a fact enhanced by the Japanese mania for information, a trait that ensures that many tourists and travellers do before, during or after travel inform themselves about their destinations, a fact attested to by the large number of titles in any major bookstore about other Asian cultures and peoples, quite excluding guide books as such which also sell in huge numbers. Unfortunately it is also true that much Japanese tourism exemplifies a less attractive model at work.

Many Japanese tours to Singapore (and a very high percentage of Japanese visitors come on such tours rather than as independent travellers) are essentially organized around consumption and as with tours to Hawaii, another very popular warm-weather destination, much of the generally short and highly organized time (partly reflecting the average shortness of Japanese vacations) is spent shopping (Nitta 1992). And although many local governments believe that tourism promotes development, in practice many Japanese tourists travel on Japanese-owned airlines, stay in Japanese-owned hotels and take their local tours with Japanese-owned tour companies which ensure that they visit Japanese stores where they buy Japanese products (often manufactured in Southeast Asia) at much lower prices than they would pay at home.

Much of the profit generated by such enterprises is repatriated to Japan. Quite apart from the lack of real contacts between the tourists and the local populations and the absence of real economic benefits to the host society, ecological problems and social tensions promoted by both the perception of inequalities and engagement in such activities as prostitution create interesting and problematic relationships between visitors and hosts.

An extremely interesting paradigm of this can be found in the problem of the spread of golf courses, mainly for use by Japanese, throughout Southeast Asia as tourist numbers grow and as large semi-permanent business communities are established. In Japan rising opposition to the construction of new golf courses – they are perceived as destroying natural habitats and useful agricultural land, as creating little employment, as contributing to pollution through the intensive use of pesticides and chemical fertilizers to keep the grass in perfect condition, and as excluding the less affluent local population who cannot afford the huge club membership fees. The same debate has spread to Southeast Asia even as golf course construction is expanding. An example of this process is provided in Ben-Ari's contribution to this volume, in which the dual influence of Japanese expatriates and tourists is examined in relation to a number of issues including those raised by golf clubs in Singapore. In that chapter, however, Ben-Ari does not dwell on the ecological impact of golf on Singapore (massive though it has indeed been), but on some of the hitherto unstudied sociological aspects. Many Japanese businesspeople who can afford to play golf only rarely, if ever, in Japan find that they can play as much as they like in Singapore, and middle-ranking company people can indulge in a lifestyle available to only very senior managers at home. Ben-Ari here and elsewhere (Ben-Ari 1998) demonstrates not only the significant part that golf plays in the ethnography of the Singapore Japanese community, but also how this translates into long-term life strategies as well as short term business contacts. This approach opens up some central questions in the study of Japanese communities, including that of the much-vaunted *kokusaika* or 'internationalization' in the light of the fact that playing golf in Singapore emphatically does not promote interaction between Japanese and locals, but if anything reinforces an enclave mentality amongst the Japanese.

With their arrival in the area Japanese business people brought with them not only management, production and service methods, but also certain patterns of leisure activities such as tennis, swimming, newspapers and books, but above all (at least for the men), as Ben-Ari notes, the pursuit of golf. At the beginning of the 1970s golf was played in local country and golf clubs (often themselves stemming from the colonial period). The entry of Japanese into these clubs coincided throughout the Southeast Asian countries with the growth of a significant local upper-middle class. This group of people have applied relentless economic and political pressure since the 1970s for establishing new golf clubs and for renovating the older ones. During the 1980s golfing tourism, again mainly Japanese, provided additional impetus for the development of new courses and the upgrading of existing ones. In Singapore, Malaysia and Thailand, the move has been from private members' clubs to profit-making enterprises based on integrated leisure complexes which include golf courses, tennis courts and swimming pools, meeting and convention facilities and dining and drinking sites (Cohen n.d. : 7). Such models have changed the leisure and consumption expectations of local people – first the indigenous upper-middle class, and later a much bigger social range of upwardly mobile professionals and business people – across a whole range of habits from reading to what to do on Sunday (see Ng and Ben-Ari in this volume). The tendency for both Japanese tourists and businessmen to set up their own ethnically exclusive zones – nightclubs, bars, pubs and restaurants – as well as shops which are largely if not entirely Japanese preserves strengthens this tendency for social segregation, a tendency enhanced by the creation of exclusively Japanese retirement communities in Thailand (and others are planned for elsewhere). Increasingly in Southeast Asia the model for leisure and consumption is no longer North America or Europe, but is Japan, the source not only of economic development, but also of fashion, foods, comics, TV programmes and all the elements of popular culture.

But as Chua points out in his contribution, the effects of such consumerism, and of models (and objects) of consumption originating from outside, are subtle and not always what one would expect. While consumer objects are of course stamped with the culture of their origin, Chua shows how Singaporeans actually 'shop the world' without actually leaving the country, and create 'defensive spaces' for themselves precisely to avoid being overrun by too much foreign influence of a kind that they have not themselves selected. Economic presence has cultural influence then, but it need not mean cultural domination, and Chua shows persuasively how Singaporeans remain very localized in their eating and dressing, two major indicators of acculturation. Despite the plethora of shops selling Japanese fashions, even female formal wear has escaped direct Japanese influence, and has rather been ethnicized according to local and regional (Southeast Asian) idioms. While Japanese food is now popular and Chinese speakers in particular watch a high proportion of Japanese TV shows, Chua nevertheless argues that 'Japan provides the concept, but not the cultural substance' behind much Singaporean popular culture, the spread of karaoke being a prime example where the form is Japanese, but the content is usually Chinese, or more specifically Cantonese. Interestingly, in the light of debates about regional identity and globalization, Chua does suggest that 'the consumption of Japanness is increasingly reframed into discourses of Asianness' rather than being simply the domination of one economy by another.

Popular Culture

The spread of Japanese culture, and especially of popular culture, in Southeast Asia is a very visible feature of Japanese impact. All over the region people, especially younger ones, are wearing Japanese fashions, eating Japanese food, watching Japanese television programmes and films dubbed in their local language, listening to Japanese pop music and reading the famous Japanese comics (*manga*) with translated dialogue. Lifestyles are consequently being transformed in numerous subtle ways, both by the widespread use of Japanese consumer products and by adaptation to Japanese models of culture.

It is in part this adaptation that makes the subject of popular culture so interesting and so ripe for more detailed analysis. Television programmes and movies clearly convey, subliminally or otherwise, numerous messages about lifestyles, mores, gender relations and acceptable forms of behaviour. Children's programmes, and in particular cartoons, have been bought in large quantities by Southeast Asian television networks. The cartoon *Doraimon* which features the adventures of a cat with magical powers is set in an ordinary Japanese suburban setting, but despite its regular depiction of bullying (usually directed at the small boy with whom Doraimon lives), of sexist and occasionally of racist

16

behaviour, is enormously popular in Malaysia for instance. Not only is the cartoon itself avidly watched, but derivative products of many kinds – pens, bags, stationary, toys, mugs and so forth – are extensively marketed as well. Childhood becomes transformed in many ways through such media. The comic book or *manga*, very widely read in Japan by millions of consumers of all ages, both sexes and most social statuses, has also made its appearance, especially in Thailand. Thai script fits very conveniently into the same area as the Japanese dialogue in the original version: the stories and artwork are left entirely unchanged.

Comics are not the only forms of popular culture which reach Southeast Asian youth in particular. Video games have also made enormous inroads, paralleling the expansion of the availability of televisions and VCR players and more recently the explosion in the availability of desk-top computers. Amongst both youths and their elders other forms of the Japanization of popular culture have occurred. Two of the most conspicuous examples are food and the enormous popularity of *karaoke*. Throughout the region there has not only been a great increase in the number of specifically Japanese restaurants, and of Japanese supermarkets selling Japanese foods which are now patronized by large numbers of locals and which have correspondingly changed local eating habits, but also what are actually Japanese dishes entering local cuisines and becoming indigenized. In Thailand for example there is a Thaification of Japanese food paralleling the earlier Thaification of Chinese food. Dishes called 'suki' have entered the diet of urban Thais (the word deriving from the Japanese suki-yaki), although for the average Thai these dishes are not associated with any Japanese origins.

Karaoke, 'empty music', the form of entertainment in which a video is played on a television screen accompanied by music, but without lyrics which are instead displayed as sub-titles on the screen and which are sung by the audience, is an extremely popular diversion in Japan. *Karaoke* 'boxes' or small salons which can be rented by the hour are found all over Japanese towns and karaoke machines are to be found in many bars, and increasingly in private homes. What began as a Japanese craze has spread like the proverbial wildfire to Hong Kong, China, Taiwan, Singapore and elsewhere in Southeast Asia where clubs specifically for *karaoke* now abound, and many affluent families have bought home equipment for their private entertainment. *Karaoke* has had a range of effects stemming from both its technical and social arrangements (special soundproof rooms and videos) and from the musical scores, styles and contents of the songs, many of which are Japanese even though the lyrics will be available in the local languages. The popularity of *karaoke* is such as to have created a genuine revolution in entertainment patterns, one which in turn has created new patterns of social interaction.

Although not usually considered strictly part of popular culture, religion, given its place in the organization of everyday life, is clearly part of or closely related to it. Japanese religions, and specifically some of the *shin shukyo* or 'new religions' (many of them actually quite old, but which rose to prominence particularly in the years immediately after the Second World War) originally spread to Southeast Asia with the expansion in the numbers of Japanese expatriates living there as business people, diplomats and members of international organizations and aid agencies. Historically however, such religions have been unsuccessful in recruiting members from exactly these social groups, and in some cases they have instead spread beyond the Japanese population into the local community. A good example of this, examined in this volume in Clammer's essay, is the Soka Gakkai movement, a form of militant and evangelistic Buddhism which has spread widely in Southeast Asia and especially in Singapore, mainly amongst working-class Chinese. As such it has not only threatened the indigenous forms of Chinese religion and drawn potential converts away from Christianity which was the fastest growing religion before Soka Gakkai appeared, but it has also greatly changed the social life of its converts, both in its daily and weekly organization and in the effect that it has had in orienting them towards Japan. Its 'Asianness', discipline, family oriented character and pragmatic ethics have attracted the favour and quiet support of the Singapore government, fitting in very well as it does with that government's 'Look East' policies. An equally interesting, if more muted example is described in Hamrin's essay on another of the major Japanese *shin shukyo* or 'New Religions', notably Tenrikyo. Whereas Soka Gakkai is a Buddhist movement and as such closer in cosmology to the beliefs of many, particularly Chinese Singaporeans, Tenrikyo grew out of Shinto and practices of Japanese shamanism. These roots, while indisputably very genuinely Japanese, make it less accessible culturally to many Singaporeans. Hamrin describes the origins and beliefs of this alternative new religion and shows how while it is a very much smaller movement in Singapore than Soka Gakkai it is a vital movement nevertheless, fuelled by its commitment to social service, especially with the very least advantaged. Hamrin also very interestingly demonstrates how for Japanese members of the religion in Singapore, its cosmology makes it a vehicle for attempting to make amends for the past Japanese record in Singapore and in particular the years of brutal military occupation.

Popular culture and religion are linked at a number of levels, some more obvious and some much less so. At the primary level they simply feed off each other: Japanese religions have become visible and attractive to Southeast Asians partly because the economic success of Japan makes it an attractive model, one constantly extolled by regional governments, but also because things Japanese have now become part of the stuff of everyday life – the food, reading material, fashion and entertainment of which we have just spoken. The transition from popular culture to religious conversion then becomes not such a great one, and indeed participation in a Japanese new religion creates the opportunity for pilgrimages, study trips and tours to Japan, combining as such things usually do, spirituality and consumption. The new religions reciprocally tend towards an ethics which promotes pragmatism and even materialism, a point of view very compatible with the get-rich policies of both local governments and their citizens.

But at a deeper level both, through these mechanisms, are implicated in the wider question of consumption. Increasingly, it can be argued, it is consumption which forms the basis of cultural behaviour in Japan (Clammer 1997) and in Southeast Asia. Other cultural forms are becoming subordinated not to the logic of scarcity, but to the logic of consumption. This applies not only to the organization of everyday life around shopping and other forms of consumption, but also to the assimilation of the 'spiritual' aspects of culture such as art and religion to the demands of consumption: these too are bought and sold, evaluated in terms of their economic value. The consumer society did not originate in Japan and spread from there to Southeast Asia, but Japan certainly does represent the most fully and intensively developed example of that most contemporary of social forms, and as such its symbolic weight as well as its economic weight is enormous and its gravitational field, culturally speaking, is proportionately power-ful. A synergistic situation indeed exists in which the multiple influences of Japan, concentrated around the focus of consumption, flow together to form a powerful field of force.

A Model to Emulate?

In today's Southeast Asia then Japan is seen – as throughout much of the rest of the world (Mouer and Sugimoto 1986) – as a model to be emulated (Yoshihara 1989). There are as we have suggested various reasons for this perception. Some of them have to do with the simple success of Japan and the emulation of a high status kind of society (as the US was and to a great extent still continues to be in the region). Where we have Coca-Cola culture, we also have Yamaha culture: an emulation of a successful lifestyle. Such emulation is the outcome of the intentional promotion of such images (by producers and marketers), and the active acceptance of products and models by local populaces.

But the issues of modelling local societies and organizations on Japanese patterns are in reality complex. Japan's success is thought of as providing a 'key' or a 'formula' that can be applied to achieve similar results in Southeast Asia. This is seen very clearly in government policies regarding industrial development, and is a favourite concern with bureaucrats and economists. In Thai economic studies for example

> one of the most popular comparative topics is the reason why the economic developments of Thailand and Japan have differed despite the fact that both countries started their modernization at more or less the same time ... Thai economists look at the Japanese economy with awe (Krongkaew 1989: 123; 133).

Closely related is interest in Japanese educational policies and institutional arrangements (Sinlarat 1989). an interest which has produced an abundant and thriving modelling of organizational, administrative, and managerial arrangements and procedures (see Stanley's essay in this volume) not only in the region, but also on the part of Japanese recommending such models to their Southeast Asian counterparts, as in Taira's case study of a Japanese company operating in Indonesia (Taira 1993).

It is also true however that alongside the stress on imitation and emulation, Japan is also seen as a country which needs to be carefully watched and monitered because of the legacy of the

Second World War and because of wariness of present-day attempts by Japan to dominate the area economically and the feeling that economic might is not yet balanced by political responsibility. So while interest in and to a great extent goodwill towards Japan are at a high level, so are the criticisms of the flaws in the Japanese model. The effects of economic domination, the misuse of aid, the half-hearted commitment to peace-keeping activities, the problems faced by Southeast Asian workers and students in Japan and the lack of integration of the affluent and self-contained Japanese communities in the region with their host societies, have all called into being a chorus of critical voices. One of the most provoking issues for many is the situation of migrant workers from the region in Japan, a point which very well illustrates the imbalances in the relationship between these northerly and southerly neighbours.

Southeast Asia in Japan

The relationship between Japan and Southeast Asia is not only a one-way road. Some large regional companies operate in Japan (banks for example, and airlines) and there is a constant flow of tourists northwards. The gravitational field of Japan however has other less desirable effects. The high visibility of Japan, its constant presence through its economic activities, aid efforts, cultural and consumer artefacts, and obvious affluence has not surprisingly implanted in many Southeast Asians the desire to go there to work and to share in the fruits of the economic miracle which their raw materials and open markets have in large part brought into being. The problem is however that Japan will not accept foreign workers, with the exception of highly qualified professionals and foreigners of Japanese descent (in particular Brazilian and Peruvian Japanese). The only way for the average Southeast Asian to work in Japan (where wages are many times that available in most regional labour markets) is to work illegally, and this many do indeed do. The numbers of illegal foreign workers and the social problems that their presence creates (human rights abuses, involvement of the *yakuza* or Japanese criminal organizations in recruitment, control and exploitation of unprotected workers, especially women from Thailand and the Philippines engaged in the sex trade, lack of access to medical and other basic facilities) has become a major issue of domestic debate in Japan (e.g. Honda 1990). These

21

workers, tolerated because of their essential contributions to building the Japanese economy, yet unprotected, without legal status, frequently living in very poor conditions (Ventura 1992) have been officially ignored despite numerous proposals from activists and academics to legalize and regulate their presence, recruitment and repatriation and to provide skills training that would make them very real contributors to their own societies on their return. This non-policy is a major cause of anti-Japanese resentment and is widely seen as evidence of lack of genuine reciprocity in Japan–Southeast Asian relations.

Illegal workers are of course not the only communities of Southeast Asians to be found in Japan. In addition to the small groups of business-people and diplomats concentrated in the large cities, and most specifically in Tokyo, there are quite large and growing numbers of students. A few of these are privately funded, some come on scholarships from their own governments, but most come on scholarships provided by the Japanese Ministry of Education. This same ministry has announced plans for doubling the number of foreign students in Japanese universities to a total of around one hundred thousand by the end of the century. Most Southeast Asian, students, however if asked to state their preference for place of overseas university education, put Western countries (including Australia and New Zealand) at the top of the list and Japan in a rather lower position. This is not only because it is very expensive and has a difficult language, but also because research facilities are often inferior (most advanced-level research in science and technology takes place in company laboratories, not in the universities) and housing is a major problem – highly priced, low in quality and often difficult to obtain as many landlords are reluctant or unwilling to rent to foreigners. The paradox of a huge economy with a poor infrastructure and an unwillingness to create policies to address this becomes, in this context too, a barrier to better relations. It is workers and students especially who, as relatively long-term residents, bring home stories about Japan (often unflattering ones) that greatly colour perceptions throughout the region.

These paradoxes, however, are not just the source of problems, but like many contradictions are the source of a fruitful dialectic. The presence of large numbers of foreigners, the pressures from within and without for a more responsible and less economics-driven set of political policies and the activities of human rights activists, environmentalists and more progressive scholars, have all placed Japan's relations with the rest of Asia squarely on the domestic agenda. Even such seemingly trivial matters as the growing popularity of Southeast Asian food, especially Thai, Indonesian and Vietnamese, have raised the awareness of the region, one furthermore visited by very large numbers of Japanese tourists every year. Within some intellectual and political circles in Japan there is something of a current rethinking of the country's wartime history and a new willingness to talk about the negative sides of the wartime presence in Southeast Asia (Otabe 1990).

The actual production of knowledge about Southeast Asia remains small scale however. Few students enrol in Southeast Asian language courses in Japanese universities and many who do take up the professional study of the region do so in British or North American universities. Very few institutions are engaged in producing knowledge in Japanese about Southeast Asia, although it is encouraging that those which do are amongst those of the highest academic standing in Japan (Kyoto University, Sophia University and the Tokyo University of Foreign Studies being amongst the most prominent). While Japanese is widely learnt in Southeast Asia and Japanese studies departments have appeared in recent years in the major universities in Hong Kong, Singapore and Malaysia, Southeast Asian languages and studies is still a very minor field in Japan. What is significant is the intensity of the debate about these relationships both in Japan and in Southeast Asia. The import indeed of both kinds of issues – 'social problems' and 'knowledge' is that they are very much discussed within Southeast Asia in various public debates. Such questions as changing (or unchanging) Japanese attitudes to the war, the fate of prostitutes and labourers, are constantly reported in the regional press and raised in political and diplomatic meetings. The issue of the relationship between Japan and Southeast Asia is very much a live and contemporary one and as such it shapes discourse and becomes one of the key elements out of which regional world views, conceptions of security and perceptions of cultural processes are formed.

Theorizing the Presence

In theoretical terms the next question must be to join the 'logics' (the terms, analytical schemes and problematic issues) of analysing

Japan with those of Southeast Asian societies. Historically each has grown up around its own 'language': early culture contact (Hindu, Islamic), colonial, anti-colonial and postcolonial in the case of much of Southeast Asia; early Chinese and Korean influences succumbing to the 'myth of Japanese uniqueness' (Dale 1995). Southeast Asian societies have thus been subject to and productive of multiple discourses of identity; Japan on the other hand has attempted to create a single image of itself as in some way outside of the world. Yet in practice today, both are linked, both through the empirical processes of 'culture contact', but more significantly for both by their encapsulation within the world system.

There is, in other words, another, a global level, to our analysis, the premise of which is that in order to understand the social and organizational activities and structures of present societies there is the need to analyse how they are related to a variety of economic, political and cultural processes summed up in the term 'globalization'. Theoretically the project reflected in this book answers recent scholarly calls for a recognition of the fact that in order to understand the present-day social and cultural world there is a need to 'go international', to theorize and conceptualize changes in the way the 'world' is now perceived and acted upon by a variety of social groups (such as states, social movements, organizations or ethnic collectivities) and individuals (Robertson 1992; Appadurai 1990). Indeed, following Robertson, we refer to the 'world' in parentheses to underline the sense of a growing consciousness of (but not necessarily consensus about) the global situation that is found among such groups.

Let us suggest a few points in this regard. The phenomenon of transnational, global flows has existed in one form or another for centuries. But today these flows have intensified. The problem is that many of the older models, explanatory frameworks and concepts found in the social sciences are no longer as apt as they once seemed: the pendulum model of cultural influence, the image of core and peripheries, or the paradigm of the nation-state are no longer as convincing as they once were. Civilizations are not as monolithic as they once seemed. Transnational flows of people, resources and information do not always circulate in the same direction or with equal force. What we are beginning to see is the emergence of a new language for talking about contemporary global processes and a vocabulary of ambivalence, difference, disjunctures and inventions has appeared. Oe Kenzaburo (1982: 50) makes this point in the context of internal Japanese cultural debate when he observes that we are witnessing a fundamental rearrangement of the Japanese cultural paradigm, a shift from the centres of Europe and America towards the 'vital cultures of our own peripheral areas ... We envision Asia as a non-unitary structure, and make Japan one of the diverse nations within it'.

There are other issues too involved in the reconceptualization of the world which are related to a more micro level (for drawing our attention to this point we thank Ehud Harari). Usually when we think about global processes we tend to consider economics or politics. But today, the direct face-to-face contact is much stronger than it has been in the past. International contact is no longer actualized only through such means as movies, newspapers and magazines. In multinational workplaces, the constraints of foreign presence are much stronger. To illustrate this by way of the Japanese case, working abroad has changed Japanese companies attitudes to such things as what makes good corporate citizens and has encouraged such trends as the incorporation of corporate philanthropy into the industrial culture of Japan. Similarly, the place of English in Japanese culture – and the added institutional infrastructure of language schools, books, tapes, and so on – is changing not only because of the centrality of the United States, but also because it is the international language of business in Southeast Asia as well.

We furthermore suggest that out of, and on the basis of, the global we can go back and try to reconceptualize what we mean by the nation-state. Thus, the thrust of our analysis lies in the contention that in order to understand contemporary Japanese society it is necessary to think internationally. In this regard we question the assumption lying at the base of many studies of Japan, that there is an isomorphism between the geo-political boundaries of the state and its social and cultural limits. Our contribution should be seen as proposing a first step towards a reconceptualization of Japanese culture itself. This culture – without assuming too much about its unitary nature – must be understood not only along the lines proposed by most social scientists who have studied Japan, but also as a set of negotiated symbols and meanings that travel *across* national boundaries (Mouer and Sugimoto 1986; Brannen 1992; Creighton 1991). To put this by way of example, just as it is possible to gain a richer appreciation of the variety of experiences entailed in being Japanese through accompanying tour groups to Europe and China, or visiting their hangouts in Thailand, so it may be possible to learn a good deal about 'Japaneseness' by observing expatriate Japanese communities and behaviour in Singapore or Vietnam. This indeed is illustrated in Ben-Ari's contribution on globalization in terms of the guiding metaphors of Japanese business expatriates as they confront this wider world. For many Japanese business people fulfilment of an overseas assignment is necessary now for their professional advancement. In this situation, the 'models' that Japanese expatriates themselves have of their overseas service in Singapore are of great interest since they force them to a re-reading of core-periphery relationships. As Ben-Ari suggests, being situated between some postulated ideas of 'East' and 'West', the Singaporean city-state raises questions for Japanese in ways that other world cities – London or Paris for example – do not. So while a Japan-centred vision of business careers and general orientation still prevails, the assumptions upon which this image of the career path are based are beginning to be questioned, as the reality of an increasingly fluid and complex world are grasped.

Internal Cultural Debates

The various Japanese presences (economic, political, cultural), and the stress on emulation, are related to a set of questions that appear in public dialogues and exchanges all over Southeast Asia, and are today regarded as at least as critical as discussions of Americanization or the Sinification of the area. These presences appear in what may be termed the 'internal cultural debates' (Parkin 1978) because of the perceived success of Japan. The Japanese 'miracle', a special combination of culture, economics and government policy, is a central axis in contemporary global discourses themselves. Maybe this situation will change in the future with the uncertainties of present-day Japanese politics. But for now it seems that the Japanese story will, as Robertson (1992: 86) notes, continue to be a central narrative for the building and development of nations because it is the society from which '"leaders" of other can learn how to learn about many societies. *That* is what makes Japan a global society, in spite of claims to the contrary'.

How does Japan figure in the internal cultural debates of Southeast Asian countries? First, it is used in many contemporary discussions of 'Asian-ness'. Historically speaking, the notion of

Asian civilization may be traced to the idea of the 'Greater East Asian Co-prosperity Sphere'. But today of no less importance are current debates about 'Asian-ness' that are appearing in such places as China, Korea and India (Vishwanathan 1975) and that are a central issue in public debates in Singapore (Chan 1993) or Malaysia (Shafie 1990). What is interesting is that Japan for Southeast Asians becomes a sort of test case through which to explore notions of Asian-ness and Westernization, a point made by several contributors and in particular Chua and Stanley.

Second, Japan figures centrally in the notion, bandied about now for the last hundred years or so in the West, of a 'civilized society'. The essential elements of this notion are of a family or group of civilized societies that are perceived to be marked by a certain level of cultivation or sophistication. Societies wishing to enter this elite group must adopt the standards of refinement and urbanity by which it is distinguished. Historically speaking as Gong (1984) has shown, this 'folk' model is related to the emergence of an international standard of 'civilization'. His focus is on the international arena and the confrontation that occured as Europe expanded into the non-European world during the nineteenth and early twentieth centuries. He carefully shows how this clash was not only political and economic but also cultural or civilizational. At the heart of the clash were the standards by which these civilizations identified themselves and regulated their international relations.

Our argument is that this international, diplomatic and elitist model has today become a 'folk' model. For many people in the contemporary world, a major image of the globe is centred on the inclusion or exclusion of societies in a family of 'civilized societies'. The criteria for incorporation are not only technological advancement, but no less importantly a certain kind of cultivation of style and etiquette, and interpersonal behaviour. Being civilized, however, does not directly imply being Westernized, a point made by Ben-Ari in his essay on globalization in the next chapter.

The social carriers of the terms and criteria for contemporary identity are a variety of actors such as cultural mediators, business leaders, politicians, media representatives, intellectuals, academics, (increasingly) expatriates, and what Robertson (1992: 61) terms 'new actors' and 'third cultures' such as transnational movements and international organizations that are oriented, negatively or positively, to the new global-human realities. Among these social groups are graduates of programmes of study in Japan found all over Southeast Asia – in Thailand in large numbers and in a variety of fields for example (Fungtammasan 1990) – who have returned to their own countries. While in Japan these students and researchers participate in government-run programmes (the previously mentioned Ministry of Education scholarships being the most famous) or programmes under the aegis of private companies such as Hitachi. Similarly, the Toyota Foundation, through its 'Know Our Neighbours' programme promotes the translation of local literary works and social science books into the Japanese language. In 1993 three Vietnamese, one Thai and one Indonesian books were translated and published under the programme (Toyota Foundation 1993). Just as there was and is a pattern to movement to north America and back by local people seeking education and training, now this pattern is being repeated in respect of Japan, bringing with it language skills, positive and negative impressions of Japan and a detailed acquaintance with her ways of life, popular culture and social and institutional arrangements.

In this respect the role of Japanese expatriates is central, for they simultaneously actualize and reinforce the actions of the other elites. Expatriates (organization men and women) who are posted abroad for a number of years are the people who are in constant contact with members of other cultures and who most acutely face the personal issues of accounting for, embodying and understanding globalization (in organizational theory these are indeed called 'boundary spanning roles'). These people are not the 'captains of industry' nor the 'international statesmen' who are seasoned veterans of media interviews and who regularly deal with (to put this point by way of the Japanese example) such issues as Japan's trade surplus or the felt need to increase its political and security presence in Asia and around the world (see for example, Mimura 1987). Rather, these are the unexceptional people who work overseas and who carry out debates about the global–human situation (although they may not use this kind of term) on a daily basis. It is also these millions of people who carry their experiences of contact (or its lack) back to their countries. The social circumstances within which the 'larger' debates about globality take place are related to and refracted through their personal life courses. The extension of expatriate service to larger numbers of people as international networks intensify and as more services and industries are moved 'offshore' is itself making the problems of accounting for globalization much more intense at this level of everyday life worlds as well as on the larger scale. While Southeast Asians working in Japan represent one end of such a network, the large Japanese expatriate communities represent the other, both bound together in a total system of interaction, a situation discussed in the case study by Ng and Ben-Ari in Chapter 5. In that instance, the 'transplantation' of a retail business, and one furthermore dealing in one of the major artifacts of culture and cultural transmission – the book – is explored against the background of debates about the transferability of Japanese organizational practices. While Chua explored the lives of Singaporeans in a cultural environment increasingly framed by Japan, here Ng and Ben-Ari look at the lives of Japanese expatriates encapsulated in Singapore. This raises a range of questions, such as do conditions of work in (Japanese) companies in Japan replicate themselves abroad? This is yet another dimension of the 'internationalization' issue, since as Ng and Ben-Ari document, such companies, whose managers are largely Japanese, have to cope with local staff, a situation involving the negotiation of barriers of language, culture, rules of politeness, ideas about work and motivation and differing expectations where the Japanese seniority-based promotion system comes into contact with the Singaporean one (fast if possible and based on productivity and educational credentials).

What is interesting about the internal cultural debate throughout Southeast Asia is that people are increasingly using a common set of terms by which to talk of themselves. The use of a rather conventional set of images and phrases for talking about the modern world is not incidental. Here we follow Robertson (1992: 135) who suggests that 'globalization involves the development of something like a global culture – not as normatively binding, but in the sense of a general mode of discourse about the world as a whole *and* its variety'. As we understand it, his proposal is that what we see today is not the advent of any kind of world-wide consensus or harmonious co-existence, but rather that the basic terms and criteria which are used in various discussions about the world are equally accepted by many contemporary groups. In other words, many nation-states, organizations, social movements and individuals today share to a great extent a common discourse about the world.

Why is this so? On the most general level, as the processes of globalization proceed there is an attendant constraint upon such social entities to 'identify' themselves in relation to the global-human circumstances (Robertson 1992: 58). With increased communication and integration there is more cultural contact (but not necessarily agreement) which leads to a situation in which people make such schemas as we have identified here more explicit.

> In an increasingly globalized world there is a heightening of civilizational, societal, ethnic, regional, and indeed, individual self-consciousness. There are constraints on social entities to locate themselves within world history and the global future. Yet globalization in and of itself also involves the diffusion of the *expectation* of such identity decelerations (Robertson 1992: 27).

It is in this sense that talk by Japanese expatriates about such societies as England, Bahrain, the United States, Italy or Singapore, coded differently though they may be, implies discussing the essence of Japanese culture. Indeed, the very term 'Japanese culture', predicated as it is on the assumption of a culture common to a nation-state, is a product (and a continual expression) of global processes over the last hundred years.

Internationalization

Globalization is closely related to one of the most debated issues in Japan: the degree, extent or quality of the country's 'internationalization'. This question, endlessly discussed in the Japanese media and by academics, commentators and public opinion formers, refers to the extent to which Japan has become a more open society with regard to the rest of the world. Although the indices of 'internationalization' (*kokusaika*) are disputed, they include factors such as, and as diverse as, foreign language learning, travel abroad, having non-Japanese friends and consuming non-Japanese products. An alternative approach to the analysis of internationalization in Japan is to examine not the internal qualities of Japanese society, but rather the lives and attitudes of those Japanese living outside of Japan and who, most significantly, will eventually return, often to high-profile jobs. Put simply, what better place to examine the extent and character of cross-cultural ties than abroad where Japanese business people and their families live among (and must face daily) the real presence of members of other cultures. In places such as Singapore it is possible to examine the ways in which the exposure to 'others' touches the lives of Japanese people. We can then investigate how the dynamics of various business or leisure related occasions are related to the creation of bonds that both affirm and cross-cut membership in Japanese groups. We can debate whether we are witnessing the emergence of a new breed of cosmopolitan Japanese (Hannerz 1990). This is precisely the issue raised by Ben-Ari and Yong in their chapter on single Japanese female expatriates. These women, marginalized both from mainstream Singapore society and from the Japanese business community of men and their families, are an interesting revelation of the way in which both aspects of Japanese social structure and of attitudes reappear even in foreign fields. The result is that female expatriates find themselves engaged in strategies of adaptation and struggles for identity quite unknown to the majority of their male colleagues. The positive side is that such women, as a result, do not inhabit either physically or mentally the enclaves of their male compatriots (and their wives), but tend to make local friends and are emancipated from the restraints of many of the Japanese expatriate networks – the golf network for example. Despite their problems, the number of such women is growing and Singapore is a favourite destination for well-educated females with language skills, especially in English, who seek a more cosmopolitan lifestyle abroad and at home than their male colleagues. Women prove to be not only the harbingers of internationalization, but also in many ways those best adapted to the realities of globalization.

Examples of the dialectic between locals and Japanese which have a bearing on the question of internationalization can be seen not only in the examples of religion, management and consumption addressed elsewhere in this book, but equally in the areas of education and leisure. The settlement of large numbers of Japanese expatriates abroad has brought with it the usual problems of expatriate communities everywhere – access to medical care, familiar foods, housing, reading material, leisure-time contact with co-nationals and perhaps above all the problem of education. Businessmen in Southeast Asia are normally posted abroad with their families, often including school age children. For some of the more adventurous or genuinely internationalized, local or international schools are options. But for many the two-fold problems of language and being placed outside the highly competitive Japanese school system (performance in which determines access to the best universities and hence to enhanced employment opportunities throughout life) mean that parents want to keep their children within the familiar system. There are two ways of doing this – either leaving the children with relatives in Japan, or placing them in Japanese schools abroad. The Japanese Ministry of Education has responded to the presence of large numbers of Japanese living abroad by setting up a network of Japanese schools throughout the world, staffed by Japanese teachers sent from Japan and following precisely the curriculum of all other Japanese state schools. The biggest Japanese school in the world is in Singapore. This policy, while it does provide high-quality educational resources to Japanese families living abroad, also contributes to the isolation of Japanese children from the society to which their parents (overwhelmingly fathers) have been posted (Hook 1989). Those children who do attend local or international schools on the other hand (and some of those in Japanese schools who, like most children, are inquisitive and experimental and who find life abroad freer than at home) and who go back to Japan as *kikokushijo* or 'returnees' are increasingly seen as a major force for the genuine internationalization of Japanese society. Although problems exist regarding their educational and cultural assimilation back into Japanese society, many enter elite universities, promote the use and spread of foreign languages, eventually enter major businesses, international organizations and government agencies, and so, together with their parents, become a significant source of social and cultural change (Goodman 1993).

Leisure activities (and the quite literal internationalization of many of them especially sports) provides another and rather different example. This is illustrated very well in the chapter in this volume in which Ben-Ari finds that neither golfing occasions nor eating and drinking with co-workers in Singapore seem to lead in practice to very much 'internationalization', in the sense of creating and maintaining contact with locals or other expatriate foreigners, or in the sense of a greater awareness of the culture of others (an awareness that is greater than could be found within Japan). Interestingly rather, going overseas is not so much a process of 'going international' as it is one of 'going national'. During their period of service in Singapore, business expatriates tend both to create and maintain ties with Japanese from other geographical areas and workplaces in Japan, and to be much more aware of the cultural assumptions and practices that they share.

Getting Reflexive: the New Ethnography and the Problems of Cultural Exchange

The 'presence' of Japan in Southeast Asia, and in particular the cultural presence and the means of representing this presence raises an interesting question relating to a controversy that emerged during the 1980s and is still a live question: the problematic status of ethnographic writing. In response to this Fardon (1990) and his associates suggested that as social scientists we situate our writings in the context of localities of fieldwork. 'Ethnographic accounts are pervasively cross-referenced, both explicitly and implicitly, to accounts both within and outside conventionalized regions of enquiry' (Fardon 1990: 22). He continues:

> the projection for nonspecialists of regional representations (often via exemplary texts or, as commonly, secondary representations of them) which establish an image of place in terms of particular problematics which it typifies. At this point we are confronted with the radical simplifications which the residually universalistic aspirations of anthropology as the study of mankind must necessitate. Appadurai's formulation is again apposite: 'gatekeeping concepts' are those 'seen to limit anthropological theorizing about the place in question, and that define the quintessential and dominant questions of interest in the region' (1986: 357). Looking historically at the succession of problematics, we see also that the burning issues of anthropological theory are regionalized, so that a particular region comes to more general theoretical prominence in terms of certain issues. Regions become exemplars of types of features and problems: lineage in Africa, exchange in Melanesia, caste in India (Fardon 1990: 26)

This observation raises an extremely interesting theoretical issue in the analysis of relations between Japan and Southeast Asia. Fardon is of course addressing the particular problems of anthropology. But very similar questions can be raised in respect of history, sociology and comparative religion. Two problems appear here: that of disciplines and that of the problematics of cultures.

Each discipline tends to bring to bear on its subject matter, which may be the same society or set of issues, characteristic approaches. Each of these approaches, while it provides insights and analytical possibilities of a certain kind, necessarily excludes others: econometrics and narrative depiction are rather hard levels to combine in the same account. The project represented by this book is a multidisciplinary one, a feature which itself goes some way in addressing the multifaceted nature of the relationship between Japan and Southeast Asia as it expresses itself in the contemporary world. However the primary focus of the project is of course culture, whether seen by the anthropologist or by the management specialist. This raises a special problem: that any culture tends to become itself represented through a set of problematics invented, with varying degrees of accuracy, by the social scientists who study it. In the case of Japan two levels of this process are discernable. The first being the formulation of a set of broad categories which tend to organize knowledge production, categories such as groupism, management practices, socialization techniques and the alleged role of aesthetics in Japanese culture. And the second being a conceptual vocabulary within these primary categories used to marshall cultural phenomena. Many of these categories (*uchi/soto*, *honne/tatamae*, etc.) probably derive ultimately from Ruth Benedict's famous, misleading and highly influential 'patterns' approach to Japanese culture (Benedict 1946) and are routinely reproduced, with varying degrees of sophistication in textbooks of Japanese culture and society, down to this day.

This situation raises an interesting intellectual problem: the typical problematics through which Japanese culture is constructed and organized come, in a situation of culture-contact, into contact with the equally typical but quite different problematics of Southeast Asian societies. Some of the larger figures here we have already identified: a long history of cultural mixing, profound cultural formation through the agency of outside forces such as Islam, the experience of colonialism, and the intense experience of anti-colonial struggles. Within these figures society-specific troupes come into play: the fact that Thailand was never (technically at least) colonized; the essential multiethnicity of Singapore; the Islamic character of Indonesia and the Buddhist one of Burma, and so on. Cultural relations between Japan and Southeast Asia bring into play not only the forces of economics and politics, but also the negotiation of these cultural paradigms, mediated as they are by local intellectuals and expatriate social scientists. Understandings, and misunderstandings, between Japan and Southeast Asia must also be seen in this light, a point that in various ways contributors have attempted to emphasize and illustrate throughout this book. The negotiation of meanings becomes the fundamental level, and our project as such as much a hermeneutical one as a sociological one.

The Shapes of Things to Come

The present moment, with its flows of information, resources, people and images between Japan and Southeast Asia, is a key one for understanding both that specific relationship with all its economic, political and social implications, and broader processes of cultural interaction within the Asia-Pacific region and between that region and the rest of the world. Southeast Asia, through its growing prosperity and settled security situation since the cessation of the Vietnam War and the subsequent calming of the Cambodian situation, has both a sense of itself as a region and a new confidence. Japan, through trade, development efforts and the export of culture has come to have the highest profile that it has had in Southeast Asia since the war. Within Southeast Asia people are interested in the Japanese language, want to understand the historical process by which Japan has risen to become an economic superpower and are very much drawn to emulating an Asian nation which has created a dynamic economy while also managing to avoid many of the social problems that so often accompany such development, and which has been able to remain within a democratic framework while doing so.

But while interest in and goodwill towards Japan are at a high level, so are the criticisms of the flaws in the Japanese model. Throughout Southeast Asia people are becoming more alert to the dangers of economic domination, cultural imperialism, mercantilist politics, segregation of Japanese expatriate communities and lack of welcome in Japan for Southeast Asian workers, all of which Japan also represents. At this point it is easy to turn programmatic and moralistic and to urge mutual sensitivity, greater research and understanding on the part of the Japanese into the history, societies and sensibilities of Southeast Asian countries with which Japan has aid, business and tourism links. Fortunately there are signs that these are beginning to happen, even when driven by the engines of self-interest. One of the most hopeful signs is the interest in Japan about Southeast Asian cultures, and not just about those societies as markets. This is paralleled by the interest amongst Southeast Asians in studying not just Japanese economics and management techniques, but also culture and society and the ways in which

Japan has managed the transition to modernity (and maybe even to postmodernity) without massive social disruptions, without revolution and without descending again into political authoritarianism. This kind of interest is not confined only to a few: its reflection in books and current thinking has spread into the wider social circles. One of the most powerful agencies in this regard is of course the media, and the way in which the media on both sides portray the relationship between Japan and Southeast Asia will be an important measure of the way in which mutual perceptions evolve and are shaped.

In the past those cultures which have most impinged on Southeast Asia and have had a lasting effect have been those based on religion – successively on Hinduism, Buddhism and Islam. Even much of what has remained of the Western colonial powers has been religious in nature – the varieties of Christianity which have taken root in Southeast Asian soil, or the social initiatives – schools, hospitals and ideas of human rights. Japan has wrought enormous changes in Southeast Asia primarily through an economic presence and the social trends which have accompanied it – tourism, consumption, administrative and organizational techniques. Whether in the long run the Japanese presence will also be assimilated, transformed and reflected back in yet-to-emerge forms of Southeast Asian culture we can only speculate. But the enormity of the contemporary Japanese cultural presence cannot be denied and is sufficient in itself to provoke the investigation of its forms and processes. In any case, the nature of the world has changed as we enter together the period of late modernity and the old models no longer work in quite the same way. As economies themselves become increasingly 'economies of signs and space' (Lash and Urry 1994) rather than of things, and as they increasingly become the circulation of images and symbols rather than of objects, so the convergence between what used to be called 'economics' and what used to be called 'culture' increases to the point where in some cases they cease to be distinguishable. This is the moment now reached in the relationship between Japan and Southeast Asia: two sets of culture, each changing and each caught up in the operation of the world system, speaking to each other, often in a new language, a situation fraught with implications personal and social for those who live through it and which forces upon us the necessity of new modes of cultural analysis to grasp an example of what is fast becoming the normal way for the world to behave.

Chapter 2

"Global Talk"? Discourse and Cognition among Japanese Business Managers in Singapore

Eyal Ben-Ari

Introduction

There has been a profusion of sociological and anthropological discussions about the complex set of processes termed "globalization" or "internationalization" in the past two decades. These debates have attempted to grapple with the implications of recent developments in the world economy and political order. Several of these developments have emerged in the wake of such processes as better communications, cheaper transport, new divisions of national and international labor, the effects of powerful trade and capital flows, and the intense activities of transnational corporations. From a cultural point of view, these processes have led to intense interactions between various "cosmopolitans" and "locals," and to powerful contentions about "global" or "native" identities (Hannerz 1992). From a sociological point of view, these trends have been accompanied by diverse forms of international migration and movements of peoples. An important group now travelling in ever greater numbers are the managers and engineers of transnational companies who converge on what Cohen (1997) calls "global cities."

This chapter centers on a group of such expatriate managers in one global city in order to uncover how the meanings that guide their mundane, everyday activities are related to their interactions with "locals" (and other "foreigners") and to formulations about their identity. Specifically, my focus is on the cognitive schemas — alternative terms are lay theories, interpretive schemes, or folk models (Ortner 1973; D'Andrade 1992: 29) — that guide the activities of Japanese business executives in Singapore. In a previous paper (Ben-Ari 2000), uncovering these schemas allowed me to show what is entailed by the unquestioned, taken-for-granted knowledge that "every Japanese business person knows[1]." In this chapter I develop my examination of these schemas in two further directions. First, I show how the interpretive models that Japanese expatriates use are derived not only from Japan's national culture. Rather, I explain how these schemas also result from a rather specific view of the world as one unit. In this respect, I follow Robertson (1992), who refers to the "world" in inverted commas to underline the sense of a growing consciousness of (but not necessarily consensus about) the global situation that is found among many contemporary groups. Second, I offer some perspectives (or speculations) on the comparative aspects of these cognitive schemas. I do so by contrasting the case of Japanese business people to those of other expatriates and to the perceptions of other national groups. In other words, my aim is to situate the case of Japanese business expatriates in Singapore within a much wider (indeed, world-wide) context of social and cultural aspects of globalization.

Why are these issues important? Groups that frame and formulate contemporary notions of cross-cultural identity include a large variety of cultural mediators, business leaders, politicians, media representatives, intellectuals, academics, members of "third cultures" (such as transnational movements and international organizations) and (increasingly) expatriates. Yet expatriates (along with migrants), who are posted abroad for a number of years, are the people who are in constant contact with members of other cultures and who most acutely face the personal issues of accounting for, and understanding, globalization. These people are not corporate presidents or political leaders who are used to media interviews and who typically deal with (to put this point by way of the Japanese example) such issues as Japan's trade surplus or the need to increase its political and security presence around the world. Rather expatriates are the people who work overseas and who carry out debates about the "global–human situation" (although they may not use this kind of term) on a daily basis.

My argument is thus simply that the increasing numbers of expatriate managers and engineers in itself makes the problems of accounting for globalization much more intense. Psychologists and anthropologists have demonstrated that an important task in adulthood is to achieve a sense of coherence: individuals need to weave disparate experiences into a comprehensible story or personal narrative of their lives (Cohen 1994; Spencer 1990; Sugarman 1986: 129–30). What seems to be happening during this historical period is that issues of face-to-face cross-cultural contacts are a central element in constructing personal accounts. Overseas secondments thus become "major life events," transition points in the human life-cycle for formulating the criteria and terms by which people ask and evaluate such questions as "who they are" and "where are they going."

Until the 1980s, an overseas assignment in many Japanese companies was seen as something to be undertaken under pressure. Yet since that period, and especially in light of the rapid expansion of Japanese corporations into countries around the world, such assignments have begun to be viewed as imperative for promotion into senior posts. Partly as a reaction to these changes, a number of scholars have begun to publish studies about such issues as executives who have returned to Japan (White 1988) or returnee schoolchildren (Goodman 1991; Kobayashi 1978). While these studies focus on the difficulties faced upon a return to Japan, as of yet, apart from some limited scholarly work (Befu and Stalker 1996; Inamura 1982; Hamada 1992) or journalistic observations (Kotkin 1993; Sender 1995), no extended study of Japanese expatriates in their host country has ever been published in English. The research I carried out between 1992–1994 and for a short while in 1995[2], is aimed at filling this lacuna.

Japanese Corporations, Expatriate Managers and a Global City

Why study Japanese managers in Singapore? An answer to the question involves the move of Japanese businesses abroad; the role of the people executing and enacting this move; the centrality of Singapore in world-wide and regional terms; and the special characteristics of this global city.

While post-war Japanese businesses began to move outside the country during the 1960s, the massive relocation to Southeast Asia (at the beginning the ASEAN countries and later Indochina) began in the 1970s (Nakane 1974; Sender 1995). At the start, this move usually embraced production and servicing facilities and firms dealing in international trade. In the past fifteen or so years it has also consisted of financial services (Soderberg 2000). Again, while the first moves into the area were undertaken by large Japanese corporations, in recent years small and medium-sized companies have increasingly come in their wake. In this context, it has been primarily in Singapore that business headquarters and facilities for many companies in the region are located (Choy and Yeo 1990). Indeed, by some calculations as much as one-fourth of Singapore's GDP is generated by Japanese companies (Cronin 1992).

By some estimates (Kotkin 1993) there are over 600,000 Japanese expatriates around the world at one specific time. Unlike tourists, these people reside in their "host" countries for periods ranging between two to five years, and are overwhelmingly business men and their families. The Japanese expatriate community in Singapore itself is very large (it is the second largest after the American community) and relatively homogeneous. It now numbers over twenty thousand people and is served by three schools and a kindergarten, shops selling various Japanese merchandise, booksellers (Ng and Ben-Ari in this volume), restaurants and bars, special markets or even real-estate agents and home-moving companies. Like such communities around the world, it comprises primarily the people who manage Japanese businesses and their family members.

But the importance of Singapore as a research site is not limited to its economic might, to the economic presence of Japanese companies in the island-state, or to the size of the Japanese expatriate community there. First, Singapore is a prime example of a global city. The placement of corporate headquarters in this city-state in wake of shifts in the world economy has been compounded by the long-term placement of financial services, production plants, and servicing facilities there. Second, being integrated into the world economy Singapore has become a multicultural, multi-ethnic, and certainly multilingual city in which managerial ideologies, tastes, and consumption patterns are drawn more from an emerging global culture than from the national culture (Cohen 1997: 167). In this sense then, Singapore provides a dense concentration of arenas for contact and interaction between different (national) business communities. Third, the very economic success of Singapore is an issue which raises, for Japanese as for others, questions about what Wee (1996) has termed "East Asian Modernity." In other words, because the Singaporean city-state combines elements of ideals of "East" and "West" and is a prime example of "Asian success," it raises questions in ways that other world cities — London or Paris, for example — do not.

Careering and Overseas Secondment [3]

Organizations design career paths in order to control — predict, supervise and regulate — the movement or flow of individuals through them. From individuals' perspectives, however, careers are uncertain and unpredictable because only some people will be promoted. This picture may contradict many popular and academic portrayals of Japanese workplaces: while the life-time employment system (applicable to men in large corporations) usually implies job security, it is nevertheless marked by uncertainties over promotion because many mid-level positions are limited and job movements are often undertaken without advancement (Skinner 1983: 68; Hamada 1992). As a consequence of these circumstances, individuals find that they must constantly and actively undertake strategies to assure promotion. Critical to formulating these strategies, however, are certain cultural guide-lines or schemas which provide the standards by which people appraise themselves (and are appraised by others), and evaluate their movement according to the organization's pathways, routes and timetables (Plath 1983: 3).

What does the schema which governs the career strategies of Japanese business managers look like? And how is it related to overseas assignments? An answer to these questions involves a cognitive schema of Japanese white-collar organizational life. At base, Japanese business people conceive of their career as a movement within the company through patterns of rotation within headquarters, and between headquarters and branch offices or facilities. According to their understandings, while this movement may take place sideways to relatively equivalent roles or upwards to more important posts, it is definitely not a smooth or automatic flow from one position to another. Rather, executives constantly maneuver and jostle for promotion to an ever-decreasing number of senior posts. Thus in competing for advancement, they must interpret their relative chances, formulate appropriate strategies and then actively pursue them by succeeding in business dealings and cultivating support networks (Ben-Ari, in this volume). Within this perspective each new assignment is construed in terms of the advantages and disadvantages for careering that it presents.

41

It is against this background that overseas assignments should be seen. While such secondments fit with the organizational logic of rotation, they are also promotions. Because (whatever their legal definition) companies situated outside of Japan are like "daughter companies," employees are usually assigned to posts that are a notch above the positions they filled in Japan: people who were department heads in Japan become division heads overseas, and section heads become department heads. Hence in comparison with postings to new positions in Japan, stints abroad present opportunities to handle greater responsibilities and more important tasks. To reiterate a point made earlier, today overseas secondment has become a normal part of many managerial careers. It used to be so in the general trading companies (Yoshino and Lifson 1988) and shipping or air companies, but now it is increasingly becoming a prerequisite for individual advancement in very many companies (including medium-sized and small firms) (Hamada 1992: 155). Yet notions about careering are refracted and actualized through more general cognitive schemas of the world.

Centers, Peripheries and Careering

Probably the most common metaphor used by the business men I interviewed is that of the globe as comprising arrays of "centers and peripheries." This metaphor centers on the relations between hubs of economic activities and various regional bases within the structure of the world's political economy. More specifically, the idea is one of Japan as a center and the various outposts and stations abroad as peripheries. According to this logic, Japanese expatriates are sent from the center to provide knowledge and techniques, while "peripherals" are more static in that they usually stay in their place to receive learning and expertise. In addition, it is at the center where power and authority reside and "the" place where things happen. I began to be aware of this when I went over my field notes. For example, when I talked to the chief of a Japanese press bureau, he referred to his superiors in Tokyo in rather conventional terms as "the people on top." A senior executive in a servicing facility with three years of experience in Singapore observed,

> It doesn't really matter if it's Europe or America or Singapore. In principle, Tokyo always looks at your performance, at how you work ... The question they always ask is how much this

person has contributed to the company. That's what they look at.

Thus by using such body-imagery as "head-quarters" or "head-office," or arboreal and spatial metaphors as "branch" or "out-post," Japanese managers underscore the preeminence, hierarchy and "mental" functions of the Japanese center.

In addition, a prevalent idea is that within the Japanese center, rivalry is played out almost exclusively between Japanese companies. Thus corporate success is overwhelmingly measured in terms of position relative to other Japanese companies. Along these lines, the general manager of Sumitomo Bank noted that

> This is the time of Southeast Asia and not America or Europe and that's why places like Singapore or Hong Kong are so important. From the bank's point of view they are strategically important and that's why it's a challenge to be here ... Especially for Sumitomo Bank we are lagging behind the other Japanese City Banks and my mission is to recover position here in Singapore.

In a like manner, while admitting that their primary competition is with the American company Caterpillar, an executive from Komatsu was quick to point out that "our business is to fight with Caterpillar, they are our big competitor; but also we compete with Hitachi and Kobleco." For a Seiko engineer, the adversaries are Citizen and Casio and "yes well, also the Swiss watch makers." One of the top managers of a furniture making firm told me:

> In Japan we are one of the four biggest companies for office furniture; everyone knows about us and even if we are a young company here in Singapore it's good to start with the brand name of Uchida because there are about 1,500 Japanese companies in Singapore.

Finally, a section manager in the Bank of Tokyo explained this idea in the following manner:

> In Japan there are different rankings for companies. If one enters a grade-one company and leaves the company, he will have to enter a grade-two company the next time. If he leaves the second company again this time he will have to join a grade-three company.

The terms people use to characterize "centers" and "peripheries" portray a vibrant globe in which their company competes with other (mainly Japanese) enterprises for markets, goods and sources. But what is of importance here is that the map of the world — the cognitive schema of the "globe" held by these executives — is arranged according to how the firm's operations bear upon an individual's prospects for promotion. It is an important point because overseas secondments represent both opportunities and dangers for interfirm promotion.

The issues that interviewees raised in regard to the potentials and hazards of a stint abroad centered on mastery of new skills, prospects for striking successful deals, and networking. The managing director of one of Sony's factories in the island told me that whereas in Japan he had concentrated mainly on design and development, the stint abroad allowed him to develop his managerial skills and to master the intricacies of finance. A manager from a printing company evoked the strong Japanese stress on organizational learning (Rohlen 1992) when he proposed that his period in Singapore offered many opportunities for study and should be seen as part of "a life-long learning process in the organization: we must study till we die." A banker noted how "in Singapore, you can make decisions, decide about new directions, implement new things." Other issues raised by the men I talked to involved learning about new markets, garnering sales and marketing skills, managing ethnically diverse employees, or mastering English. An engineer from Kitamura told me that while in Japan he participated primarily in small projects, in Singapore "I am the number two man in the company and take care of basically everything that comes here as well as sales, negotiations, worker salaries, planning, and import and export."

While a period in Singapore (or any other place outside Japan) is usually seen as useful, many expatriates pointed out the dangers of secondment. Time and again I was told that from the point of view of careering, personal resources acquired overseas may hinder prospects for advancement because they may preclude accumulating knowledge and expertise within Japan. The engineer from Kitamura told me that he would have to "get used and adjust to the different pace of working in Japan." The most common issue related to overseas secondment, however, centered on the possible "disconnection" from networks of personal supporters (superiors, peers and underlings) in Japan (see also Hamada 1992: 146ff).

Accordingly, many men talked about how their careers depended on Tokyo and about the need to constantly monitor their relations and contacts with important people at "head office". An executive from a heavy machinery firm put this point in rather stark terms:

> [T]here is a danger [to overseas postings] because you don't know what will be in the future. If you will be here too much time, then they may not know you in Tokyo; and so you constantly have to show Tokyo that you are working hard, and that they will constantly say Yamamoto is in Singapore but he works hard. Everything is controlled from Tokyo, your salary, your promotion. If I stay here for twenty years maybe I will have a lot of power but I am finished in Tokyo because they will not know me.

Overseas secondment is thus integrated within an understanding of the dynamics of intra-company competition for promotion. In this manner, global centers and peripheries are personalized: what interests people are their relative standings *vis-à-vis* their organizational consociates. Looking at things from Singapore (or, again, from any such world city) the conclusion Japanese business executives reach is that one way to "get ahead" at the center is to succeed for the company abroad.

A Unique Japan: Boundaries and Cultural Mediation

The second schema, wielded by the business expatriates to interpret their stint in Singapore is based on a popular view of Japanese uniqueness termed *Nihonjinron* [lit. theories of the Japanese] (Dale 1986; Befu and Manabe 1991; Manabe and Befu 1992). Manabe (1992) suggests that *Nihonjinron* theories tend to stress the following characteristics: the singularity, uniqueness and homogeneity of Japanese society; the (essentialist) need for Japanese "blood" for mutual understanding and communication: the utter incapacity of foreigners to fully master Japanese culture and language; the coextension of Japan's territorial, social and cultural boundaries; and the exclusion of non-Japanese in areas of marriage, employment, teaching, and political and artistic leadership. In Singapore this schema is utilized to explain cross-cultural contacts within the workplace and to reason about the long-term significance of overseas secondment.

In more candid interviews, managers explained that despite the formal division of labor or legal distinctions within their work-places, the most significant differentiation centered on an "invisible" boundary between Japanese and Singaporean members. To put this point rather starkly, for Japanese expatriates the "real," personally relevant and culturally shared, organization is the one in which only Japanese people participate. To take an example from my field notes, when an executive of Toyota's trading company accompanied me to the door at the end of our interview, he stopped and told me to look at the employees sitting in one large hall:

> You see, there are maybe eighty employees here. You can't see it, but only about ten of them belong to the real company; the Japanese belong to the real company.

A similar instance was encountered by Kotkin (1993: 128) when an executive in one of the giant trading firms told him: "we are not really with the others. Every morning my manger says 'Good morning,' and at the end of the day 'Good-bye,' to the British staff but that's the extent of it. In Japanese and with Japanese we talk about all our other interests."

At one level, focusing on the "real" company fits with expatriates' interest in pursuing successful careers at the head office in Japan. At another level, however, such depictions involve an assumption about the distinctive understandings and connec-tions that only Japanese people can have. This schema then, is basically essentialist, for it is predicated on the substance, the embodiment of Japanese-ness. Japanese culture, according to this schema, is so unique, so special that only some people can participate in it. A 40-year-old sales manager at Matsushita talked about Japan having a "mono culture," he emphasized that "being homogeneous, we need special training in the company to make us aware of the existence of other cultures." The organizational implications of this model, in turn, predicate Japanese expatriates as cultural mediators. The notion of mediation was very often phrased in humorous terms as when I was told that the principal role of Japanese in Singapore was to decode documents or telephone messages for local staff[4]. A related, and more serious, aspect consists of instructing locals about Japanese practices and etiquette. A manager at a servicing facility for a large manufacturer told me about how uncomfortable he and his colleagues feel when called by their name without the addition of "-san." He went on to tell me how the staff have to teach each newly recruited local employee to add "-san" to Japanese people's names.

The significance of these issues was made clear to me when the managing director of a large manufacturing firm called his role that of "domestic diplomat." He maintained that his aim is to promote goodwill and to intentionally and consciously interact with the locals. In the organizational literature, mediators have usually been conceptualized as "boundary spanners" between the organization and its environment (Aldrich 1979; Aldrich and Herker 1977) with their function including the recruitment of resources, gathering information, and managing public relations. But as the case of Japanese executives in Singapore underscores, such mediators also translate between different cultures and languages within an organization. They may mediate two boundaries: the (national) cultural and the organizational.

In explaining the uniqueness of Japanese culture and its distance from local (Singaporean) culture, many executives invoked attributes of Japanese corporate culture. Thus for example, the lack of "teamwork," "interdependence," "cooperation," or "loyalty" of Singaporeans came up time and again in the interviews. A section head in an electronics firm told me that the local staff tended to report for work late, to lack enthusiasm and initiative, and to be over defensive when their mistakes were pointed out. In addition, he added, these people often wasted time on "personal grooming during office hours: they spend half an hour in the bathroom putting on make up or something . . . and idle or talk to each other during office hours". The director of Fuji Xerox told me that drinking with non-Japanese is difficult because "in Japan we have nomi-communication [lit. drinking communication]," which by implication only Japanese can understand. Similarly, the manager of the Sony factory reported that as the Japanese expatriates had encountered various problems of communication, they had instituted a weekly meeting exclusively for the Japanese whatever their official title or position. While he stressed that this was purely a forum for communication and not for decision making, the implication of excluding non-Japanese was clear. A manager at a giant electronics firm evoked another Japanese "quality":

> When something goes wrong, Japanese say "sorry" first and then carry on with the job. Singaporeans say "its not my fault" — they push the blame to others . . . Singaporeans also

47

think about resignation when they want to improve their job prospects. Japanese workers are like sumo wrestlers: they *gambaru* [persevere] to the end. They don't give up easily.

In a similar manner, the chief of the local office of a major Japanese newspaper told me:

> In Singapore, things tend to work out in a contractual way, unlike Japan; we work things out through human relationships between people (*hito to hito no tsukiai*). In Japan, we emphasize human relationships (*ningen-kankei*). In a company, no matter what job you are assigned, nobody will complain. We are like a family, however, Singaporeans only do what they are assigned ... I think many Singaporeans consider work in monetary terms. Many Singaporeans like to job-hop just because they can get a better salary ... As I've said, a Japanese company is like a family. If you transfer into a new company, it is very difficult for you to merge into the new circle. The people in the new company will treat you like an alien (*yoso no mono*).

Corollaries of the stress on the uniqueness of Japanese culture are views about the risks of losing ones's Japanese essence: to appear to "have gone native," to be seen as too localized. Thus a consistent stress in the interviews was the sense that expatriates must maintain the appearance — the demeanor, language and attire — of Japanese. A high-level executive in one of the securities firms noted that he dressed differently when meeting Singaporeans and when meeting other Japanese: "When I meet Japanese guests I always wear a suit. If I don't I will feel awkward, very uneasy. Maybe they will think that I am too localized, too relaxed. So in order that they don't get that impression I dress this way." In contemporary Japan these seem to be rather important issues as Merry White (1988) and Roger Goodman (1991) point out. Overseas secondments pose threats to people's "Japaneseness" through overexposure to "other" cultures. Accordingly, I was sometimes told by my interviewees of their being "rehabilitated" or "reeducated" upon returning to Japan.

Civilization, the "West," and "Asia"

The third schema is based on an explicit conceptualization of the globe as a whole unit. This is not a view of the world, as Robertson

(1992: 78) proposes, comprising a symmetrical or asymmetrical series of relatively closed societal communities. Rather, the focus is on groups of societies and the ordering principle at base of this view is that of "civilization." According to this schema societies around the world either belong to, or are situated outside of, a family or company of "civilized societies." This is not a static model, for societies who wish to enter this select company can and must adopt certain standards of refinement and urbanity by which it is distinguished. As Gong (1984) explains, this schema is related to the emergence of an international standard of "civilization" at the end of the nineteenth century and the beginning of the twentieth century. While his specific contentions center on the emergence of international law as the mechanism for regulating inter-state relations, he is careful to point out that this legal framework entailed not only political or economic implications, but cultural or civilizational ones as well. As Wallerstein (1991: 223–4) explains, the idea of "civilization" which emerged out of the European centers of the time was an ideological construct which implied both inevitability and desirability. According to this view the capitalist world-economy in itself represented progress because it was "civilizing."

Today, this historical model has become a rather widespread interpretive schema found around the "developed" world. Concretely, this model provides criteria by which such people as the Japanese business expatriates that I studied (and others) appraise whether certain societies should or should not be included in the family of "civilized societies." These standards include both technological advancement and the cultivation of style, etiquette, and interpersonal behavior. In Stephen Mennel's (cited in Robertson 1992: 117) evocative metaphor this schema is based on what can be called "the globalization of manners." Moreover, as I will presently demonstrate, this schema intersects, reinforces *and* weakens the previous two models I have outlined.

The following passages underscore these contentions (also Ben-Ari, 2000). When I interviewed the vice-president from Nomura, he explained that during an earlier phase in his career he had been assigned to Bahrain:

> I don't want to sound prejudiced, but they are less cultivated like in their language ability or mathematics ability so we employed people from other countries like India and didn't

rely on the Bahrainis; In London, the British are very similar to the Japanese in their mentality.

Along similar lines, when I asked a senior manager at one of the city banks about the kind of preparation that he thought would benefit employees before going abroad he answered:

> Listen, language is important, but I would also like young Japanese to learn the culture and customs of overseas countries; like how to dine. For example, I often feel shame that they don't know which glass of wine to use, how to eat with a knife and fork, how to offer bread to clients.

These examples underscore something that Gong (1984: 245) pointed out over a decade ago: such countries as Thailand, China and Japan have long been the sites of debates about fusing desirable European standards with their own notions of historical "civilization." From our perspective, such passages accent the complex manner by which Japan's location is interpreted in this schema. Japan is concurrently a "civilized society" that other societies must try and emulate, and one that itself must emulate more advanced countries.

Yet the full complexity of this schema is revealed in regard to how Singapore is construed. From our perspective, what is interesting is that for Japanese expatriates Singapore becomes a sort of "test case" through which to explore notions of Asian-ness and Westernization. Take the ambivalence toward "Japanese" and "Western" standards of civilization as they bear on organizational behavior. One manager noted the individualism of the Singaporeans: "It is usual for the Japanese to ask a colleague or friend 'What did you do last night?' To show concern and as a form of a greeting. But this may be misunderstood by a Singaporean as an infringement on their privacy." Evoking the general category of "development" (and hence progress and cultivation), a banker observed, "I think that Singaporeans job-hop too much, if they would not do so then maybe Singapore can also be a developed country (*senshinkoku*)." A manager at an electricity works company was more specific when he said:

> I think Singapore is not so different from Japan. Singapore has a Chinese Asian kind of culture, so it's not so different from Japan ... [But] there are some differences. For example,

when the phone is ringing and the person at the desk is not in, nobody wants to pick up the phone. They say it's not their job to pick up someone else's phone. But Japanese will pick up the phone even if it's not theirs. A Singaporean friend says Singaporeans don't like others to do their job, so maybe that's the difference. I think it's a Westernized way of thinking.

Another manager at one of the Japanese banks linked individual action to a society's history:

Japanese will not job-hop for a twenty or thirty dollars increment in their salary ... If you ask Singaporeans to do something new, they will say "Sorry, that's not my job"; unlike Japanese ... Perhaps it's because of the short history of Singapore.

The director of Fuji Xerox echoed these points:

If you go to England, a lot of countryside, there's a lot of history, there are castles, lots of museums. But come down to Singapore's museum, not so much; one time is OK, unfortunately. Really history is very important, Japan has a lot of history. When I am in Japan ... any time I can visit Kyoto, I can visit Nara by bus tour ... Much history and very interesting, But Singapore, not so much interesting, maybe only sports life.

Such observations, which came up in a number of interviews, linked the lack of appreciation on the part of Singaporeans of "who they are" (of their tradition and roots) to the very potential for civilizability.

Global Talk

But there is more here. Take the following two passages: one related to the workplace and one more general in its nature. A senior engineer from Seiko who had been in Singapore for four years, talked about group orientation: "As you know the Japanese like working in groups and here they are relatively individualists. You have to change their way of thinking and to teach them how to work in groups like in the new production system we brought here about three years ago." Evoking both the exclusivist Japanese model and the schema of civilized societies, a personnel manager at a large firm ruminated:

Let me say this directly. Maybe you as a European feel that we and the Singaporeans are the same thing: we have the same black hair, brown eyes, or color of the skin. But I feel that although we all look like orientals as though we are similar to each other, the Singaporeans are very different. They have names like Desmond or Tom, and this creates a very strange feeling for me; as though they are in some way Western. It's funny, their roots are in China and in this way they have a relation to us Japanese. But the younger generation here have lost their identity because they don't speak good Chinese, they have lost their Chinese [language] ... The personal philosophy of many of them is very Western so many times I feel I don't understand them. Many times they will say what they think as a logical opinion and then I don't have the same feeling of understanding them like I do other Japanese.

At one level these two passages focus on differences: on attitudes to work and about outlooks on life. Yet they also belong to what Robertson (1992: 113) refers to as "global talk": "the expansion of the rhetoric of globality, globalization, and internationalization ... across the world as a relatively autonomous mode of discourse." The very terms that these men use — "groups," "individualists," "orientals," "European" — are indicators of cultural identity and belonging which can be found anywhere around the contemporary world. Such expressions draw upon familiar world-wide parlance for clarifying and explicating issues involving both singularity and sameness.

The use of a rather conventional set of images and phrases for talking about the modern world is not incidental. Robertson (1992: 135) suggests that "globalization involves the development of something like a global culture — not as normatively binding, but in the sense of a general mode of discourse about the world as a whole *and* its variety" (emphasis in original). Thus what has developed over the last hundred or so years is not a world-wide consensus about the location of various cultures and societies. Rather there is a very basic commonality in the actual terms and the criteria used by different groups, organizations or movements in discussions and contentions about the world.

Seen in this light, the models that I examined — centers and peripheries, a unique (Japanese) society, and "civilized societies" as they bear upon personal careering — take on a different perspective. My contention is that while "colored" by Japanese attitudes and the special circumstances of Singapore, they nevertheless all draw upon (and contribute to) world-wide models and discursive terms. Let us examine this realization in regard to each model in turn, and then move on to some comparative issues that undergird them all.

Corporate Culture

In the first model Japan, America and Europe (and increasingly China) are conceived of as being centers or cores while their business outposts are thought of as peripheries. The idea here is that centers provide managerial personnel and knowledge while the periphery supplies such things as labor, resources and goods. In addition, it is the center that has the power to bestow or withhold recognition and acknowledgment of the success of peripheries. This model is probably the most common to executives, managers and engineers the world over. Take notions like "organizational" or "corporate culture" which have been bandied about in the past 25 years. Whether used as a prescriptive device for improving organizational performance (Bartlett and Ghoshal 1995) or a critical means to deconstruct how corporations control employees (and managers) (Kunda 1992), these terms are rooted in what could be called a model of modern (and post-modern) organizational life in which elements of careering, advancement, networking and success are central. This is not to deny that in its Japanese guise this model is more company centered, but it is to state that the very terms with which executives around the world interpret and plan for their careers are derived from a world-wide culture of corporations.

Cultural Nationalism

As we saw, the second schema is based on the *Nihonjinron* notion in which Japanese culture is considered to be a delimited and unique entity. The main idea here is of cultural contact and mediation between the bounded Japanese entity and other cultures. Japanese expatriates (and to a lesser degree other persons) translate and negotiate the understandings and expectations of these cultures. But if one sees, as Befu and Manabe (1991) suggest,

Nihonjinron as a version of Japan's cultural nationalism, one begins to understand that the very term "Japanese culture" is based on the assumption of a culture common to a nation-state. This idea of the nation-state as the locus of identity is, in turn, a modern one which is the product (and a continual expression) of global processes over the last 200 years (Cohen 1994: chapter 6).

International Standards

The third model involves a picture of a family of "civilized societies." The central image is one of certain international standards of advancement and cultivation which a country must meet before being recognized (by others) as civilized. In this view Japan is contradictorily perceived as belonging and as not (just yet) belonging to a set of advanced civilizations. This model is the most explicitly global in its perspective and contents. It reflects developments that have been taking place in the last hundred years with the spread of European (and later American) cultural standards to virtually every country and region around the globe.

Sociologically speaking, the development of such "global talk" in which issues of similarity and difference are debated is itself related to the rapid diffusion of ideas through various media. The Japanese business expatriates that I interviewed gather their ideas not only from interpersonal contacts. They also use ideas from a variety of intellectual products — books, magazine articles, radio and television programs — to make sense of their worlds. To put this point by way of the second schema, people use new technologies to push the old traditions of *Nihonjinron* (Manabe 1992). I encountered a revealing illustration of this point towards the end of my fieldwork. During our interview, the director of an office equipment manufacturer told me how he had read and begun to apply the ideas of Kenichi Ohmae (Japan's "management guru"). He constructed his personal narrative by using Ohmae's ideas of company leaders breaking down economic barriers and overcoming state intervention.

Yet while all these models are predicated upon a common world-wide discourse, they categorically do not imply a homogenization of views. Cohen (1997: 169: also Hannerz 1992, Appadurai 1996: 188–90) suggests that "a perverse feature of globalization at the cultural level is that it has brought about the fragmentation and multiplication of identities." And, as Robertson

(1992: 27) reminds us, "globalization in and of itself also involves the diffusion of the expectation of such identity decelerations." More specifically the spread of globalization has entailed an attendant constraint upon various groups to "identify" themselves in relation to global-human circumstances (Robertson 1992: 58). With increased communication and integration there is more cultural contact (but not necessarily agreement) which leads to a situation in which people mobilize such schemas as I have examined here in order to explain where they stand in regard to such things as world history and the global future.

Comparative Perspectives

In what respect do the models I have set out for the Japanese expatriate group differ from the schemas used by other such groups? In what way, for example, is *Nihonjinron* different from the strong Chinese (Dikotter 1990) or Jewish sense of distinctiveness based on a sense of venerable and noble beginnings? Or, to take another example, are Japanese views of the world different from the perspectives of other "Asians" — like Koreans, Thais or the Chinese — where the world's races are depicted as a hierarchy where the yellow race has a particularly uneasy power position in the middle? Given limits of space, in what follows I can only offer some speculations or hypotheses about the comparative aspects of this chapter.

Economics and politics

As I reviewed the interviews, I found that issues related to military strength and standing, or to international political relations, were altogether missing from people's stated interpretations of the world. For the overwhelming majority of the people I talked to, international politics, and especially security matters, seemed to be a sort of "invisible" issue. By the term "invisible" I do not mean that the expatriates I interviewed were not aware of politics. When prodded, they could often make rather penetrating analyses of various developments in the world's political order. Rather, the Japanese expatriates hardly used political or military terms to account for their personal circumstances or the circumstances of their companies. This "invisibility" seems to be a peculiarity of contemporary Japan (and perhaps of Germany): national security in this society is usually formulated in comprehensive "economic" terms. Thus, to put it simply, if Americans tend to view the world order of centers and peripheries in terms of military might *and* economic power, the Japanese do so primarily in terms of economics (Samuels 1994; Katzenstein 1996).

Overseas secondment, individuals and the state

Many languages contain terms denoting long-term residents outside their country of citizenship. In English the word "expatriate" means a resident of a country in which one is not a native. Its slightly archaic connotation is negative as in "to expatriate," meaning to expel or banish. The word in Japanese, "*chuzaiin*" is more neutral and means to be resident overseas, or personnel that are placed in a foreign country for some time. In Hebrew, however, the term "*shlichim*" which is used to refer to expatriate managers and representatives of different companies was (and still is) originally used to allude to state representatives. Hence, it carries the undertone of being a representative of a collective, of the whole nation-state or organizations within it. In contrast to the English or Japanese terms, the stress in Hebrew is on going abroad to achieve some collective aims. Hence, in contrast to stereotypes of Japanese employees as being group oriented, it may be much easier to explicitly link overseas secondments to personal advancement and careering in English or Japanese speaking circles than in Hebrew speaking ones.

The Nation-State, Peoplehood and Identity

Similarly, while there are cross-cultural equivalents of *Nihonjinron*, they differ in emphasis. Singapore has a small Jewish community (roughly 400 people) who are citizens of that state and an Israeli community of about 300 people (who are all Israeli citizens). In addition there are hundreds of American, Australian and European Jews on the island. Based on a small research project into the Israeli community and numerous conversations with members of the other two groups in the island, I initially thought that a possible parallel of *Nihonjinron* theories of uniqueness were various models of the essence of Jewish-ness. In my interviews in Singapore I often heard about stereotypical Jewish traits such as the "Jewish mind" or the "Jewish proclivity for business."

But when I began to look for the organizational equivalent of Japanese management methods I found that it made very little sense to talk about a Jewish model of organizational techniques. It seems that for each of the three different groups of Jews that I had met, the link of culture and organization was different: for Singaporean Jews it centered on Singaporean methods (a strong business orientation), the Americans spoke about American corporate culture (for example, efficiency and a "can do spirit"), and the Israelis consistently invoked Israeli organizational principles (like initiative or flexibility). Thus from this point of view, the identification of Japanese traits with peoplehood and specific national and organizational characteristics seems to be a rather special construct.

National identity and international encounters

These findings are echoed in Befu and Manabe's (1991) suggestions. They propose that when *Nihonjinron* is placed in a comparative perspective, it becomes clear that in Japan cultural identity is synonymous with national identity. Historically speaking, the remarkable fact about Japan is that in the process of creating a modern state the Japanese government faced little need to suppress the primordial sentiments embodied in *Nihonjinron*, but instead exploited them to the full (Befu and Manabe 1991: 108). Paradoxically then, it seems that it is outside the country that this isomorphism between peoplehood and the nation-state is most strongly reinforced. In other words, for many Japanese, the very experience of being expatriates, or more generally of travelling abroad, strengthens these concepts.

There may be two interrelated reasons for this situation. First, intercultural contact in and of itself carries demands for identification and self-identification. Thus in their daily lives, expatriates are constantly forced to define who they are and who they are interacting with. In this process they "naturally" tend to fall back upon models readily available to them such as *Nihonjinron*. Second, as Befu and Manabe (1991: 110) note, when compared to Americans (for example) foreigners have always been very important for self-definition in Japan. Whether through the sale of bestsellers by foreign experts or more humdrum questioning of outsiders about their opinion of Japan, the opinions of "aliens" has always been important in Japan. Thus, to return to my case, the very process of deterritorialization that these expatriates undergo leads to a strengthening of imagery linking territory, culture and nationhood. To put this point rather picturesquely, many Japanese travel to Singapore (and other places) to discover their Japanese-ness.

"Internationalization"

This imagery is related to another phenomenon. When referring to "globalization" many Japanese ordinarily use the term *"kokusai-ka,"* which, strictly speaking, means "internationalization." This denotation is not a simple matter of incorrect or sloppy translation. For in underscoring the relations between nations, *kokusaika* clearly predicates the cultural power of the nation-state as a political entity with clear geographical boundaries (Befu and Stalker 1996: 102). Accordingly, when Japanese expatriate managers in Singapore deliberate issues related to the "internationalization" of Japan, they assume that the relevant "culture" and its derivatives (like personal or organizational identities) is the national-culture. This assumption is based on an unproblematic notion of the distinctiveness of societies, nations, and cultures. Indeed, in Japan, as in some other societies, this "fact" is so taken for granted that each country is seen to embody its own distinctive culture and society. Thus the Japanese men I talked to take the very common modernist view in which "the terms 'society' and 'culture' are routinely simply appended to the names of nation-states, as when a tourist visits India to understand 'Indian culture' and 'Indian society'" (Gupta and Ferguson 1992: 7).

From a theoretical point of view, this understanding may expose how at the base of many scholarly studies of Japan is an unstated assumption about an isomorphism between the geo-political boundaries of the state and its social and cultural limits (Ben-Ari 2000). In other words, many such investigations unreflectingly accept the taken-for-granted model which many Japanese use to interpret the world: the unstated postulate about the link between language, culture and territory in Japan. The assumption has been that if one wants to study Japanese culture then that it must be done in Japan. But my proposition is that this culture — without assuming too much about its unitary nature — could be understood not only along the lines proposed by most social scientists who have studied Japan, but also as a set of negotiated symbols and meanings that travel *across* national boundaries (Mouer and Sugimoto 1986; Brannen 1992; Creighton 1991).

Deterritorialization and the nation-state

The travel of this culture across national boundaries suggests another, more subtle, view of current predictions about various processes termed "deterritorialization." Running through the literature on globalization is a concern with how production, consumption, communities, politics and identities "become detached from local places" (Kearney 1995: 552) and work to reform the role of the nation-state. In its more radical guise, this view theorizes the dissolution of the nation-states in the face of global pressures (Cohen 1997: 156). My findings appear to contradict such a view.

For the Japanese business expatriates that I studied, there is no substantial deterritorialization of social identity; their experience does not seriously challenge the nation-state's claim to make exclusive citizenship a defining focus of allegiance and fidelity in favor of overlapping, permeable and multiple forms of identification. The Japanese nation-state (and its various appendages) extends its hold over citizens who live outside its boundaries. That the Japanese state has such a hold in political or economic terms is well understood (in granting passports or withholding taxes for instance). What my chapter underscores is the cultural hold of Japan over its citizens. As I demonstrated, deterritorialization paradoxically leads to a strengthening of "Japanese" identity in the sense of an identity which is rooted in, and derived from, a geopolitical entity (the nation-state). On a micro level then, "Japan" is constantly created and recreated through the minute, everyday activities of expatriate managers who must make sense of, and act upon, the reality within which they live. On a macro level, these practices serve to reinforce the division of the entire globe into separate nation-states (Kearney 1995: 553), and to contribute to the idea that an enduring locus of individual and group identity is the nation-state.

Behavioral implications

The cognitive models that I have examined in this chapter have a number of concrete organizational implications. Probably the most serious ramification involves the "invisible" boundary found in most Japanese companies between Japanese nationals on the one hand, and locals and other non-Japanese members on the other hand. A number of comparative investigations have found that Japanese overseas affiliates do not, on the whole, promote non-Japanese to senior managerial positions. Thus for example, Shiraki (1998) carried out a large-scale study of foreign companies in Southeast Asia. He found that American companies were most likely to promote locals, European firms were somewhere in the middle, while Japanese enterprises were least likely to undertake to offer such promotion. Similarly, Kotkin (1993: 152) found that

> Japanese firms ... generally employ expatriate Japanese managers at a rate ten to twenty times greater than their rivals from Europe or North America. In many cases, Japanese executives seem to view foreigners as barely capable of performing the most basic managerial tasks, with even supposedly high-ranking executives frequently overruled by Japanese "shadow managers," who actually exercise control over critical decisions, and in some cases are even prohibited from contacting Tokyo without consulting a Japanese staff member.

It is not surprising then, that in numerous interviews I found Japanese expatriate managers alluding to this situation. While not directly addressing this "sensitive" issue, I was told time and again that a large part of the work undertaken by the Japanese managers in Singapore entailed "following-up" on the locals and their assignments.

Homogeneity and discordant Voices

My final point involves the fact that I found almost no discordant voices, no critical appraisal of the models I have examined. The reason for the relative uniformity of views that I encountered may lie in the relative homogeneity of the expatriate population in Singapore. In his study of *Nihonjinron*, Yoshino (1992) found that of all of the groups he investigated, business people were most likely to hold such tenets. Similarly, Manabe and Befu (1992: 89) found that it is the middle class that tends to believe in the validity of *Nihonjinron* theories. The Japanese community in Singapore, in turn, is very uniform in these respects: almost all of its members are related to business and are solidly middle-class. In addition, their demographic similarity — they are in their late thirties, forties and early fifties — seems to indicate that they have all grown up and been educated during a similar historical period and thus been exposed to roughly the same ideas about the "world" and about "Japan."

Conclusion: Japan, Singapore and Global Talk

This chapter has focused on the cognitive and discursive dimensions of the Japanese business experience in Singapore. As such it should be seen as a modest corrective to ongoing studies of "globalization" or "transnationalism." While these studies include fascinating inquiries into the social and cultural aspects of migrants and immigrants, of diasporas and refugees, or of tourists (Kearney 1995), as of yet there is very little in the way of systematic examinations of expatriates in general (Cohen 1977) or of Japanese expatriates in particular. In this conclusion let me underscore a number of more general points that link the Japanese presences in Singapore to "global" issues.

Roland Robertson (1992: 86) proposes that Japan will continue (along with other Asian societies) to be global in the sense of being a society from which "'leaders' of other societies can learn how to learn about many societies. *That* is what makes Japan a global society, in spite of claims to the contrary" (emphasis in original). In this sense, Japan and (to a degree) Singapore are very different from Angola or Uruguay (to take but two extreme examples). They are different because the Japanese and (latterly) the East Asian "miracles" — a special combination of culture, economics and government policy — have become central models in contemporary and world-wide debates about the development and transformation of nation-states.

Given the uncertainties of present-day Japanese politics and economics this situation will perhaps change in the future. But as for now, it seems that the Japanese story will continue to appear in the "internal cultural debates" (Parkin 1978) of various countries. To put this point rather crudely, debates about Japan may not be about that country at all. Rather, through addressing Japan or its attendant qualities, people in other countries constantly promote or denigrate certain visions of what their societies were, are, or should be like. Thus in contemporary America and Southeast Asia, for example, Japan is used as a case through which to legitimate the pacification of labor, and as a justification for promoting teamwork, reducing discontent, and developing workers' strong emotional attachments to firms (Dore 1987; Raz and Raz 1996; Stanley 1988). Goodman (1998), to cite another instance, shows how Asian educational models are used by a variety of politicians in Europe to justify their programs.

My final point derives from this consideration. In contemporary Southeast Asia, fears of "Japanization" are part of a larger debate about the cultural identity of the area and are akin to concerns about possible "Americanization" or "Sinification". Part of the appeal of Japan is its very "non-Western-ness" and the perceived suitability of its qualities and characteristics for "non-Western" societies. Along these lines, current debates about "Asian-ness" and "Asian-values" that are appearing in such places as China, Korea and India (Vishwanathan 1975) and in Malaysia and Singapore (Chan 1993: Shafie 1990) all encompass references to Japan as the leading model positing an alternative to the West. Hence, in a curious way, Japanese businessmen trying to make sense of themselves and of their activities in Singapore contribute to much wider debates about the world, about Japan's place in it, and about a wider contest between "the West" and "the Rest."

Notes

I would like to thank Lise Skov, Brian Moeran, Boas Shamir, and Oded Shenkar for comments on earlier drafts of this paper. This chapter has also benefited greatly from conversations with Harumi Befu.

[1] It is these schemas that provide deep-rooted, implicit assumptions concerning such things as relations between individuals and organizations, in-groups and out-groups, and the manner by which the "world" is ordered.

[2] I carried out research through interviews and participant observation. While I interviewed over 90 individuals, about 60 were business people (almost all of them men). Typically, they were almost all white-collar managers and executives who had been posted to the country for a period of between three to five years and in their late thirties to early fifties.

[3] The following sections draw on Ben-Ari (forthcoming).

[4] I found another interesting indicator of this role in the custom some managers have of adopting informal English names. They would sometimes print names like "Todd" or "Mike" on their name cards but in parenthesis.

Chapter 3

Japan as a Model for Economic Development: The Example of Singapore

Thomas A. Stanley

Studies of modern Japan have concentrated on Japan's use of Western models for its development, but a new relationship between Japan and the world has emerged in recent years and the outside world is now interested in emulating Japan. The emergence of Japan as a major economic power has led many corporations in Europe and North America to consider learning Japanese methods which may improve their own competitive position in domestic and foreign markets. Even governments see the Japanese example as instructive.

This is particularly true in the Pacific area, where the newly industrializing nations are increasingly turning to Japan for inspiration and advice. Japan's position as the dominant trading partner of some of these nations and its record of high growth are only part of the reason; the use of a distinctly Asian model, with morals and social values presumed to be more amenable to Asian situations, is also strongly appealing.

The Republic of Singapore is one country in which the Japanese model of economic development is a major influence on governmental and public thinking.[1] To be sure, the government encourages the emulation of other countries in other fields, such as the US for business and finance, Israel and Switzerland for defence and Britain for education. The Japanese model, however, is used especially in the area of industrialization and social values.

This chapter explores ways in which Singapore has been influenced by Japan's model of industrialization, and especially by the social and moral values presumed to be an important part of

Japan's industrial success. Japanese institutional and ideological efforts to minimize conflict and direct it into economically productive channels have received special notice in Singapore and, accordingly, the adaptation of these methods in the Singapore context is the main focus of this study.

Singapore's Accomplishments and Problems: An Overview

Singapore's leaders have effected vast changes in the quarter-century they have been in power, especially Lee Kwan Yew, Goh Keng Swee and their successor Goh Chok Tong. Singapore is rightfully proud of many accomplishments: a per capita GDP higher than Japan's and second in Asia only to Hong Kong in 1998 (*Far Eastern Economic Review* 1998) and so high that in 1985 New Zealand moved to reclassify it as a developed nation; public housing projects far superior to the slums they replaced; efficient harbours, roads and a rapid rail transit system; sophisticated shipbuilding, petroleum, petrochemical and computer industries; political and social stability; and a sense of nation developed in the midst of very difficult circumstances.

Each accomplishment can, of course, be denigrated because solutions to old problems have created unforeseen new problems. For example, in the high-rise public housing projects, the racial segregation of the old neighbourhoods has been broken, reducing the likelihood of racial rioting. The government formalized racial quotas in public housing in 1989 for the additional political purpose of preventing the re-emergence of concentration of Malays or Indians who voted against the government the 1988 general elections in disproportionate numbers (*Far Eastern Economic Review* 1989a). A negative consequence, however, is a high degree of social isolation, resulting in new forms of social discontent and anti-social acts that are of increasing concern to residents and government alike (*The Straits Times* 1979). The primary concern of the government, and probably of the people, has consistently been material well-being. The high-growth rates of the past decades have gone far to satisfy everyone's wants. Again, however, there are problems. The national wealth is not equitably distributed, income gaps are larger than in the past, and leaders complain about the population's materialism.

Singapore has a very good image outside Southeast Asia as well. Tourists are generally pleased by Singapore's combination of modern efficiency and a taste of the exotic East without the 'dirt' and confusion of other Asian cities. The country is stable, is aligned with the anticommunist world powers, avows democracy and supports a regional strong military, diplomatic, and economic presence by the US and Japan. Being much smaller than the other three newly industrializing countries of Asia (Hong Kong, South Korea and Taiwan), Singapore has generally missed being singled out as a major trading threat to industrialized nations.

Labour Policy

To the outside investor Singapore has been attractive for three decades because of its labour peace and political stability. But Singapore has not always had a labour force acquiescent to the government.

At the time of independence, in 1963, Singapore suffered chronic unemployment combined with a vigorous labour movement often controlled by left-wing elements identified now as pro-communist or communist by the ruling Peoples' Action Party (PAP). In 1955, when radical elements in the labour movement frequently led strikes for political reasons, Singapore lost 946,000 man-days to strikes. By 1965 the PAP had driven the left-wing out of its own ranks and established its own labour union movement (the National Trades Union Council, or NTUC) to compete with that of the leftists. In the same year 46,000 man-days were lost to strikes and by 1977 only 1,000 man-days were lost. There were no strikes from 1977 until 1986 (*Far Eastern Economic Review* 1982).[2] Indeed, strikes are virtually illegal.

The National Trades Union Council, a national umbrella organization for unionized workers, has significantly helped to avoid conflict by reining in individual unions and by transmitting the policies which the government sees as essential to political and economic goals. Although NTUC was originally built on the aggressive model of the British labour movement, it has lost all the considerable power it once had, and, while it calls itself an independent organization which supports the PAP, it is in fact subordinate to the party.[3] Wage guidelines are set by the National Wage Council (on which NTUC is represented) and usually strictly observed. The government has said it is in favour of a system in which labour and management bargain directly, with the government present as a secondary party. In the mid 1980s, however, in response to economic contraction, the government imposed a two-year freeze on wage and salary increases. In 1998, the government condoned cuts in pay and in employers' contributions to the retirement system in order to adjust Singapore's competitiveness in view of the economic turmoil in Asia that began in 1997. Thus, the government's interests are paramount, with management's interests usually next and labour's interests last, but with economic growth and stability foremost in government thinking.[4]

The disfavour with which the government looks on industrial action by any union was typified by the direct intervention of Lee Kwan Yew in a dispute between Singapore International Airlines (SIA) and the SIA Pilots' Association (SIAPA) in 1980. One flight was cut short in Zurich instead of its destination in London when the pilots refused, in accord with an SIA-SIAPA agreement, to work for more than twelve hours at a stretch. Lee intervened and ultimately the flight crew of four was fired and fifteen of the twenty-man committee directing the SIAPA were charged with instigating an illegal strike. All pleaded guilty.

Several months later, Ong Pang Boon, who was both Minister of Labour and Secretary-General of the PAP, was demoted to the less important Environment Ministry for attempting to handle the SIA-SIAPA dispute in a 'British manner'; that is, through arbitration by an independent arbitrator who strikes a bargain acceptable to both sides (*Asiaweek* 1981a). Lee complained that his approach lacked 'productivity', which he defined as 'total cooperation [and] confidence between workers and management'. The then President of the Republic of Singapore and former head of NTUC, C. V. Devan Nair, warned menacingly that 'the next time you or any other group of employees in SIA indulge in arm-twisting tactics, you will be smacked down, good and hard' (*Asiaweek* 1981b).[5]

Singapore and Japan

If Lee found the British system of industrial relations inappropriate for Singapore, his visit to Japan in 1979, one year before the strike, left him strongly impressed with Japanese labour relations. Not long after demoting his Minister of Labour, he promoted Wee Mon Cheng, then Singapore's Ambassador to Japan, to three consecutive year-long appointments as chairman of Singapore Broadcasting Corporation, the government's public television and radio monopoly, touting him as an expert on Japan.[6]

Use of Japan as an explicit model began after Prime Minister Lee Kwan Yew's trip to Japan; thereafter, there was a virtual barrage of pronouncements eulogizing Japan. Lee returned not only with his own enthusiasm about Japan, but with promises of help. The Japanese undertook to establish a Department of Japanese Studies at the National University of Singapore and to improve the engineering faculty at the computer training facility. Lee was particularly impressed with Japan's long-range economic planning and the high degree of consultation among representatives of government, management and labour. To help understand this new model, top economic officials went to Tokyo in 1980 to study how Japan formulates policy (*Far Eastern Economic Review* 1981a).

In the 1980s 'co-operation between management and labour', 'house unions' and 'teamwork' became catch phrases with constant publicity. Since 1980 there have been month-long campaigns to encourage teamwork. Sponsored by the National Productivity Board, a statutory board established by the government, the campaigns gained public attention with a cartoon strip featuring, as symbol and mascot, a busy bee named 'Teamy'. Teamy originally encouraged workers to be productive, but in the 1984 campaign concentrated on management practices that limited productivity by infuriating or hindering workers. Unreconstructed workers and managers were criticized through comparison with their ideal Japanese counterparts.

There was considerable reason for action to reduce tension between workers at the end of the 1970s. The so-called second industrial revolution initiated under the leadership of Goh Keng Swee in 1979 was designed to push Singapore from labour-intensive industry to capital and knowledge-intensive industry. In part this was accomplished when the National Wage Council raised wages about 20 per cent each year in 1979, 1980 and 1981; the stated intention was to make labour-intensive industry in Singapore uncompetitive in the international market, thus forcing workers and businesses to invest in better skills, capital equipment and technology. In 1980 and 1981 better workers were to be given even higher wage increases to encourage better attitudes and higher productivity. This was felt, however, to be so divisive and threatening to so many workers that the government had added stimulus to turn to the Japanese labour model to seek additional ways of promoting teamwork and reducing discontent (*Far Eastern Economic Review* 1981a).

In addition to the measures mentioned above, other Japanese-inspired devices and institutions for enhancing peaceful labour relations and increasing productivity were established at the government's behest. By the mid 1980s, quality control circles were established to increase quality and productivity. Work Improvement Teams (WITS) were organized to encourage workers to study production methods and make suggestions on improving them. Companies were encouraged to undertake welfare programmes for their workers. They were allowed to retain part of the joint company–employee payment to the Central Provident Fund (CPF), invest it at returns higher than CPF paid and, after the amount increased sufficiently, begin providing employees with welfare benefits similar to those for which large Japanese corporations have become famous in the post-war era. The hope was that workers would develop a strong emotional as well as pecuniary attachment to their firms.

An impediment to developing worker loyalty towards employers is the high frequency with which Singaporeans change jobs. Their 'job-hopping' is so famous that passing reference to it brings a knowing laugh from any audience, whether labourers, students or bankers. Officially, of course, it is viewed with displeasure since it results in labour instability and is a distinct disincentive for employers to provide on-the-job training to employees, be they plastic intrusion machine operators, machinists or computer programmers.

Various ways of limiting job-hopping were proposed, all of them based on increased benefits to workers who stayed with their employers. Wee Mon Cheng objected that these plans amounted to materialistic incentives for loyalty to the employer while materialism was the root cause of job-hopping or disloyalty. Drawing on his knowledge of Japan, he emphasized that job-hopping could best be reduced by cultivating the workers' sense of belonging in their company and by stressing professionalism and pride in their work (*Far Eastern Economic Review* 1981b). Nevertheless, job-hopping remains common – mute testimony to the difficulty of fostering the kind of employees' loyalty to the company that is such a remarkable feature of Japan's labour relations, even during the collapse of the 'bubble economy' in the early 1990s and the long recession of the late 1990s.

In the mid 1980s, the government made another step towards the Japanese labour relations system by encouraging the establishment of company or house unions. In Japan's case, these have been praised for facilitating management's goals while reducing worker recalcitrance, resulting in better productivity and profits; the better profits are supposedly returned to the workers in higher wages and benefits over the long term. House unions in Japan have also been criticized by critics for exposing the workers to exploitation by their companies and so the debate repeats itself in Singapore.

The NTUC and the government itself were the focus of changes in union structure away from industrial or trade unionism to house unionism on the Japanese model. House unions in a number of statutory boards and government agencies were established in the absence of any union. In 1982, under the guidance of Japanophile Wee Mon Cheng, the Singapore Broadcasting Corporation established a house union which newspapers quickly labelled the 'new model' (*Far Eastern Economic Review* 1982). In 1984 the NTUC initiated the first major step towards house unions when it imposed them on workers at Changi Airport.

When the question of dissolving the Singapore Air Transport Workers' Union (SATU) and creating new house unions was put to the leaders of the existing union, however, significant dissent arose. Several prominent union leaders questioned or opposed the changes. Letters signed by 300 members addressed to Prime Minister Lee Kwan Yew and President Devan Nair requested a referendum on the issue in order to establish a mandate for or against the change. Immediately the chief leaders of the NTUC forced SATU to bring charges and pressure to bear on the opponents, threatening them with expulsion or other sanctions (*Asiaweek* 1984b).

The cudgelling of opponents to accept the principle of house unionism and the related one of co-operation between labour and management also raised questions about the purpose of house unions: in whose interest were they being created and what was their purpose? In the case of the campaign to raise productivity, the same questions arose. A 1982 survey showed that although 94 per cent of respondents had heard about productivity, 70 per cent felt that the company and not the worker would benefit (*Asiaweek* 1982).

By 1986, one review of Singapore's labour union situation concluded that the attempt to emulate Japan's model was a failure. Since the government legislates almost all employer benefits, unions 'have little, if any, role to play in helping to better their members' livelihood.' In any case, union membership was only 16 percent of the workforce (192,394), down from a peak of 25 percent in 1979. There were 39 house unions with a quarter of all unionized workers in them (51,950) (*Far Eastern Economic Review* 1986).

Conflict Control

Many of the Singapore government's actions have been directed to achieving high growth, the area where the Japanese model was so effective until the mid and late 1990s. Other actions of the government have been dedicated to controlling or reducing conflict, an emerging area of interest among students of Japan too.[7] In this area, parallels are pronounced and the Singaporean use of the Japanese model is often explicit. For example, the Singapore police have sent missions to Japan to study the *koban* (local police box) system, employed Western consultants familiar with the Japanese system and invited Japanese police to Singapore to lend assistance. Whether a *koban* system can work well in a nation of high-rise apartment blocks is debatable. To support the system, Singapore planned to add 4000 officers to the police force, nearly a 100 percent increase in the 5400 officer force (*Asiaweek* 1983).

To a larger degree, however, the Japanese experience serves to legitimize Singaporean programmes that began before the 1979 watershed in choice of Japan as model. A case in point is ethics education. When Singapore became an independent state in 1965, it had to promote loyalty to the state. Consequently, the schools increased the emphasis on patriotism in ethics education, reminiscent of pre-war Japan's *shushin*. As the population came to identify with Singapore, explicit nationalism was reduced.

In the late 1970s and early 1980s concern about declining moral values and personal behaviour rose at the same time that patriotic loyalty was felt to be firmly established. Increasingly, Singaporeans were warned against the permissiveness, 'unfettered' individualism, decadent materialism, and 'soft options' of the West. Lee Kwan Yew and other leaders have also frequently voiced concern about cultural rootlessness and its dangers. It was dogma that education in English alone increases rootlessness, while education in Chinese (or Tamil or Malay, depending on race) preserves cultural traditions and morality. In Parliament in early 1977, Lee said, regarding the possibility of eliminating Mandarin in the primary and secondary schools, 'If you lose that Chinese education and you go completely English-educated, you will lose that drive, that self-confidence. That is what is wrong.' (*Far Eastern Economic Review* 1984a:23) In 1979 Goh Keng Swee, then Minister of Education, initiated a study which listed desiderata for moral education in the schools: '"Sense of belonging to the community" must be taught as part of "social responsibility" and must contain elements such as "civic consciousness, respect and care for others, care for public property, respect for law and order, safety, harmony, group spirit, love for the school, cooperation, friendship, neighborliness and generosity."' (*Far Eastern Economic Review* 1980b) Lee himself was quoted as saying

> Unless we make a concerted effort and sustained effort at inculcating into [younger Singaporeans] the virtues of group discipline and the overriding calls of society upon their individual rights, more and more will be consciously influenced by the concepts of Europeans and Americans: that the rights and liberties of the individual are the first charge upon society. ... The generation now in school are nearly all in the English language stream, where the philosophy and doctrines taught are less Confucianist than the Chinese language schools; hence the importance of imparting the traditional values in moral education in the schools. (ibid.:83)

The thrust towards moral indoctrination is concentrated on Confucianism. This is not surprising since Singapore is about 76 per cent ethnic Chinese. Moreover, the disproportionate percentage of the political, economic, educational and medical elites – indeed all elites are Chinese; moral decay among the Chinese would presumably have immediate irreversible impact.

To be fair to all Singaporeans, the government also emphasized Islam, Hinduism and Buddhism. It even lauded Christianity, because 10.3 per cent of the population was Christian and even more in some elite groups in 1980; 22 per cent of the members of Parliament, four of the government's seven 'second-generation' leaders, 30 percent of all university students and 70 per cent of the medical students were reckoned to be Christian. By 1988, 18.7 per cent of the population was Christian, including 38.5 per cent of those with tertiary education (ibid.: 77; 1989b).[8] Accordingly, the government promised by the mid-1980s a compulsory moral education course under which students would study either Islam, Buddhism, Christianity, Confucianism or World Religions (a catch-all) (*Far Eastern Economic Review* 1984a).

Confucianism, however, received the greatest attention and publicity. It was presumed to be of 'natural' interest to the Chinese majority. The 1980 Census revealed that nearly all who professed no religion (13 per cent among those over ten years of age, rising to about 20 per cent among those with upper secondary education or better) were Chinese (*Asiaweek* 1984c). In 1982 and 1983 a series of prominent Confucian scholars from Taiwan and the USA were brought, amidst great publicity, as consultants on the Confucian curriculum. Particularly emphasized were themes in Confucianism familiar to the student of pre-war Japan: obedience, loyalty and service to the state; care of parents; esteem for the three-tiered family (children, parents and grandparents living under the same roof); and disdain for materialism. Although it was claimed that these values were universal to all religions, political leaders became specific when discussing Confucianism.

The promotion of values useful to a government interested in control and manipulation of the population requires no special explanation. In the case of Japan in the Meiji and pre-Second World War periods, these same moral values were encouraged in an effort to promote Japan's modernisation while easing the resulting dislocations.[9] Confucianism also served to reduce threats against the regime by encouraging loyalty and obedience to the state. These points, especially the latter, are hardly unknown to Singapore's leaders.

Some effort has been made to provide institutional support for Confucian values. In early 1982 Lee Kwan Yew, expressing shock at callous disregard of aged parents, said the government would introduce legislation requiring children to care for their parents. The plan was dropped at that time, but changes were made in the administration of the public housing programme which gave significant preference to three-tiered families, greatly shortening the 18- to 36-month wait for a publicly constructed apartment (*Far Eastern Economic review* 1984a:26).[10] In the early 1990s, the plan was revived and implemented in the 1994 Maintenance of Parents Bill.

At times the urge for control exceeds the possible, especially when it seeks to promote behaviour which appears to run contrary to the general course of development in modern societies. In a television National Day rally speech in 1983, Lee Kwan Yew complained that university-educated women tended to have few children or did not marry at all. Noting that in 1980 married women who had graduated from the university had an average of 1.65 children, while women with no education averaged 3.5, Lee, accepting the hypothesis that intelligence is based 80 per cent on hereditary factors and only 20 per cent on environmental factors like education, worried that the number of highly educable people would fall, while the uneducable population would sharply rise (*Far Eastern Economic Review* 1983c).[11] Since government figures showed that of 117,000 women graduates, only one-half were married, efforts were made to encourage educated women to marry sooner and have more children. (One is reminded of Mori Arinori's brief hope in the 1870s of improving the Japanese race through intermarriage with Caucasians (Hall 1973). Goh Keng Swee, Lee's right-hand man, lauded the success that Japan experienced with arranged marriages and computerized match-making. An official mission was sent to study Japan's computer match-making and bring back the software necessary to begin a similar programme in Singapore. Goh also suggested a university course on courting (*Asiaweek* 1983b; 1983c).

Although Lee promised that no compulsory measures or disincentives would be instituted, within six months the government established incentives to encourage graduate women to reproduce while efforts to discourage others continued. The children of graduate women with three or more children were given top preference in determining school registration while 'extra' children of unsterilized, non-graduate women with three or more children were given the least preference (*Far Eastern Economic Review* 1984b). In order to encourage other female graduates, favourable publicity was given to graduate women who decided to have a third child.

Other programmes were instituted in accord with Lee's genetic concept. The Curriculum Development Institute of Singapore was set to work producing materials to teach junior college and pre-university centre students, many of them university-bound, the importance of marriage and having children (*Far Eastern Economic Review* 1984a:10). A very large tax deduction was given to graduate women who were working and had children. In early 1984 a Social Development Unit was quietly established to identify graduate women who were unmarried or university students who might not marry. These were to be taught basic social skills and the virtue of marriage and children, and many were placed in social situations alongside potential mates – boat cruises, vacation trips abroad or within Singapore and other short-term get-togethers. As of March of 1985, S\$300,000 had been spent by the Unit; 4600 people were introduced to each other and two marriages had resulted (*The Straits Times* 1985). There were also rumours that unmarried graduate women were not being hired or were being passed over for promotion in the civil service. In 1990, Lee Kwan Yew reported that 50.3 per cent of male university graduates married women graduates in 1989, down from 51.8 percent the previous year, but up from 37.6 per cent in 1983 (*Far Eastern Economic Review* 1990a). There was considerable protest against the programme, especially by the educated elite and the university women who stood to benefit. Ultimately, in 1985, the school registration preference for prolific graduate women's children was withdrawn, leaving in limbo the few third children of graduate women conceived under the programme's stimulus, but it was re-implemented within three years. The other programmes were continued and in 1987 then First Deputy Prime Minister Goh Chok Tong was quoted as saying 'Have three, and more if you can afford it'. He also added more benefits for women having three or more children including large tax rebates, child care subsidies, priority in housing and, for civil servants, up to four years unpaid leave to women staying home to raise their children (*Far Eastern Economic Review* 1987).

The genetic interests of Lee Kwan Yew must be considered not as an aberration of some kind, but as part of the concern of the leadership with the quality of future leaders. The PAP leadership is very worried about differences between itself and the younger generation. Lee Kwan Yew constantly refers to Singapore's 'rugged' society, but worries that the younger generation appears entirely different – softened by materialism and seduced by Western decadence and individualism. The Party's worries were given reality in a 1981 by-election when, for the first time in 16 years, a member of the opposition party, J. B. Jeyaretnum of the Workers' Party, was returned. Later, when he was on the verge of handing the prime ministership over to Goh Chok Tong, Lee worried in public that Goh was too soft for the job.

Confucian moral education, combined with patriotism cemented during compulsory military service, might be an excellent tool for regaining the loyalty of youth, judging from pre-war Japanese experience. Government control of the media is also put to use; SBC television has broadcast the Japanese series 'Oshin', and its own production, 'The Awakening', both in Mandarin. They are dominated by the theme that 'the young are constantly reminded of their parents' suffering and hard work, without which the Economic Miracle ... would never have occurred'. The director of 'The Awakening', Hong Kong expatriate Leung Lap-yan, admitted that the programme necessarily reflects government policy and said, 'We hope that after watching the show [the youth] will appreciate the good life they have' (*Far Eastern Economic Review* 1984c; *Asiaweek* 1983d).

By 1988, Goh Chok Tong said that 'Singaporeans have superimposed [upon the British system of government] the ideal political leader as a Confucian gentleman, a *junzi*, someone who is upright, morally beyond reproach, someone people can trust'. Two years later, Lee Kwan Yew was quoted as saying 'Asians are in little doubt that a society with communitarian values, where the interests of the society take precedence over that of the individual suits them better than the individual rights of Americans' and 'Asians see Japanese achievements as higher and the Japanese are not pushy or self-proselytisers at least not yet' (*Far Eastern Economic Review* 1990b).

Conclusion

Part of the appeal of the Japanese model for Asia is that Japan is Asian. It is assumed this model is more suitable to Asia than European or North American alternatives. In particular, it is assumed that the values and social factors of Japan and Asia are so similar that adoption of Japanese systems will significantly reduce the strains and dislocation of change. Certainly the Singaporean example reflects this belief. Such thinking, however, ignores several important differences between Japan and Singapore.

In Japan, there was historically a strong concept of service to the nation, but the concept of nation is new in Singapore and service to the nation is an idea the government constantly endeavours to instil in the population. Japan has a relatively high degree of social homogeneity, notwithstanding minority populations of perhaps three per cent of the total, but Singapore has a pronounced mixture of races; the races strongly differ in traditions and harbour deep antagonisms towards each other. Despite the conflicts and divisions recently documented by historians, such as peasant revolt, class conflict, labour strife and individual or local community resistance to the central state, Japan by and large has a group-oriented society in which school class, place of employment and university or school affiliation are common foci of identification, gained by effort and merit rather than birth. Singapore's group orientation extends primarily to family and racial or linguistic group in most cases. These differences suggest that merely being Asian will not make adopting the Japanese model easy.

The Japanese model attracted Singapore's attention because of Japan's economic and social success, not because Lee Kwan Yew saw the development pattern as one that harnessed and muted conflict in the past 100 years. It is, however, just this harnessing and muting process where the Japanese model has been particularly effective in Singapore. The labour scene offers strong testimony to this. A new system of labour relations, artificial in the sense that it has no immediate indigenous roots and is based on the Japanese system, was being imposed on workers, primarily by the government, in a broad attempt to eliminate conflict, promote productivity and increase the freedom of management to act in response to the market without constraints by an active labour movement.

The Japanese experience was quite similar. Its labour relations system can be traced back only to around 1900. It was developed by industrialists and government officials interested in capturing expensive skilled labour, stabilizing and pacifying management-labour relations, and preventing political radicalism among workers. Although ties to Japanese traditions were professed, it was 'artificial' in the same sense that Singapore's use of the Japanese model is; it had no historical precedents in the labour market. Indeed, it was created for modern industry and bloomed there particularly after 1945; traces are virtually impossible to find in small-scale traditional enterprises.

If Singapore successfully adopts a Japanese-style labour relations system, one would have to conclude that, notwithstanding cultural and historical differences, Japan's system is transferable in form, if not in spirit. Although the government, party and labour union are all willing to impose the system with a measure of force, the company union model remains a small component in the labour union movement which is itself shrinking.

In the area of values a similar process appears to be under way. Confucianism continues to be promoted as a bulwark against decadent Western values, a brake on individualism, an inspiration to hard work, and a buttress for the authority of the state. Whether Confucianism can mitigate the extremely individualistic, commercial, materialistic environment of Singapore is questionable. While it does have its roots among the Chinese majority, they are shallow roots in a society that is hostile to certain aspects of Confucianism that were important in Japan, such as service to the state. At best, it appears to be useful primarily in restricting individuals and enforcing the acceptance of authority.

The authoritarian side of Confucianism draws frequent cautions from observers of Singapore who are familiar with Japan in the 1930s and 1940s, when Confucianism often served the same purpose. Like Singapore's use of Japanese-style labour relations, in the short to medium term, the Japanese model will be successful primarily as a means of increasing the state's authority and control over society and the economy and less as a blueprint for industrial development. And, as in Japan at least until 1945 – constriction of democracy and of individual freedom and happiness is pronounced. Whether this is an inevitable result of the Japanese model may be debatable. What is certain, however, is that at least in Singapore, such a result is deliberate; indeed, it was one of the main reasons for using the model.

Afterword

This chapter was originally written a dozen years ago after a period of residence in Singapore during which Japan was often in the newspapers as a model for development. I have added substantially to it to draw forward in time the continuing patterns. I consider the conclusions reached still valid. Two additional observations are worth adding: one dealing with Singapore's use of the Japanese model and one dealing with Confucianism and traditional values in Asia today.

First, the Singapore government continues to turn to Japan, making this discussion of continuing interest both with reference to Singapore and to the nature of the Japanese model. For example, on July 12 1995 it was announced that NHK (Japan Broadcasting Corporation) television would be one of the few foreign channels initially permitted on Singapore's cable television experiment

(*International Herald Tribune* 1995). The article noted that the 'authorities were adopting a conservative approach to cable television'. A government spokesperson said

> cable television should be used to strengthen civil and grassroots organizations in Singapore so that Singaporeans have a strong sense of belonging to local communities and caring for each other. ...

> 'With cable TV, it is possible to take this a step further and provide channels which monitor goings-on in the immediate neighborhood,' he said. 'Residents can keep an eye on activities at public parks, neighborhood centers, carparks, open areas, corridors and even lifts.'

NHK itself would not, of course, contribute to public surveillance in Singapore, but the conservative social values put forth on NHK parallel the government's use of the Japanese model and the model's presumed base in Confucianism. Like other countries, Singapore is cautious and suspicious of the effect of television (or other media) from Western nations beaming directly into the masses' homes via cable or satellite. The leadership is more comfortable with local or Asian programming, or with the Japanese model, because the values presumed to be present are also presumed to be similar to the local ethos.

Second, the discussion of the role of Confucianism continues throughout Asia. For example a commentary by Professor Wang Gungwu in *The Times Higher Education Supplement* discussed traditional values in Asia. It cast some doubt on the relevance of Japanese Confucianism to the rest of Asia, noting that 'it is one thing for Japan to adapt what it borrows from the rest of Asia, but quite another thing for the rest of Asia to try and take from Japan what it had uniquely shaped through its own chemistry'. (Wang 1995) How much more true, I would argue, for South and Southeast Asia which experienced Confucianism mediated through the Chinese Overseas minorities rather than as a social, intellectual and political system instituted with the full power of the state over centuries of time (Vietnam is an obvious exception to this statement).

Professor Wang expanded his essay into a discussion of the mixture of Asia's traditional values with government leadership of business and the role that higher education can play, reminding

78

Japan specialists of Bryon Marshall's (1967) view of Japanese capitalism and nationalism before World War II. He concludes that

> The modern universities should stop thinking of traditional cultures as something exotic and belonging to the past. In the new context, they should begin to turn to the great traditions of Asia in order to understand what the new generations of Asian businessmen hope to achieve in the 21st century.

Numerous other authors, political commentators and political leaders have addressed the question of values in contemporary Asia, especially in terms of what Confucianism in particular and traditional values in general can or cannot contribute to development in Asia. Almost any newspaper or weekly news magazine that deals extensively with Asia will have an article or commentary on the question every month. Singapore's use of the Japanese model and Confucianism, however, typifies the tension between conservative, even authoritarian, manipulation of the model and the desire for efficient progress with stability. When the question of values becomes linked to religious fervour, nationalism, and discussions of regional security or trading blocs, it may become alarmingly explosive and not just academically interesting.

Notes

[1] It is not easy to define 'the Japanese model', for even experts are not agreed. For my purposes, however, I will use the model that Singaporean authorities emphasize. The model centres on factors which have fostered Japan's high-growth economy since 1945. These factors include the guidance provided by the government to the economy and to individual industries; the 'Japanese employment system' of lifetime employment for permanent employees, extensive fringe benefits and salary based on seniority, the Japanese industrial relations system that minimizes labour–management conflict through company unions which co-operate intimately with management; and the sequence of development of industries of increasingly higher capital or technological investment. Social stability is seen as an important contribution to economic performance. Therefore, factors like the family system, paternalism and Confucian ideology are incorporated into the model.

[2] There was, however, a strike in early 1986.

[3] In 1983 the secretary-general of the NTUC, Lim Chee Onn, was one of the rising stars of the PAP's 'second generation' leaders and a technocrat appointed to NTUC from the bureaucracy. Lim was suddenly removed from his office in April 1983 in a public exchange of letters with the prime minister, Lee Kwan Yew, who appointed Ong Teng Cheong as a

replacement (*Far Eastern Economic Review* 1983a). While Lim's sudden disgrace and elimination from the 'second-generation' group underlined the penalty of political missteps, it also underlined how little independence NTUC has. It was Lee Kwan Yew and the PAP who appoint and remove NTUC leaders, not the NTUC itself. The NTUC does 'elect' leaders after they are designated by the government. *Far Eastern Economic Review* 1983b.

4 An interesting sidelight on the question of wages arose from a letter to the editor by Chan Heng Wing, Singapore's consul-general to Hong Kong. Responding to hints by Hong Kong's Financial Secretary that Singapore was interferring in the economy more than Hong Kong, the consul-general wrote 'The Singapore Government makes no dictation on wages. We have no minimum wage. The National Wages Council comprises representatives of labour, employers and government. Its annual wage guidelines are the result of negotiations in the council and so reflect the views of all three parties. These guidelines help individual companies make their own wage settlements expeditiously. But companies are not compelled to follow them. Several small and medium enterprises ... have already stated that they will not cut wages this year. ...' *South China Morning Post*, 1998.

5 Devan Nair was himself 'smacked down, good and hard' for alleged misbehaviour with women and use of drugs. He was forced to resign from office and a good number of details were made public.

6 Wee was tried and found guilty of tax evasion on 31 January 1984, the final day of his tenure as chairman of SBC. His son later faced related charges. This kind of disgrace following political patronage led Goh Kian Chee (son of Goh Keng Swee, Singapore's economic wizard and Lee Kwan Yew's right-hand man) to observe that he could not recall anyone leaving the higher echelons of the PAP 'without (a) having defected to the communists, (b) having gone crooked, (c) having been pronounced incompetent, unreliable, weak, brainless, lacking in intellectual depth, enjoying laxity in amoral lifestyle, reckless and ambitious, and (d) having gone somewhat gaga' or dying. *Far Eastern Economic Review* 1980a. Later Goh Keng Swee did withdraw from politics, to concentrate on advising China's leaders on economic reforms, without suffering any of his son's four dire possibilities. Wee Mon Cheng was replaced with another former Ambassador to Japan, Wee Kim Wee (*Asiaweek* 1984a).

7 For example, see Ellis S. Krauss, Thomas P. Rohlen and Patricia G. Steinhoff (eds), *Conflict in Japan* (Honolulu: University of Hawaii Press, 1984); Tetsuo Najita and J. Victor Koschman (eds), *Conflict in Modern Japanese History: The Neglected Tradition* (Princeton, N.J.: Princeton University Press, 1982); and George de Vos (ed.), *Institutions for Change in Japanese Society* (Berkeley, Calif.: Institute of East Asian Studies, University of California Press, 1984

8 The 1980 Census recorded Christians as 10.3 per cent of the population over 10 years of age. Among those with tertiary education, 35.9 per cent were Christian. See Asiaweek, 1984c. The 1988 figures are from *Far Eastern Economic Review* 1989b.

9 See virtually any study of late Tokugawa and Meiji Japan, especially Byron K. Marshall, *Ideology and Industrialization in Japan, 1868–1941:*

The Creed of Prewar Business Elite (Stanford, Calif.: Stanford University Press, 1965).

[10] Over three-quarters of Singaporeans own or rent apartments built by the public Housing Development Board. For all but the elite, private apartments and houses are prohibitively priced. HDB is an efficient instrument for enforcing officially condoned behaviour since there is no viable alternative housing for the vast majority and since the government retains broad powers to evict even those who purchase their living quarters.

[11] Ultimately, the school registration programme was also offered to women with A-level examination qualifications (equivalent to high-school education) and graduates of non-university tertiary institutions like the Institute of Education, a teacher-training facility.

Chapter 4

Twice Marginalized: Single Japanese Female Expatriates in Singapore

Eyal Ben-Ari and Yong Yin Fong Vanessa

In this chapter we examine the social position and individual experiences of single female Japanese expatriates in Singapore. Our contention is that these women are marginalized both from the host Singaporean society and from the large Japanese expatriate community in the island. On the one hand, as expatriates they are positioned on the periphery of Singaporean social structure. They tend to live out their lives — like most expatriates from affluent countries — on the margins of this society and in their own social enclaves. On the other hand, as single working women they are at the margins of the Japanese expatriate community. As women pursuing their occupations and careers they are alienated from most Japanese businessmen who tend to have rather conservative views about the place of women at the workplace. As unmarried women they are also estranged from the wives of these Japanese businessmen who tend to be organized in rather homogeneous and tight-knit circles. The outcome of this situation is twofold: single Japanese working women in Singapore tend to create informal and semi-formal networks of mutual support with each other (and to a very limited extent with a few other expatriate women); and, these networks are situated outside both Singaporean social formations and the organizations of the Japanese expatriate community.

Why study such individuals? Empirically speaking, single Japanese women working overseas have not been studied either abroad or upon their return to Japan. Thus some studies of Japanese expatriate families (White 1988), married women (Nakano 1995), children (Goodman 1990) and men (Ben-Ari, in this volume) have been carried out. But we know of no systematic inquiries into the social character and personal lives of single Japanese working women living abroad. Theoretically, this group of people seems to offer a fascinating case for investigating how the dynamics of expatriate communities interact with patterns of female employment within and outside of Japan. In other words, an examination of the experiences of such women may shed light on how the forms of male–female relations in Japanese workplaces are reproduced or transformed within the context of Japanese expatriate communities. Along these lines, in this chapter we address three sets of issues: the patterns of "push" and "pull" factors leading to the move of these women to Singapore; the workplace environments within which they are employed; and, the patterns of social contacts and networks that emerge out of this situation.

We interviewed 26 women between 1993 and 1995 for this project (11 people were interviewed by Ben-Ari and 15 were interviewed by Yong). The wide-ranging interviews included questions about the women's employment, manner of obtaining their jobs in Singapore, language use, expertise at the workplace, social interactions and ties, club membership and participation in informal networks, and residential choice and neighboring. The interviewees were contacted through a snow-balling method based on the authors' diverse personal networks, and through inter-mediaries in the Japanese business world of Singapore. In addition to the interviews, in the framework of his larger study of Japanese living in Singapore, Ben-Ari exchanged information with numerous other such women in activities held by Japanese organizations and businesses (for example, during lectures and conferences, receptions and parties, golf tournaments, and tours of offices and plants).

The Japanese Community and the Women

Erik Cohen (1977: 16) notes that "expatriates all over the world create their own 'enclaves' which shelter them off from the environment of the host society." He calls these "enclaves" "environmental bubbles" which encompass typical expatriates who tend to be reluctant to expose themselves to the host surroundings. Physically the "bubbles" are manifested in areas into which expatriates retreat to live in close proximity, and within which they feel safe and comfortable. While they may interact with locals at work, the social networks and leisure activities of expatriates are "normally always monopolized by fellow expatriates" (Cohen 1977: 29–77). In addition, they frequently patronize services, organizations and facilities that cater solely or primarily to their needs. This exclusiveness is reinforced by the presence of expatriate associations, clubs and schools. The encapsulation of expatriates within their "bubbles" is to a large extent due to their transience in the host country, their relatively privileged circumstances (for example, they receive such benefits as large salaries, housing, and educational allowances), and their hesitation to enter the native society.

Cohen's generalizations well characterize the Japanese presence in Singapore. There are over 20,000 Japanese expatriates in the city-state. The vast majority of these people are families comprising male business expatriates (managers and engineers) and their (normally non-working) wives and children. The men are typically representatives of large, medium and (since the mid-1980s) small Japanese companies who are posted to Singapore for a period usually ranging between three to five years. While a small minority of the men are "straw widowers" (*tanshin funin*) who have left their families in Japan, the great bulk of the businessmen come to Singapore with their families. As anticipated in Cohen's model, these families tend to congregate in three or four particular residential areas around the island. The relative affluence of these expatriates means that they live in the more well-to-do areas of Singapore (usually upper-middle class precincts).

The expatriate families are served by a range of educational services: a kindergarten serving nearly 400 children, a primary school serving 1900 children (which will soon be divided into two institutions), a junior high school serving about 700 children and a recently established high school serving about 500 youngsters. All of these establishments teach in Japanese, and are run according to curricula determined by the Japanese Ministry of Education. In addition, there are at least 12 *juku* (supplementary afternoon schools preparing children for university examinations in Japan) dotted around the city. The existence of a large Japanese expatriate community has spawned an extensive range of services: supermarkets and speciality shops, restaurants and cafes, clothing stores and boutiques, book shops and hobby stores, real estate and travel agents, and shipping representatives. In addition, a number of locally printed or produced Japanese language newspapers cater to their needs and tastes. Finally, for many people, the Japanese Association (the chief expatriate club on the island) is the hub of many activities. The buildings of the Association include meeting and reception halls, study rooms, a karaoke lounge, two restaurants, a library (for books and videos), and a medical clinic. Its activities include such things as English and Mandarin language lessons, Ikebana circles and traditional Japanese poetry recitations, lectures and lessons on contemporary issues, and customary Japanese festivals and golf tourneys.

The composition of the community in Singapore is the outcome of formal and informal policies in Japanese companies. First, most companies continue to recruit males to managerial track jobs. Second, these companies often (informally) encourage these men to marry early in their careers as a sign of maturity and responsibility (Edwards 1989; Rohlen 1974). Third, for many executives and engineers a posting abroad is becoming a common part of careering in management or engineering. And fourth, a placement overseas does not occur at the point of entry, but usually happens after a few years in the company. Consequently these patterns imply that it is married male employees (usually during the middle of their careers) and their families who are sent overseas. In a related manner, wives, it is still thought in many Japanese companies, are there to support the husband and to bring up the children. Thus even if wives worked in Japan, as expatriates they tend to evince conservative — or, more correctly, neo-traditional (Pharr 1981) — patterns of behavior: many of these women tend to retreat from the labor force and take up their "traditional" role as supporters of men and as nurturers of children (Nakano 1995).

Despite these trends, in the last decade a growing number of single Japanese women have begun to work outside the country, and one of their destinations is Singapore. The reasons for this development have to do with the interrelations between the Japanese labor market, the self-perceptions of these women, and the skills and capacities they bring to overseas markets. Basically,

> though there are more women working in Japan these days, mere numbers do not tell the whole story. Most are still in low-paying jobs, and more than a third are self-employed or working in family businesses. Almost all of the women

returning to work after raising their families work as part-timers without the security and few of the benefits of full-time employment (Whitehill 1991: 76; see also Kawashima 1995: 285).

Present-day Japanese women, and especially the well-educated, are less likely to want to work as one of the "office ladies" whose careers within Japan are severely limited (Lo 1990), or as part-timers. Within Japan, the continued difficulties many women face in pursuing long-term job opportunities in large firms has led to a move of females into specific sectors (the media and retailing, for example) and into smaller sized companies where they have a chance of pursuing a career.

Closely related to this "freeing" of female labor within Japan, is the move of many women into temporary contract work with personnel placement agencies. Temporary staff agencies began to proliferate

> when large numbers of women began to enter or reenter the work force, and they have recently begun to attract many of those women who have left their first job for various reasons and who have particular skills to offer ... Working through such agencies offers women greater freedom: They can accept or reject requests to go to this or that company, and as transient workers, they do not have to conform to menial tasks like tea service and tidying up. They can determine how long they will work in any one job, allowing them to reject work when they have other plans (Iwao 1993: 170).

It is in this light that the single working women that we studied should be understood: in ways similar to women working for temporary staff agencies within Japan, a sizeable minority of females are now considering and opting for openings overseas.

Who are these women? The 26 women we interviewed range in age between their mid-twenties and early forties with the biggest group being women in their late twenties and early thirties. The bulk of this group consists of women who have been in Singapore for about two years with a few individuals nearing four years. Of these, 20 had previously been outside Japan for substantial periods of at least one year in such places as the United States, Australia, Canada, Hong Kong, Taiwan and European countries. Except for two women who have only a high school certificate all of the other individuals have pursued higher education either in universities (some rather prestigious like Keio and Waseda) or in junior colleges. Finally, while the majority have never been married, two individuals (one in her late thirties and the other in her early forties) were divorced.

Workwise, the women are divided along the following lines: the biggest group work in the private sector in administrative and executive positions in the banking, finance, tourism, electronics, and manufacturing industries; the second group comprises five Japanese language teachers (three at the National University of Singapore, one within the framework of Singapore's Ministry of Education and one in a private language school); and the third group are two women who are employed respectively, in JETRO (Japan External Trade Organization, a government agency) and in a JETRO-affiliated organization as administrative staff. Of the 19 who work in the private sector, 15 work in Japanese companies with the rest employed either in Singaporean companies or in other foreign companies in Singapore. Not surprisingly, in the framework of the Japanese companies these women tend to be employed in service industries (like financial firms, personnel agencies, or real estate offices) and thus to an extent to replicate their presence in the service sector of Japan. In addition, many women (including the two individuals who work for the government agencies) fulfill support roles: they are employed as administrators, public relations officers, accounts clerks or personnel managers. As we shall see, their jobs require them to be fluent in both Japanese and English.

No less importantly, the great majority of these women have applied independently for positions in Singapore. In other words, they were not sent there by the companies in which they are employed. Three exceptions are the woman belonging to JETRO, the person sent by the JETRO-affiliated organization (to a joint computer development project signed between Singapore and Japan), and a Japanese language teacher assigned by the Japanese government to teach Japanese in Singaporean colleges. While this situation implies that the majority of the women are "independent" of their companies or organizations, it also implies that they are employed locally and thus receive local contracts and pay packages. For Japanese male executives, expatriate benefits include such things as housing allowances, two salaries (one paid in Singapore and one in Japan), medical insurance, educational subsidies, tax breaks, and yearly bonuses. Except for a few women who receive housing allowances and three who teach at the National University of Singapore and who have obtained university residences, none of the other women receive any kind of expatriate benefits. The fact that they do not receive expatriate packages serves to set these women apart from their Japanese male compatriots.

Taking up Work in Singapore

The limited opportunities that the Japanese labor market provides for women forms the general background for a more personal set of motives for moving to Singapore. The women interviewed often furnished intertwined accounts of escape and adventure of their relocation to the island: escape as a strategy for avoiding the negative aspects of Japanese society, and adventure as a quest for new experiences. Quite naturally, almost all of the women told us that the move was accompanied by much trepidation and anxiety, although a surprising number also mentioned that they perceived a cultural affinity between Singapore and Japan as Asian societies. Rather typical were the words of Sayoko (we use pseudonyms), a financial officer in a medium-sized Japanese company:

> I went back to Japan after finishing my education and working for years in the US. I worked there [in Japan] for three years but I couldn't get used to it. I used to travel an hour and a half each way to and from work; and I used to get so tired, and didn't like the trains and was tired all of the time. I decided I had to leave Tokyo; I felt that I had to escape. At the beginning I thought of going to such places as America or Australia, but when I studied in the States I had made friends with a Singaporean woman, and I visited her here twice. I thought this would be a nice place to work and English is spoken here; and this is an Asian society not far from Japan, and I thought that the prices in Japan were ridiculous and this would be a nice place. My friend also said she would help me to get into this place. I came here and sent my résumé around and finally got this offer which is to work mainly with Japanese clients.

Along similar lines, a real estate representative told us that after being in the United States for eight years she returned to Japan. She did not feel comfortable in the Japanese working environment and was soon recruited by a company looking for someone to run their Singapore office. She decided upon Singapore as she was looking for something interesting and somewhere where she could utilize her English language ability. The restrictions of Japanese working places were most explicitly remarked upon by Nabuko who works as a public relations officer for a precision instruments company. She graduated from university and worked in a number of companies in Japan but came to realize that they were "dead end jobs for women; no chances for advancement." Understanding that she could not change the working environment in Japan, she decided to do something drastic and leave for another environment:

> Singapore is Asian and more like Japan. At that time America didn't appeal to me and Europe was too varied. I came here and found this job through a personnel agency.

For a number of women, personal reasons were a prime "push" factor out of Japan. One divorced woman told us that going abroad was a way to build a new life without the difficulties a divorcee encounters in Japan (Iwao 1993: 113–21). A mother of two young daughters said that not only was it easier to be out of Japan as a divorcee, but found it easier to fulfill her role as a single parent by employing a maid in Singapore. A third woman, Takako, lived with her parents in Japan and felt that she always had to be "her parents' daughter." As they and many of her relatives pressured her to get married, she applied (via an advertisement in a trade journal) and was accepted to work as a language teacher at the National University of Singapore.

The stories told us by the women employed by the Japanese government were different. Emiko who works in JETRO did a year of her undergraduate work in America and upon graduation wanted to return there. Her parents opposed the idea and she looked into the possibility of employment with foreign companies in Japan. After understanding that she would not be allowed to participate in decision-making and be offered few career options in these firms, she decided on JETRO (she was recommended by a university friend). This was the time that the Equal Employment Opportunity Law was enacted in Japan (Lam 1993), and Emiko was told that in contrast to private companies, salaries for men and women were identical for government employees. Emiko went on to tell us that after a few years working for JETRO she approached her supervisor about the possibility of a stint overseas:

At the beginning at JETRO they never thought of sending women overseas as they did not really pursue careers. Then they started sending them to different parts of Japan as part of building their careers and later on they sent women on business trips outside of Japan ... Things started to change slowly. I came in wake of someone who had "paved the way." Another woman had been assigned abroad before me. She also was assigned to Singapore which they [her government bosses] think is safe and secure for a woman, and they talk English here. Today there are only two women in JETRO who are on overseas assignment.

Indeed, it is only these women — employed, for example, as staff of the Ministry of Foreign Affairs or as representatives of Japanese financial ministries — who receive full expatriate benefits in Singapore. This situation is an extension of the circumstances found in Japan as the

> most important early predictors of a woman's employment career are whether she started out as an employee and whether she started out in a government position ... Government workers make up a disproportionate share of the few women who started out in internal labor markets, and these women are less likely than any others to quit working upon marriage (Brinton (1993: 187).

In this respect, the words of Sachiko, a economist working in Nomura's research institute in Singapore, underline well the different conditions governing the work of women employed by private Japanese companies. Her words are worth quoting at length:

> I work here on a local contract despite the fact that the position is a professional one. There are 18 people who work here with seven Japanese. Of the Japanese, five are on expatriate contracts and they are all men, and two on local contracts: another Japanese woman and myself ...
>
> I graduated from Keio University's faculty of economics. After graduating I worked in a number of banks and then in a patent making company. A few years ago I decided to leave Japan [later it turned out that she had divorced] and came here to Singapore. I worked as a translator and interpreter

and from the beginning was awarded only local contracts. After some part-time work I worked full time for about six months as a Japanese language teacher in a company that worked with Singaporeans in Japanese businesses. I taught Japanese to Singaporeans from such companies as Sony or TDK so that they could work with their Japanese counterparts on new projects. I was a language teacher, but because this was a program for business people I found myself explaining such things as Japanese culture, organizational behavior and Japanese management methods ...

Here I was initially accepted through a "temp agency." The managing director here interviewed me. He is also a graduate from Keio University but he finished the faculty of commerce which has a lower ranking than the faculty of economics. I guess that may have been a factor for accepting me for the position. One of the Japanese expatriates had to return to Japan and since no one replaced him they asked me if I would take over his job. I prepare various kinds of reports in Japanese about the economic situation in South East Asia ...

I like my job as it involves my profession as an economist, but if I look at the future then my prospects are limited here. When I look at my career all the options are closed. There is a constant uncertainty about what will happen in the future. Someone may come from Japan and take up this job and then ... I think that this is because I am a woman. If I were a man I think that there would have been a chance to find a job like this in Japan.

I always feel that I am a "pinch hitter." Last month I wrote a report for the monthly review of the Japan Chamber of Commerce. It was about the new goods and services tax in Singapore, but the only reason they asked me to do it was because the man who was supposed to write it was too busy. I was lucky to get this opportunity, but it was only an opportunity that came my way, not because they recognize my ability.

Nabuko's words (she works in a precision instruments company) echoed many of these themes:

Through the "temp agency" that I applied to, I heard that many Japanese companies abroad become even more

Japanese, and when I arrived here I definitely felt it. This is a very Japanese company. There are many rules and they interfere in your personal life. Like they tell you when to take leave; you can't choose yourself. Benefits are also lower for women who are employed on local contracts. Maybe this is because in Japan they are a male-dominated company: they have many engineers and only a few women in administrative jobs.

Along similar lines, a number of women added that these differences in expatriate benefits, were "unfair to us" as the male Japanese expatriates "receive privileges that we don't get." Thus while many women have moved overseas in search of new opportunities, for the majority Japanese workplaces in Singapore reproduce the same kinds of male-female relations found in Japan itself. Furthermore, their working environment determines to a great extent the resources at their disposal, their residential choices, interactions with (Japanese and local) colleagues, and membership in local associations and networks.

At the Workplace: "Service", Mediation, and Support

Like all professionals, so the female expatriates that we studied work long hours. For example, Sachiko (Nomura Research Institute), told us that although the working hours are from nine to five, she actually works from eight to about seven or eight in the evening. In addition, if there is an urgent deadline to be met then she even works Saturdays and Sundays. Her account was duplicated by all of the other women including the language teachers. In making sense of this part of the women's working lives we initially followed Atsumi (1979), who found that for male workers in Japan, the workplace was a prime site for initiating and maintaining social ties. Accordingly, of the 26 interviewees, half said that *at work* they interact mainly with other Japanese, seven mainly with locals, and four equally with locals and Japanese.

What we found however, was that what mattered to the women we studied was not socializing or the national affiliation of their "interaction partners" in the workplace. What was significant to them were the contents and quality of the interactions. To be sure, the assignments of the 16 women who work in Japanese companies usually require them to come into contact with other Japanese quite frequently. Usually holding executive or administrative positions, their duties largely involve liaising with Japanese clients and assisting their Japanese bosses. But there are two distinct features that characterize this kind of work: one involves the "traditional" female or "support" role, the other embraces the function of cultural mediator. In both cases, women are delicately but clearly excluded from the male centers of organizations.

Typically, Chiaki, a sales executive in an electronics firm, comes into frequent contact with other Japanese. Verbalizing a number of assumptions about proper "female" business behavior, she observed:

> In my job, because I can speak Japanese, I deal mainly with Japanese, like calling Tokyo HQ to get information or meeting Japanese customers here. It probably helps that I know the Japanese etiquette as well, you know, like the bowing, using the polite language and all that.

Familiarity with Japanese business customs and Japanese language competency were also cited by Tomoko, a personnel executive in another electronics company:

> My work mainly involves seeing to the accommodation and transportation needs of new Japanese expatriates who just came to Singapore. My company thinks that a Japanese is more suitable for this job. First, I can speak Japanese. Also they think that as a Japanese, I am supposed to more or less know what Japanese want, their preferences, their tastes — sometimes even without them saying so.

While subtle, her words reflect the general Japanese cultural expectations that women should be able to "anticipate" the wishes and needs of their interaction partners.

Many women employed in Japanese companies work closely with their Japanese superiors and are formally or in practice, personal assistants to the chief executive. Norie, a senior executive in a manufacturing firm, wryly commented that her boss,

> delegates me jobs he can't spare time for. In fact, sometimes I do mainly paperwork for him, so that he can spend more time playing golf.

These patterns should be seen as part of a general set of expectations that many Japanese executives have about the "proper" responsibilities and demeanor of Japanese working women. Mariko, who works in a personnel placement agency, noted:

> I think it may even be an advantage to be a woman in the services sector. I always tell my workers that it's like being a mother to children. We need to think about what the clients need: it's like thinking that the children need food and drink and providing them with it.

The words of Takie, a real estate agent at a Japanese agency, corroborated this view. When meeting clients she makes a point of talking very politely and noted that

> maybe the men prefer to talk to me about apartments to rent; maybe it fits the conservative, traditional image of what women do and what they are in charge of.

We then talked about the kinds of clothes used in Japanese companies. She observed that the men in the sales and service industries (banking, insurance and finance) come to work dressed in dark suits or keep a jacket in the office. She went on to note:

> I usually don't wear heavy clothing but I do wear a skirt and a shirt. But when I go to certain companies — the more conservative Japanese companies like banks or Matsushita — then I dress in a more Japanese manner: much more conservative, like covering my neck and so on. I think that is what they expect.

Where to these expectations come from? Despite some rather slow-moving changes, the vast majority of women in Japan, and especially in the large companies, continue to perform peripheral roles. According to McLendon (1983; see also Carter and Dilatush 1976; Pharr 1984) "OLs (office ladies) are expected to support men in their work by preparing tea, making copies and running errands." These expectations, moreover, are also shared by many women (Kawashima 1995). As Whitehill (1991: 77) concludes, such

> important management concerns as supervisor-subordinate relations, patterns of leadership, promotion decisions, and development programs clearly are influenced by the accepted, conventional male-female relationships ... In the workplace, too, women are on a different track to men and frequently are considered little more than *shokuba no hana*, or office

flowers. Many top Japanese companies continue to select all of their female recruits from high schools or junior colleges. In too many cases, the major selection criteria are that the graduate must be younger than 24, attractive, well-mannered, obedient, and totally lacking in ambitions.

In short, our findings are that in numerous companies situated in Singapore, Japanese executives expected Japanese women to behave as they do in Japan. A number of women we talked to noted that this situation was especially true of the larger and older Japanese companies. Sachiko of Nomura Research Institute, works in a very conservative office:

> There are many problems regarding the fact that I am a woman. For example at the beginning, my colleagues asked why I work overtime, whether I don't have to go home early. There's a "funny" thing here. They [the Japanese executives] usually go to have lunch together. They asked me once to go with them, but they never asked me again after that time. It doesn't matter whether I want to or not, they just don't invite me. It's the same when visitors from Tokyo come and they all go out. They tell me that they would rather go out in the company only of gentlemen, so I never go out in the evenings with them. Only once, when a delegation from Japan arrived with some women then the managing director asked me to come with them to dinner.

She went on to talk about "tea service":

> At the beginning I prepared tea and coffee when I came here, but now that I have this new job then I don't; the secretarial helpers do. Now I only prepare for myself. When you came [to interview me] I thought of preparing you coffee, but I asked one of the secretaries to do it. Maybe in this company I have to behave this way or else they won't understand my position and status. Listen, as far as I see things, I don't mind preparing tea even if I were the managing director, but in this company and in Singapore in particular it is important to maintain your status. There is a Singapore woman here who heads a research team. She never prepares tea and I learnt from her that maybe I have to copy the style of the Singaporeans in terms of professional behavior.

When we asked her about sexual harassment, she replied:

> Well something direct, like touching or talk about sex, I never encountered in this office. But for example, when the Japanese men talk they say things like how they want a younger [Japanese] woman here. They need, they say, to talk to the head office to send a younger woman so that she can prepare coffee and tea. I never react during these situations, but I've heard them on the phone and that's the way they talk ... In the previous places where I worked in Japan these things happened more directly like touching my body, my face; and these things happened at the office. At the beginning I didn't know how to behave, but with time I learnt to treat the men like children, like kids. In general, Japanese men don't know how to relate to women on an equal basis. They treat women like mothers, daughters or women but they don't know how to treat them as colleagues.

In contrast, Sayoko who works as a financial officer, presented us with a minority view. One of only three Japanese at a medium-sized company, she observed:

> I've never had any problem as a woman here or in Japan. First within the company my MD and his deputy [the other Japanese man] are young and don't give me any problems. Second, the Japanese businessmen who come here soften up. [Laughs] Maybe its the climate, or maybe they come here with the expectation of meeting strong Singaporean women, but they never give me any trouble ... Maybe I also make a point of not meeting those people who have a more conservative attitude. Listen, the atmosphere at this workplace is very good, maybe the best among the Japanese companies working in Singapore. I don't know if this will continue, but the two Japanese men who are here are very easy-going, don't give orders and rely on us to do the work. Even when I make a mistake they are willing to help.

She encountered the same kind of attitude in regard to entertainment:

> Usually the MD and his deputy do the hosting, but he invites me along about once a month. I then go out with the clients

to enjoy dinner or something. Of course it's important, the social side to business, but there is no feeling that this is formal. I even go to karaoke lounges and hostess bars. I don't mind going to such places. I feel comfortable. The hostesses there are nice because they see me as a client and they ask all sorts of questions about what I do and so on. In addition, we have outings here for all the staff and we have a good time. We go out on trips to Thailand and Malaysia, for example.

Nabuko (from the company making precision instruments) has mixed experiences:

The men usually behave very nicely during work. But sometimes when they drink they use the fact that this is Singapore and nobody speaks Japanese and make comments. Sometimes when they drink they ask me all sorts of things like to take my clothes off or to drink some more. It embarrasses me but they don't think they are doing something wrong; they do it in a sort of innocent way. They just don't understand that this is a sort of discrimination against women. Once or twice I said something about this and the following day they said that I spoil the drinking occasion and that I am not entertaining. And I said "if that is so then don't invite me." And consequently lately I don't go to these occasions.

Mariko, from the personnel agency, explained:

I am very careful when I organize *tsukiai* [entertainment] with clients. Of course it's important to go to such activities to create proper ties and relations. But because I don't know what expectations men have of such activities, what they think about these activities, so when a number of men invite me together then I go, but if it is one man then I always say that I will bring along a friend of mine, a woman.

The woman employed in JETRO told us that she encountered no difficulties among the ten Japanese she worked with. But her exclusion is more subtle. When entertaining guests she joined her colleagues for the "first party," usually dinner, but never joined them for the "second party," held in drinking establishments and where much of the office politics are played out (Ben-Ari, 1993).

In-Betweeners: Cultural Mediation and Ties With Locals

The other role the women carry out involves cultural mediation. At one level this role is related to their language proficiency; at another level it is the result of their being outsiders to both the male Japanese executives and to the locals. The majority of the women we talked to are relatively adept in English: all of them have learned English for at least six years in Japan, and (as we have noted) most have spent at least one or two years studying or working in English speaking countries prior to their sojourn in Singapore.[1] Consequently, many find themselves helping their bosses when they run into difficulties with English. Tomoko, a personnel executive, addressed this issue directly when talking about her Japanese bosses:

> They don't really like to speak to the local colleagues — maybe they feel shy because their English is not too good. So they ask me to pass the message instead.

Ayako, a production control executive in a Japanese manufacturing firm, noted:

> My Japanese bosses, and, in general, Japanese don't speak good English — they speak 'Japlish'. Because I have studied in the States for a year, I often help them to interpret, especially when they get the meaning wrong.

In contrast to her Japanese colleagues, Tomoko's (the personnel executive) facility in English helps her to mingle with her co-workers:

> With English, I can talk and joke with my local colleagues. But for many of the Japanese in my company, except for those who can speak a little better English, most of them usually talk among themselves in Japanese.

Cultural mediation also goes on at a more "macro" scale: for example, Takie, who works in the real estate agency, sees herself as mediating between the needs of her Japanese clients and the local market. She said that as many newcomers lack proficiency in English they prefer to talk to her and have her understand their needs. In a similar vein, Mariko of the personnel placement agency, observed that especially smaller companies are coming to Singapore and their representatives do not speak good English. We can help during the first period when they arrive here. We are a bridge between the Japanese companies and Singapore.

The confidence some women feel in using English was brought out in the interview with Megumi, a broker in an American brokerage firm:

My job is fast-paced and stressful. I have to be good in both Japanese and English. My Japanese clients tell me what they want over the phone and I have to immediately yell across to my colleagues in English.

Nevertheless, despite the informants' proficiency in English, they did encounter difficulties with the "Singlish" used by Singaporeans: a mix of English, Malay and local Chinese dialects. Kimie, an operations co-ordinator at a medical service center, related:

I had culture shock initially at the languages spoken here ... and they are all mixed together. When my colleague asked me "Let's go *makan*," I didn't understand, so she explained that *makan* means "eat" in Malay.

A few of the women we interviewed found the English spoken in Singapore to be "puzzling" and "funny." Etsuko, a teacher at a private Japanese language school, noted:

The way Singaporeans speak English is a little different, isn't it? I think you call it "Singlish" here? You use a lot of "lah" at the end of sentences ... Also, the accent is quite clipped and the accent is quite different from American English.

Along these lines, a few women reported that while they initially had some difficulties in understanding Singapore English, they became used to it after a period.

Against this background, while most of the women working in Japanese companies reported a high level of interaction with other Japanese at work, they said that they get along better with their local colleagues. The difference in work-status between these working women and their Japanese (male) managers explains this situation. Chiaki, a sales executive in an electronics company, pointed out:

At work, the Japanese I interact with are either my Japanese clients or my bosses. They are all my superiors. Apart from work-related matters with them, I prefer to interact with local colleagues. Also, because I am employed as a local employee, I identify more with my local colleagues in the office.

Consequently, many of the women mentioned feeling more relaxed with their local colleagues. For example, while several told us that they take lunch with their local co-workers and frequently joke with them, none mentioned going to lunch with their Japanese colleagues. In general then, women employed in Japanese companies who have fostered good relations with locals and are not always seen as "one of the Japanese". In one case, Yuki's colleagues (she is an accounts clerk) even complained to her about how difficult it was to rise to managerial level posts in the company because one is not a Japanese.

Ties Outside Work

But the question still remains as to what kind of ties these women foster outside of work. First, it is not surprising that the women we studied rarely interact with their Japanese colleagues or with their wives outside work. Alluding to the Japanese style of cultivating social ties, Ayako (the production control executive) explained:

My association with them [her Japanese male colleagues] stops after work. If we go to golf together, we have to care about the relationship. In Japan, we are very strict about elder or younger, boss or subordinate. I have to care about each other's relationship. If he is a superior — you always say, "*Hai, hai, hai*" [Yes, yes, yes]. It makes me very tired.

This view was also voiced by a number of other respondents who found it "taxing," "difficult," and "takes a lot of energy" to interact with Japanese as a heavy emphasis is placed on social formalities, obligations and the cultivation of workplace related status. In addition, the twin themes of gender and age often came up in informal socializing with Japanese co-workers: questions about their reasons for not marrying made some women "very conscious of age". This kind of situation is very similar to that found in Japan. To a great degree, work is still a "way station" on the road to marriage for many women in Japan (McLendon 1983):

100

a very large portion of women in Japan leave work when they marry or have their first child. More concretely, various forms of social pressure are exerted on those who do not get married and stay in the company: they may be labeled as spinsters and subject to various forms of ridicule about their age (Hamada 1989). Hiroko, an assistant manager in a German bank, related:

> Back in Japan, colleagues say "Why don't you get married?"; The boss asks, "Why don't you get married?"; Neighbors ask, "Why don't you get married?". I don't want it to happen in Singapore again! I think it is [chuckles] sexual harassment!

In addition, many of the women felt that "Japanese here don't understand us." Miwako, who works as an executive in a Japanese bank, echoed the views of many of the women:

> They don't understand why I want to come to Singapore to work; why can't I be like the "typical" Japanese women in Japan — stay in Japan, work for a few years, find a husband, get married, stay at home and be a housewife. They don't understand why a woman wants a career.

Encounters with the wives of their Japanese colleagues also put the single working women on the defensive. A woman working as an economist noted:

> We get many opportunities to meet them at company dinners but I always feel uncomfortable. This is only a feeling, nothing comes out specifically, but it's as though we have nothing to talk about, no common subjects and maybe our different life styles.

"During these engagements," Nabuko told us, "one does not know exactly how to interact and everyone is very careful." Consequently, almost all of the informants said that apart from work they do not come into contact with Japanese businessmen or their families.

But contact with locals outside the workplace is also limited. Most of the women have only a few local friends. This point was illustrated by Megumi (a broker at an American brokerage firm) who could "count the number of local friends on one hand." For many persons, local friends consist of colleagues who sometimes go out for dinner together, and the one or two Singaporeans that they knew before coming to Singapore. Accordingly, while a few of the women do mix with locals and other expatriates, by far the most common pattern is for them to interact with other Japanese working women outside work. As we were told, these friends and acquaintances are mostly confined to a small circle of single Japanese women who are "easy to get along with" and "can understand us," or, in a few cases, to Singaporean women who can speak Japanese. As friends these women go out to dinner, play tennis, swim, do other sports, go to movies, and host each other in their homes. Takie, the real estate agent, for instance, said that almost all her friends are other Japanese women and that she has only one Singaporean friend. Along with a few other women, Sachiyo, a language teacher, is the exception in that she interacts both with the family of a businessman and with other expatriate friends (Indian, American and Canadian). In general then, the women prefer to limit their contact to working Japanese women who are like themselves, and who are perceived as being able to understand each other.

Residential Choice and Neighboring

These findings are replicated in terms of the women's residential choices and neighboring patterns. As noted earlier, expatriates tend to form their own enclaves by living in close proximity in the same residential areas (Cohen 1977: 29). Of the 26 women, 9 stay in condominiums, 8 in other private apartments and 9 stay in public (ie. Housing and Development Board) flats[2]. The criteria used by the women in choosing their current residences are principally rent and location. As the majority receive no housing allowances, they give high priority to affordable rent, while the minority who do receive such allowances tend to live (as other expatriates) in the well-to-do areas of Singapore. Consequently, the women who stay in HDB flats (and the language teachers securing university housing) all told us that they were not aware of any Japanese staying in their neighborhood. Ayako (the production control executive) explained:

> The Japanese businessmen in Singapore are sent here by their companies in Japan. Most of them stay in condominiums as their companies pay. In my case, I applied for a job here and must pay rent myself as I don't get any housing allowances. Renting an HDB room is much cheaper.

A related consideration is location near public transport. This point reflects the fact that in contrast to male expatriates who have cars these women are dependent on accessible means for commuting to work. As one woman told us "it is easier to take a train than a bus, just like the subway in Japan."

What is of significance, however, is that none of the women mentioned the nationality of their neighbors as a consideration in choice of residence. This point contrasts with Ben-Ari's findings in regard to families of Japanese expatriates who generally choose to reside in areas populated by their compatriots. Indeed, it is generally true that even those respondents who stay in areas populated by Japanese families, told us that their interaction with their neighbors is minimal and in some cases nonexistent. As in work, most women see themselves as "different" from their Japanese neighbors and as having nothing in common with them. For example, despite the fact that Sumiko, a language teacher, lives in an area (Newton) where there are many expatriates, she has almost no contact with her Japanese neighbors. Hiroko, who lives in a condominium and receives housing allowance noted:

> When I come back from work in the evenings, I always see them [her Japanese neighbors] at the club house in our condo, but I hardly ever join them. They are mostly housewives and they talk, talk, talk ... mainly about their children, their husbands. I am different from them, no children, still single ... Nothing in common to talk about.

For Miori, a senior officer in a Japanese securities company, her single status was also keenly felt in such circumstances. She somewhat self-consciously commented on her Japanese neighbors:

> They might even be talking about me ... [laughs] This strange Japanese woman who doesn't get married but comes to Singapore all alone to work.

Consequently, the single working women living in such areas try to minimize their contact with their Japanese neighbors. They confine such meetings to the occasional tennis game together, or when they are invited for dinner are "sometimes reluctant to go" and "try to turn down tactfully." Hiroko aptly summed up the interaction with her Japanese neighbors:

> I don't really interact with the Japanese in the condo. When I happen to bump into the housewives, we usually make "small talk" — like the weather — "*Atsui ne ...*" [It's hot, isn't it?],

or about the sale at the department store — "*Yasui ne* ..."
[It's cheap, isn't it?]. Other than that, we don't really interact.

Indeed, to many of the women we interviewed, it is not important to have Japanese neighbors. As Junko, a language teacher living in an HDB flat, said "I'm independent and can do everything myself." When probed directly about their residential preference, the majority of women indicated that they would avoid staying in Japanese residential areas as far as possible and prefer to live among Singaporeans who respect privacy and are not "nosy" neighbors like the Japanese. Junko noted,

> With Japanese neighbors you have to socialize with them. The Japanese are a rather closed community. Also if I come home late at night, they will know [pause], something like a watchdog, you know. I don't like this kind of troublesome things.

Her views were repeated by Reiko (public relations executive) who did not relish the thought of Japanese neighbors saying among themselves that "this girl came back real late last night and appeared drunk." In one extreme case Norie, who felt a distinct lack of privacy where she lived, decided to move to another apartment because "there are just too many Japanese where I stayed."[3] Thus most of the women believed that living among Singaporeans gave greater privacy because "unlike the Japanese, Singaporeans don't really bother about those around them" and as Reiko observed, "Anyway, in Singapore, neighbors don't really interact, do they?". To be sure, what is of importance here is the perceived lack of interaction with the Singaporeans rather than what actually happens: it is the perceived intrusiveness of the Japanese nationals which is of significance to the women. Indeed, only one person, Chiaki (sales executive), who stays in an HDB flat conceded that she would like to have a good mix of Japanese and Singaporean neighbors. Not so much because she gets along equally well with both groups, but more because she sometimes feels "odd" being one of the rare Japanese living in HDB estates:

> I don't know what my Singapore neighbors think of me, a Japanese staying in HDB as most Japanese stay in condos here. Also, when my Japanese boss found out that I'm staying in HDB, he told me, "Chiaki, why are you so miserable?"

This feeling was voiced by some other the women who told us that "the Japanese here are rather snobbish" as "they live well here because of company pay": receiving no expatriate benefits makes them "feel poor" by comparison.

Membership of Clubs and Associations

In a new culture, clubs and associations often act as buffer mechanisms aiding adjustment. Expatriate clubs provide not only recreation activities and information about the host society but, more significantly, help to maintain a sense of belonging and cultural identity. As Cohen (1977: 41) points out, "internally they focus and structure the life of the expatriate community, externally, they symbolize its separateness and exclusiveness from the surrounding host society." What about the single working women that we studied? Except for two who belong to small Japanese clubs and three who belong to local clubs, none of the women have joined any formal club or association. Particularly striking is the fact that none have joined the Japanese Association which caters to the Japanese expatriate community in Singapore. Kuniko, a travel assistant at a Japanese airline agency, explained:

> I will feel out of place there. Those Japanese in the Japanese Association are either the businessmen, housewives or their children. I don't think there is any single Japanese like myself.

The feeling of not fitting in was related more directly by Norie, who, when asked if she was a member of the Japanese association, answered:

> Japanese Association? No! I don't feel comfortable with Japanese. Yes, it's easy to communicate — language, culture, behavior — everything. But I'm single, independent and working as a local employee. They are rich, I'm poor.

Thus the differences exposed by membership of the association are family situation and employment status. During her two years in Singapore, Miki, an administrative officer in a hotel, said that it never occurred to her to join any Japanese club as she does "not belong to the Japanese clique here." She went on to sum up her views:

> I'm not like the Japanese here. First, I'm single. Second, I don't get any expatriate benefits. Third, I'm not their typical

"kawaii" [cute] type of girl ... You know, the kind who likes Mickey Mouse, Donald Duck ... and who nudge each other and giggle at every little thing.

Along these lines, we found a perception that the Japanese association was a "family-club" with activities catering mainly for housewives and children and which are conducted mainly during the day-time and on weekdays. In this way, the women reasoned, the association was not suited to them as they have to work. As we found in regard to patterns of residential choice and social interaction, apart from the mandatory interaction at work, most women do not want to come into contact with the Japanese in Singapore and thus do not join the Japanese clubs.

Of the two who do belong to Japanese clubs, association with other Japanese is limited as these clubs cater mainly to locals. For example Junko who belongs to the *Ikebana* [Japanese flower arrangement] club, noted that except for the teacher all the club members were locals. Her situation is similar to Etsuko's, one of three Japanese in the *Chanoyu* [Japanese tea ceremony] club at the school where she teaches Japanese language. Similarly, only three respondents have joined local clubs. One is Norie who volunteers at the Chinese Orchestra Society. She goes there once a fortnight and helps in translating pamphlets into Japanese as well as collecting donations for the society. Another woman, Kimie, is a volunteer at a local hospital where she helps feed the sick during weekends. The rest of the women generally cited lack of time or feeling uncomfortable at being "the only Japanese" as reasons for not joining local clubs.

Another type of circle to which a small number of women belong are groups of university alumni. Replicating the Japanese tendency to create and maintain alumni associations, some graduates of Japanese universities meet regularly, if infrequently in Singapore. While men tend to be more active in these circles, some women (including married women) participate occasionally. For example, one of the language teachers told us that in her three years in Singapore she went twice or three times to meetings of graduates of Tokyo Joshi Daigaku (Tokyo Women's University). She revealed that about 20 of them meet for lunch once or twice a year. Yet here again, the general attitude we found was that formal club membership, whether Japanese or local, was not important for them.

But there are other types of groups, more ephemeral and less institutionalized than the Japanese Association, in which many of the women participate. A primary example is the *Sankakai* (lit. Third Thursday Association). While this association of working women includes married individuals, it overwhelmingly comprises single females. The association meets every third Thursday of a given month for what are formally defined as study meetings (*gakushukai*). These gatherings include presentations (by invited experts) about such matters as the stock market or types of insurance, but also less mundane topics as the hole in the ozone layer. A language teacher who teaches Japanese at a number of local Singapore institutions of higher education explained how the *Sankakai* was founded:

> The aim of establishing this organization was not only to study, but more importantly, to create a network [uses the English word] for the exchange of information. Through the network we get to know various people and then we can invite them to give talks.
>
> We are all scattered (*bara bara*) around Singapore, isolated. So in order to be able to share information, and in order to be stimulated intellectually we decided to meet. Today there are already 50 women who belong to this organization and it grows all of the time ...
>
> The organization itself was set up two or three years ago by a few women. The first year there were ten women who attended the meetings, but with time it grew slowly. We always meet at the Pan Pacific Hotel in a fancy meeting room. One of our members knows someone from the management so we meet there. We basically get the room for free and have to pay only for the coffee.
>
> The majority of the women are career women. Although there are more and more of us, in comparison with men we are still a minority. We just don't have access to the kind of information that Japanese men have for a number of reasons. The leading reason is the in Japanese companies women are still excluded and men don't pass information to them. It's true not only in Japan but also here in Japanese companies.

Nabuko, the woman who works as a public relations officer at the firm making precision instruments, observed:

The *Sankakai* is important for two reasons; one is the exchange of information; like we talk about the work conditions of local companies and other American, French, and European companies and see what kind of packages they have. We can then compare the packages we get not only to other Japanese companies in Singapore but to other kinds of businesses. Second, we help each other and suggest things to each other; like how to handle different situations at work.

Interestingly, the very replication (in Singapore) of Japanese patterns of male-female relations in the workplace has led to the creation of an organization aimed at ameliorating the very weaknesses of these patterns. This semi-formal network thus serves not only instrumental aims but also provides mutual support and opportunities for making friends and acquaintances. In a similar vein, Sachiko of Nomura Research Institute told us that while she belongs to the *Sankakai*, she has also recently joined the "International Business Women's Association." In the framework of the latter organization she meets local business women and women from the Monetary Authority of Singapore primarily to exchange information: "You can make friends there and some women have even been to Japan and so understand what it is like to work in a Japanese company."

In her interview, however, Nabuko, went on to tell us about another kind of grouping to which she belongs:

I belong to another organization. Well it's not an organization with a name, but it's a gathering of young Japanese, men and women. We meet casually for eating and drinking. We have a few people who direct the organization and make all of the arrangements and about 60 members ...

It's all very open and you can invite anyone, even non-Japanese. But because we speak in Japanese then maybe people who don't may feel uncomfortable ...

Lately many of the large Japanese companies send young single men here. At the beginning they went primarily to lounges and all they had were hostesses to talk to and they told me that they were miserable ... Then we started two years ago and now we have about 50 or 60 members. You also have to understand that the Japanese Association has no activities for young people ... Many of the members, and especially men, live in condominiums with pools and we organize barbecues in these places. We meet once a month or once in two months, it all depends if there is someone willing to organize it. The whole atmosphere is very casual.

These social gatherings seem to be important for a few of the women we interviewed. Sayoko, the financial officer, told us that Singapore was very limited in terms of finding a potential Japanese partner. Citing the "ticking" of her "biological clock" she was candid when saying that she was even considering going back to Japan for this reason.

Conclusion

Let us recapitulate our findings. The workplace interactions of the single working women we studied depend largely on the type of organization in which they are employed and the nature of their work. Individuals working in Japanese companies have greater opportunities for contact with other Japanese nationals, while the women employed in other organizations tend to interact with Singaporeans or with other expatriates. But as we saw, the kinds of roles which the women actually carry out serve to exclude them from the male centers of these firms and companies. Whether they perform the "traditional" female work of aid and assistance, or are cultural mediators these women are marginal to the male preserves of organizational decision-making and higher status. Thus while many women expected the move abroad to involve new opportunities for advancement and careering, employment in Japanese firms (and the majority are so employed) signals a reversion to patterns found within Japan.

While many persons interact with other Japanese nationals during a substantial part of their work days, this mingling does not "translate" into social ties outside work. In general, the women studied usually belong to, and draw support from, small circles of friends comprising other single Japanese working women. The women rarely socialize with Japanese business expatriates (except in the context of the office) or their wives (barring office parties), and only a few have a small number of local friends. Overall a sizeable minority said that they felt estranged both from locals and from other Japanese. These same patterns are replicated in terms of residential choice and neighboring. In this respect, even the minority of individuals who do receive housing allowances and stay in Japanese residential areas tend to severely limit their interaction with families of Japanese nationals. In a related manner, the women who live in regular Singaporean residential areas also keep to themselves and do not interact with their neighbors. Finally, while the women hardly participate in any Japanese or local clubs many are members of either the *Sankakai* which provides a network of support and the exchange of information, or the informal circle of young single Japanese which provides an arena for finding potential partners.

In general then, the women are doubly marginalized. As expatriates they are distanced from local Singaporean society. Being foreign nationals who speak their own language and whose allegiances and future plans lie elsewhere, they are (like most expatriates) at the margins of Singaporean groups and networks. But as single working women they are also estranged from their male colleagues and from their wives. This point is especially important given the demographic "skew" of the Japanese expatriate community in Singapore. For all of the talk about the creation of a "little Japan" in Singapore, the community is definitely not a miniature version of Japanese society. As it is made up of nuclear families (ie. married couples and their children) evincing a neo-conservative life-style, single working women find it difficult to find a place for themselves. Furthermore, as most of the single working women have arrived in the island independently and as they have considerable English language skills they have less of a need to maintain an orientation to their compatriots. Thus because they see themselves, and to a large extent are also seen, as somehow "different" from the Japanese expatriate managers and their families, these women have created their own limited and specialized environmental bubble in Singapore.

The marginal status and the specialized environment bubble which these women inhabit has both advantages and disadvantages. On the one hand, like working women in Japan (Iwao 1993: 171), their marginal status gives them greater mobility and freedom. This flexibility allows them to move between countries and jobs and to explore various adventures. But on the other hand, because they are marginals, they cannot fully enter the cores of the companies where they are employed and cannot pursue careers like their male colleagues. Ultimately, the women employed in Japanese companies are temporary staff members who are "outsiders" in the places where they work, and who tend to feel alienated from permanent Japanese workers and from local employees.

Are the women we studied harbingers of change in Japanese society? In a qualified sense they may well be. If the pattern we discovered in Singapore continues, then single women working overseas may be role models for other women striking out on their own. Perhaps the most significant aspect of the move outside Japan is that the majority of the women have decided and applied on their own for jobs in Singapore: because they were not sent there by their firms they are independent of their companies. But as we have seen, this independence carries with it limits for many women in terms of socializing, benefits, and careering.

Notes

[1] In addition, four or five individuals have a good working knowledge of Mandarin having studied it before or after their arrival in Singapore. One woman who works in a German bank can speak some German, and one who previously worked in Hong Kong can speak Cantonese. None attend English language classes in Singapore.

[2] A public organization established in 1960 to construct and sell public housing and solve the housing problems of Singapore. By 1985 84 per cent of the population in Singapore resided in HDB flats (Quah and Quah 1990).

[3] This pattern is consistent with Nakano's (1995) study of the Japanese community in Hong Kong. She found that the wives of businessmen created *fujinkai* (women's associations) which functioned as small groups exercising semi-formal control.

Chapter 5

Books, Consumption, and the Movement of Japanese Business to Singapore

Mien Woon Ng and Eyal Ben-Ari

Introduction

This chapter explores two sets of issues related to the operation of a Japanese book company — which we call Yomitakunai — in Singapore. First, the case of this book company allows us to examine the "transplantation" of a retail business from Japan to this national context. This kind of analysis is important because it has been primarily production facilities and (more recently) financial services which have been systematically studied by social scientists (Hayashi 1986; Blumenthal 1987). Thus against the background of previous studies of what has been termed the "transferability" of Japanese organizational practices we can better see the distinctive characteristics of retail businesses.

Second, the case of Yomitakunai permits us to examine the interrelationships between a large Japanese expatriate clientele and an ongoing commercial concern catering to it. In effect, the company caters to two distinct clienteles: on the one hand, like all the chains of books companies in the island, it sells books to Singaporeans and to tourists. On the other hand, like many other specialized businesses (for example, real estate agents, restaurants, and supermarkets) it caters specifically to the large community of Japanese expatriates based in the country. Given this situation, the case at hand is suitable for exploring how the consumption patterns of this expatriate community influence the internal processes and structures of the company.

112

The Book Company: Yomitakunai

Yomitakunai was established over 70 years ago in Japan. It now has close to 70 full-scale retail branches and another 30 stores in schools throughout Japan. A few decades ago it began to manage stores outside Japan, and today has over 20 branches around the world (it recently opened an outlet in London). As the marketing manager at Yomitakunai noted, his company is among (and therefore competes with) the "high class" (*joojoo*) book companies in Japan.

The expansion into Singapore should be seen against the background of the general trends of establishing Japanese business interests abroad. While Japanese business interests began to shift out of Japan in the late 1960s, the move to Southeast Asia began in the early 1970s. At its beginning, this movement comprised mostly production and servicing facilities but in the last decade or so it has increasingly come to include financial services and retail outlets. In this context, Singapore stands at the forefront of Japan's move into Southeast and South Asia. A wide range of Japanese factories, headquarters, and financial and sales centers are now located in the country. Indeed, by some estimates as much as one-fourth of Singapore's GDP is generated by Japanese companies (Cronin 1992). The Japanese expatriate community which now numbers over 20,000 people overwhelmingly comprises the people who run these businesses and their families.

The first branch of Yomitakunai in Singapore was opened in 1983 near a residential area which is heavily populated by Japanese expatriates. Initially, the bulk of the books sold by the company were in the Japanese language, and Yomitakunai saw itself as catering primarily to a clientele made up of these expatriates and to Japanese tourists visiting the island. However, in order to pick up sales after the recession of 1986 and to exploit the demands of locals, the store started to sell more non-Japanese books. Subsequently three other branches were opened around the island, the last one in 1991. While the first branch still caters primarily to Japanese expatriates, the latter stores all sell more non-Japanese than Japanese books.

The company in Singapore is quite autonomous. Only monthly reports and annual sales reports are sent to the headquarters in Japan. Once a year, the president of Yomitakunai in Japan visits Singapore to inspect local operations. Moreover, as we were told by the company's Japanese directors, looking to the future, the company expects to use Singapore as a base from which to expand to Malaysia, Thailand, and Indonesia.

According to these directors, the company has been doing well in Singapore and has expanded its sales eight-fold since its first year of operation. The company has also continually increased its staff, and today has 60 permanent employees including 8 Japanese nationals. All of these people are males on expatriate contracts and their ages range from the late thirties to the early fifties. Moreover, reflecting the general pattern of Japanese presence in Singapore, almost all of these men are white-collar managers and executives who have been posted to the country for a period of between three to five years at the end of which they return to Japan. The company has promoted local female staff to the position of store manager in all four of its branches. About 35 employees work in the retail outlets while the rest are employed in the head office (in the book divisions, and the direct marketing and administrative departments). Apart from these workers the company employs about 35 part-time workers. Due to the high turnover rate that the company experiences, it has no orientation program or in-house training.

We studied Yomitakunai between July 1993 and January 1994. Fifteen people were interviewed for this study (mostly by the first author) and these interviews were supplemented by numerous visits to the company's retail outlets and headquarters. Of the people we talked to, five were Japanese and ten Singaporeans; again, of the fifteen, seven worked at the head office and eight in the retail outlets. Our interviewees included division managers, managers of retail outlets, assistant managers, sales staff, and staff from the marketing, personnel and accounts departments in the head office. In our interviews we asked about the variety of experiences the employees had in different positions and working environments. We reasoned that only by examining this variety would we be able to fully understand what was going on in the company.

At the Workplace: Japan

The salaryman's allegiance to his firm is perhaps the most common image of the large Japanese corporation. The guiding picture of the company-as-family has made its way into numerous assessments of Japanese economic life (Van Wolferen 1989: 214; Abegglen 1984: 94). Rodney Clark (1979: 41) feels that while in contemporary

114

Japanese industry "one hears less of the particular analogy with the family, largely because the family itself has changed. There remains, however, an influential ideal of harmony and co-operation in relations among employees and between employees and their firms." A few words about the organizational attributes of Japan's large enterprises may help to place our argument in its proper theoretical context.

Two decades ago, Dore (1973:370) coined the term "welfare corporatism" to denote the central characteristics which mark many large business companies in contemporary Japan: long-term security and stability of employment, integration of (permanent) manual workers as full members of the organization, welfare programs, recreational facilities, a "familial" or corporate ideology, and company-based unions and bargaining structures. While the essentials of "welfare corporatism" developed out of the circumstances which surrounded Japan's surge towards modernization (Cole, 1979:21–22; Fruin 1983:7), it was during the post-war period that "welfare corporatism" was fully institutionalized.

By the late 1960s employees of the larger firms were enjoying such benefits as pensions, yearly bonuses, loans, company accommodations, stores, subsidized meals, health insurance, educational facilities, sports amenities, and sometimes even holiday sites. No less important, it is also during this period that the "familial" or corporate ideology has continued to be propagated by management and — to a large extent — also accepted by workers. Evidence of this propagation can be found in almost any sampling of statements by middle-level and high-level managers, or in company mottos and slogans which abound, for example, with such imagery as "trees and saplings," "the cycle of goodness," JAL's "we are one," or the well-known "harmony and strength" (Rohlen 1974). A not untypical example of the extent to which workers have adopted these ideological emphases are Kiefer's (1980:439–440) comments about white-collar workers who "typically seek companionship among their co-workers, with whom they may spend upward of 60 hours a week, including a good part of their leisure time. This is a stable, functionally diffuse group which serves many of the functions of the family for them."

Thus, although the older, pre-war legal, political and genealogical scaffolding is gone, the "firm-as-family" as an analogy and as a cultural ideal still remains viable today (Fruin 1983:8). Indeed the larger the firm the greater the chances that this analogy holds.

Because of the scale of the large firms, problems of interpersonal tensions and organizational friction are more salient. Thus these kinds of enterprises tend to invest more of their earnings in welfare benefits and in socializing their employees. Paradoxically, therefore, the firm-as-family analogy has the greatest urgency in large rather than small Japanese firms today (Fruin 1983:9). This situation applies not only to the substantial material reliance of employees on their companies, nor just to the propagation of a familial ideology. Perhaps more importantly the appropriateness of this analogy is related — as many studies show (Cole 1979:253; Kiefer 1980:436; Rohlen 1974:263) — to the emotional and intellectual identification of workers with their workplace, and especially with their workmates. As Fruin (1983:131) observes:

> Psychological bonding in Japanese organization often occurs within the context of pseudokinship ties. Even when there is no biological or ideological basis for describing organizational affiliation in such terms, the family-based mode of organization seems to resonate with the cultural and emotional proclivities of the Japanese. ...[T]he elasticity of the concept of family, as well as its universal currency in Japanese society, have allowed notions of interpersonal trust and harmony based on the family model to be widely circulated outside of actual kin-based groups. Organization, not genealogical, boundaries delimit the sphere within which cooperation and commitment expressed in terms of a family metaphor are encouraged and expected.

Moreover, as he (Fruin 1980:447, emphasis in original) puts it in a different essay:

> The Japanese display a cultural preference for affective as well as instrumental work commitment which large firms are more easily able to take advantage of through their considerable emphasis on corporate welfare and paternalism. In this cultural sense, therefore, the firm *as* a family, when used to describe the spirit or feeling of a firm has certain validity in postwar Japan.

Reinforcing this holistic concept or analogy of "corporation-as-extended-family," as Dore (1984:xxxiv–xxxvii) well underlines, are both a widespread sense of trust in the fairness of the whole system, and a sentiment of "belonging to" (rather than "working for") the company. Moreover, the picture of managers cynically manipulating workers by pulling at some hidden cultural principles is but a caricature. As De Vos (1975), Dore (1984:xxxi) and Hanami (1979) note, management feels internal commitment to keeping up their side of dependence relationships. Whether this be expressed in a readiness to "hear-out" workers or to provide them with many of the necessities of life, this is recognized by workers and at times used by them for instrumental gains.

Thus, the firm-as-family analogy well captures the major peculiarities of Japanese enterprises: a strong coupling between commitment to and identification with workmates, and a high level of material dependence on the firm. As Ben-Ari has shown elsewhere (1990:101; 1993) however, such a depiction does not imply — as indeed the depiction of the "traditional" business family does not imply (Hamabata, 1990:Ch.4) — an idyllic or untroubled existence for the employees of these companies. In the past few decades workers have increasingly come to recognize, openly express, and question the strains and tensions, and the coercive potentials that characterize relations within these firms.

At the Workplace: Singapore

Can one find similar conditions in Japanese companies who have set up operations abroad? In the context of this paper we focus on three aspects of Yomitakunai's success (or failure) in fostering the corporate family environment within its Singapore operations: work relations and interpersonal communication, organizational control and decision-making, and work benefits and motivation. While there are, to be sure, other features which are of importance to Yomitakunai's performance, we have chosen these three because of their centrality in linking individual behavior and attitudes to organizational arrangements.

Work Relations and Communication

In the purported "typical" *kaisha* (Japanese company), much emphasis is placed on creating good working relationships among workers by assuring smooth communication. It is this communication, it is reasoned, which engenders the cooperation and mutual responsibility which are important for enhanced work efficiency. The consensus within the scholarly literature, however, has been that communication in 'transplanted' Japanese firms is problematic ((Hazama 1978: 133; Higashi and Lauter 1987: 117). What is the situation in Yomitakunai's Singapore businesses? Here the majority of employees are not only non-Japanese, but also diverse in themselves: they are comprised of different Chinese groupings and Malays and Indians.

We found that the major communications problems at Yomitakunai arose out of the different ways that workers and managers relate to each other and their different expectations of the workplace. The grievances of the local employees centered on the "intercourse" style of the Japanese managers. Many of them complained that the Japanese do not directly tell them what they expect from them and what mistakes they have made. One person told us that she and her friends are sometimes frustrated as they have to "guess what the Japanese expatriates are thinking." An assistant manager at one of the stores noted that while the Japanese do not like to confront other people verbally, it is nevertheless "better for them to tell [the locals] their faults so that the same mistakes will not be repeated." Another interviewee who had been working at the head office for about a year and a half, said that "the Japanese do not like to confront verbally. They always just show their face." A store manager who has worked in the company for almost nine years holds the same opinion and remarked that "even something that the Japanese don't like, they don't tell [the locals]. They just keep it to themselves."

The Japanese managers, on the other hand, often said that they felt the locals to be too direct in voicing their opinions and demands. A manager who had been in Singapore for almost seven years remarked:

> Singaporean employees are quite direct compared to the employees in Japan. Sometimes, when the management or manager gives them a job, and they are not happy, they'll just say they are not happy; you know, that kind of attitude.

In a related manner, the Japanese marketing manager noted in regard to name appellations: "It will depend on the positions of the workers. In conversations between the Japanese staff and locals we usually use dare-dare-san. As for between the locals, I think they don't use san, It is too formal." A Japanese division manager at the head office noted that "one thing I find here is the way staff talk to each other; it's like very rude, very rough. You know what I mean?

It's like very nasty. I don't think the mean [to be] so hard, it's their way of speaking." Another division manager who has been in Singapore for four years noted that when Singaporeans "work more, they want more salary." A related problem was raised by a local store manager who has been with the company for more than five years. She contended that another difficulty lay in the way "Japanese men still believe that males are first, females are second." Thus for the Japanese employees who still adhere to the importance of showing due respect to one's superiors, and the "traditional" division of labor between men and women, the directness of the locals (most of whom are women) is rather aggressive.

A store manager mentioned that "language is a big problem. Normal working talk is still OK, but to go into deeper talks, it's difficult to communicate with the Japanese. They have difficulty understanding the locals and the locals might misunderstand them." An assistant store manager said:

> The Japanese, they can't really understand us because we speak too fast. So sometimes, we have a communications problem. When the staff talk, the [Japanese] manager doesn't understand and I don't speak Japanese. But when I repeat the same thing to them, they understand because we have worked here long, and we kind of speak the Japanese–English, instead of Singlish [Singapore English]; so they understand what we tell them.

There are yet other barriers. An assistant manager noted that most junior staff are afraid to talk to the Japanese: "The Japanese are like strangers to them, so they don't really want to approach them." A Singaporean with a year and a half experience at headquarters said that the sense of humor of the Japanese is different and that they don't like to joke as much as local Singaporeans. Another store manager with nearly nine years of experience agreed "communication-wise, there is a problem. Maybe it's because of a different culture and customs, that's why the Japanese are not used to communicating with the locals."

The situation is worsened by what the Japanese managers see as a lack of willingness on the part of Singaporean workers to cooperate. Expatriates think that this lack of cooperation is based on the Singaporeans' view that they are employed to carry out only what is within the domain of their specific job and responsibility. Thus a Japanese manager at the head office remarked that Singaporeans

> don't want to interfere in other people's work, and they don't want to be interfered. This is Japanese thinking. Of course if you are a painter or a writer you can do you own work by yourself. But for company work, we have to cooperate. Of course you will have your own work experience, but there might be another better or good way, another way of thinking. So if you have another person's cooperation, in that case you can do your work better. For the company to work, we have to cooperate.

He went on to note that Singaporeans often complain that they lack time to carry out tasks but are unwilling to ask their fellow employees for help. In a similar vein, another manager noted that "private time is important to Singaporeans. Some are quite Westernized, like duty is duty, off is off. It very clear [the boundary between them]." The English book division manager at head office, a Japanese who had been with Yomitakunai for twelve years, mentioned that Singaporean employees take leave very readily, while for the Japanese it is only on special occasions and the two peaks of New Year and Golden Week.

While the Japanese find the locals to be uncooperative, locals find the Japanese to be rigid. An assistant manager who has been with the company for seven years mentioned that "the Japanese are more systematic and they follow their rules all the way. That sometimes means that they are not flexible. For the Japanese managers, when they say 'no', means it's strictly 'no'." A Singaporean store manager in her eighth year in the company remarked,

> We have a lot of clashes when we are at work; we argue with the Japanese manager. Sometimes their practices are different from ours. What they do in Japan, they try to bring it here also.

A Singaporean supervisor at one of the outlets said,

> They'll say that this is their style, so somehow we must follow them. But we'll tell them 'right now you are in Singapore, so you must follow the way we work'.

She went on to tell us of the arbitrariness associated with transfers within the company:

> When they want to transfer some staff to another store, they will not tell you till the last minute: "I need you to go to that store." They only give you about three days. Of course when they ask for your opinion what can I say? Only "Oh, why do you want to transfer me out? What have I done?." Then, of course, they will say, "No it's just to let you learn more things from other branches." Somehow, they've already made the decision. So what can I say; I have to go.

The situation marked by difficulties in achieving a clear common understanding of work attitudes and goals is made worse by the characteristics of retail employment. Take company outings and group activities. Such practices are common to many Japanese companies in Singapore as they are seen (as in Japan) to promote understanding and group spirit and to improve worker morale. But in Yomitakunai due to the arrangements of the retail branches, employees work in shifts and it is therefore difficult to find a occasion when the whole company can get together. Even at the head office, no activities are organized for the workers. It is usually up to the initiative of locals who plan (rather rare) informal outings and *karaoke* sessions to which the Japanese expatriates are "invited." This point is echoed from the Japanese perspective. One Japanese manager noted that communication poses a problem due to the differing likes and habits of the expatriates and the locals:

> Japanese like to drink, Singaporeans don't like to drink ... Japanese like cigarettes, but Singaporeans don't.. So communication, well ...

Control and Decision-making

There is a surprising degree of unanimity among many scholars who have dealt with decision-making in Japanese organizations: managers attempt, as far as possible, to reach consensus and to impart a feeling that they make active efforts to take workers opinions into account. The case of Yomitakunai is interesting in this regard. Not only does it not conform to this ideal picture, but two factors make consensual decision-making difficult to implement. In our case, the "usual" tensions which mark any large retail organization in and around the distribution of power and decision-making between the head office and outlets, are exacerbated by the divide between Japanese and non-Japanese.

Given the workings of retail chains, power has been devolved in the company down to the retail branches. The outcome of this decentralization is a lack of uniformity in the way the different branches are run. One interviewee, a Singaporean sales representative at the head office, said that because the branches are bringing in the profits the Japanese directors of Yomitakunai have given too much power to the local branch managers: "The head office should hold the rein and not bow down to too many demands from the branches." Most Singaporeans in the head office feel this way and think that the management gives preference to the branches. This kind of view is rather typical of such companies around the world.

At the branch level however, we encountered another form of problem in regard to the distribution of power and control. Here the difficulty lies in the relations between the local store managers and the Japanese managers who are under their formal authority. All four branches of the Company have locals as store managers who are expressly designated as being in charge of running the stores. The Japanese employed at the store level are division managers in charge of Japanese books. From the point of view of the company's directors however, the role of the expatriates who work in the outlets is one of consultation. One Japanese director thus noted: "We promoted the locals to be store managers, in all the four branches. The Japanese there just act as consultants; the initiative lies in the locals and we [Japanese] only give our opinions or suggestions." Our aim, he continued is to help "the Singaporeans. Of course we give them a kind of Japanese mind; you know, give Singaporeans some kind of Japanese mind."

Consequently, because there is no clear demarcation line between the store managers and the Japanese expatriates problems constantly arise. For example, it is often unclear who has the right to make the final decision when it comes to matters concerning the store or the staff. Formally speaking, it should be the store managers who have the final say. In effect however, the Japanese managers (at the store level) seem to hold certain power just by their presence in the store and by virtue of the fact that they are Japanese and that this is a Japanese company. A Singaporean store manager who has been with the company for nine years explained that "the staff get confused; who they should listen to and who they should go to." This situation, as we shall later see, is aggravated by the behavior of the Japanese consumers.

Some locals feel that they are seldom included in the decision-making process. A store manager who has been with the company for nine years used the metaphor of up and down to observe that in "any discussion, the Japanese will discuss among the Japanese and after that, if the Director feels that the issue has to be discussed further, then he will bring it down to the locals." Locals feel that on the whole the Japanese directors prefer to listen to other Japanese although sometimes some senior Singaporeans are included in their discussions. With respect to the much heralded *ringi* system, it is virtually non-existent at the head office. Basically, reports are submitted upwards, from a boss to his boss; it is seldom passed around to the various departments. Very often, only a memo will be circulated to inform the staff about what has been decided. A local in the personnel department noted in regard to such a memo that "it is only informative, something that informs the staff what is going to happen. It does not actually ask the staff for their opinion." Decision-making in Yomitakunai, to put it succinctly, is seldom based on consensus.

Work Benefits and Motivation

As any large company so Yomitakunai is keenly aware of the importance of its reward system in managing employee motivation (Griffin 1993: 383). Like many (but not all) large Japanese firms, so Yomitakunai links benefits with the concept of seniority (basically conceived of in terms of number of years served in the company). This system is based on the reasoning that workers will be motivated to work because they know that their present loyalty and investment in the company will be paid off over the long run. But the working arrangement that has been instituted in Yomitakunai, however, is a mix of Japanese and Singaporean systems. A Japanese division manger at the head office explained it thus:

> [Here we have] a mix of Japan's system and Singapore's system. Singapore's system is like even though a new worker is young, but if she has good education then she'll become a

manager. Something like that. In Japan, it's not like that ... So in our company if she's new and has good education or experience, in that case she'll enter at a higher position; but not as high as in Singapore companies. And if a worker has worked very long but is not that remarkable [in performance], but still good, of course she'll also have a chance to be promoted. Our company is more flexible.

This combination of Japanese and Singaporean patterns is exemplified in the following story. A supervisor told that when she entered Yomitakunai, the company was looking for graduates with "o" levels. She tried anyway and despite having only "n" (that is, a lower degree of academic achievement) levels, by making a good impression she was recruited (and eventually promoted).

Certain work benefits however, are based on the seniority concept. One clear example is the fact that annual leave is proportional to the number of years that the worker has served the company. For example, the first year in the company does not entitle one to any leave. Beginning with the second year of service, a worker is entitled to ten days of leave and this will increase as the years of service increase. This situation, it should be stated, does not go down well with most of the locals as it is very rare that annual leave is determined in this manner in Singaporean workplaces. "I can easily get 21 days of leave if I was working for the Times Bookshop," remarked an interviewee who has only ten days of leave now as it is only her second year with the company.

In promotion prospects, seniority (years of service in the company) is not the only, but certainly a major factor that is taken into account by Yomitakunai's Japanese directors. These practices tend to clash with the expectations of the Singaporeans who tend to be more concerned with rewards based on performance. A local store manager who does not support promotion by seniority said: "There is no training, or probation. They just judge on the number of years of service. People will feel it's unfair." Her criticism centered on the difficulties of motivating employees. She contended that despite putting up a better performance some workers were passed by for promotion by others on the basis of seniority. The Singaporeans, as a Japanese division manger in the head office noted, are "more demanding, they work more than those in Bangkok and Kuala Lampur but they want more salary."

Arrangements for the annual bonus are also similar to Yomitakunai's policy in Japan. Beyond being based on position and years of service, the bonus varies according to the number of days an employee has taken medical leave in a specific year. In this manner, by cutting the bonus workers receive at the end of the year, the company discourages workers from taking medical leave too often. For example, we were told of how one Singaporean worker who contracted chicken pox and was absent for a month, had her bonus drastically cut that year. A Singapore store manager said:

> One thing I don't like is that whatever MC [medical certificate, ie. leave] the staff has taken, they will get a deduction from the bonus ... This is a way to discourage them from going on MC ... We cut their bonus if they go on very frequent MC ... So I think it's not fair. But the Japanese practice it that way, so we have no choice ... I have heard from my director that in Japan, Yomitakunai, they practice it this way. So we have to accept it.

Another aspect related to the seniority principle is the fact that some senior Singaporean workers are given a chance to register with company headquarters in Japan. The criteria for selection include performance, leadership qualities and usually at least five years of service in the company. The advantage of being a registered member with headquarters lies in eligibility to receive bonuses when workers in Japan get theirs. The actual amount of a specific bonus is determined however, by the job title held under headquarters' membership. For instance, a manager in Singapore may hold only a job title of supervisor in Japan.

But there is another underlying factor which came up time and again in the interviews: the gap between the benefits the Japanese and the Singaporeans receive for the same work. We began to understand this point when a shop assistant remarked that it was only "natural" that the company treat the Japanese better. This naturalness underlined how the most decisive dividing line in the company is the one between expatriates and locals. The Japanese managers, being expatriates, receive a better salary, relocation and housing allowance, education allowance, and leave pay. The woman who runs one of the branches observed, "if you compare things like salary, it's different because they are from Japan, and with Japanese knowledge and because they are serving the Japanese community, of course they will get more. ...They will get more priority, even though they may not be the store manager." An assistant shop manager in her eighth year at the company talked about the benefits received by the Japanese managers:

> I don't think this is unfair because after all they are Japanese and they come all the way here to work; we cannot compare with them. We are locals here. It's not that they get special treatment but they get more chances. Sometimes we do complain, like "Oh, they go for golfing with the Director and we have to work so hard and don't get anything." But sometimes in a month, when the sales are good, we request a dinner from the management, yah, we do get it ... Yah, we get a lot of frustrations, like the Japanese always getting special treatment, and we are also managers but they get special allowance, they get their houses, apartments' maintenance fees; they have everything, they can even drive the company car.

A Singaporean assistant to the General Manager in his third year with Yomitakunai noted that "this is a company with two groups of people, the Japanese and the locals. So somehow there is a dual practice, dual standard." He went on to note that while promotion was based on capability and that the directors would not want somebody who is incapable just because he is Japanese, nevertheless the differences between the two groups were "very subtle."

This situation is related to the different career structures of the expatriates and to their loyalties and interests. With the expansion of Yomitakunai's interests beyond the borders of Japan, and with the establishment of stores and regional headquarters abroad, an assignment overseas has come to correspond to the patterns of rotation within the company. But such an assignment, as we saw, is also a sort of promotion: because companies situated outside of Japan are like "daughter companies" (*kogaisha*, although their exact legal definition may vary), people who were (to give two examples) department heads (*ka-cho*) in Japan become division heads (*bu-cho*) overseas, and section heads (*kakari-cho*) become department heads. This point was put to us by one of the Japanese managers who had been in Singapore for about four years.

> In Japan, I started off as a trainee, and step by step going higher. But here I came as a manager. So the management

level is different. In Japan where I was junior staff I worked 9 to 6 and then "bye, bye." But here I am management level and so cannot be like that. At six o'clock I cannot go back home. No overtime pay. Even for an off-day. I have to come back here; here I am the boss, so I have to decide myself. So I have less time compared to Japan.

Hence in comparison with posting to new positions in Japan, the stint abroad very often presents opportunities to handle greater responsibilities and more important tasks. In this context, however, it is important to note something that was not a taken for granted matter in most Japanese firms like Yomitakunai until a few years ago: a tour of service out of Japan has by now become a normal part of many managerial careers. It used to be a part of "normal" career development only in the general trading companies (*sogo shosha*) (Yoshino and Lifson 1988) and in other internationally oriented businesses like shipping or airlines. But now it is increasingly becoming a prerequisite for individual advancement in very many companies (including medium-sized and small firms) (Hamada 1992: 155). Thus for expatriates, careers depend on the head office in Tokyo and thus they must constantly monitor their relations and contacts with important people at headquarters (see Ben-Ari, 1995).

The Clientele: Consumer Trends and Organizational Dynamics

As portrayed up until this point, the case of Yomitakunai does not differ in any basic manner from examples of other multinational retail chains. Yet because this book company caters not only to a general Singaporean and tourist clientele, but also the Japanese community in the island we find an added factor that influences its internal organizational dynamics. Theoretically speaking, this expatriate clientele forms an important factor in the company's external environment that influences its internal management and labor relations.

With their arrival in this city-state, Japanese business expatriates brought with them not only management, production, and service methods. They also brought with them certain patterns of leisure activities such as golf, tennis, swimming, and reading. Indeed, according to an interview with the general manager of Yomitaku-nai (Lianhe Zaobao, 6 June 1993, our translation)

Compared with Japan, each Japanese in Singapore reads five to eight books more per month. The reason for this is closely related to television programs. [The general manager] said that in Japan people can see programs on six or seven channels from 6 am to 2 am daily. In Singapore there are very few Japanese programs on television and unless they rent video tapes everyday, they will not have a chance to watch television. This situation makes the Japanese in Singapore read even more.

Staff whom we interviewed noted that reading is one of the favorite hobbies of the Japanese expatriates. The Japanese customers themselves are diverse. They range from salarymen and housewives to school children. The salarymen visit in the evenings while on weekends it is usually whole families who browse in Yomitakunai's outlets. We were told that housewives can sometimes buy up to ten books per visit and return the next week to buy more. Many of the company's customers order their weekly magazines on a long-term basis. Every Friday, when the shipment of the magazines comes in, many customers would already be at the store, asking for the magazines long before the staff are able to get them ready. Yomitakunai's also accepts customer's orders for books that need to be purchased overseas (overwhelmingly in Japan). In addition, most staff noted that while the Japanese often come to the stores on purpose, the locals tend to enter because they happen to be shopping nearby.

The proportion of Japanese customers varies between retail outlets depending on whether they are located near areas populated by Japanese expatriates or in the city's center. The indicator used within the company is the percentage of Japanese language books kept in a particular store: for example, one branch reported about 75 per cent Japanese books[1] while another reported between 30 and 40 per cent. On average, we were told, about 50 per cent of the company's customers in Singapore are Japanese. Indeed, all of Yomitakunai's outlets include Japanese language sections, arranged (in the Japanese manner) with open stacks of books and magazines about almost all conceivable subject matters. The marketing manager told us that expatriates tend to read business books, magazines and journals, best-sellers (which they read about in the Japanese dailies), comics, travel books about Asia, maps, and many language learning books (primarily English and Mandarin). In addition, the Japanese dailies (two are printed in Singapore) are distributed among the expatriate community all over the island.

In general, it is the Japanese adults (rather than the children and teenagers) who are most demanding for high-quality service. Based on comparison with the kind of service provided in Japan, these people bring with them a high level of expectations from the company. In this manner when going abroad and encountering a Japanese firm, they expect that the cultivated consumption patterns and reading behavior to which they have been accustomed to in Japan will be met. This stress, is congruent with other findings that Japanese consumers in general are, comparatively speaking, very demanding (Higashi and Lauter 1987: 145). A Japanese expatriate manager in his second year in Singapore noted: "because this is a Japanese company, [we] have to follow certain customs. The Japanese here will expect the same kind of service from the company as they would in Japan." A local assistant manager voiced a similar sentiment:

> the Japanese here have very high demands and this is a Japanese company. It is not small in Japan and the Japanese expect the same kind of service that they have in Japan. For example, out of ten times, nine times I would reserve the books for the customer correctly and on time, and he doesn't say "thank you." The one time that I forget, that's it.

We would contend that while Japanese customers make up only 50 per cent of the total customers, they are perceived by staff to be much more salient and important in terms of the demands they place on the company. A store assistant in her eighth year at the company observed,

> Before they join the company, I always tell [the new staff] that the Japanese here have very high demands and we are a Japanese company. Yomitakunai is not small in Japan and the Japanese expect the same kind of service that they have in Japan. We really have to try our best to serve them.

Moreover, besides expecting a high level of service from the staff, Japanese customers tend to demand to see the Japanese manager whenever something goes wrong or when they are unhappy with the staff. Said a Singaporean store manager,

> Especially the fussy Japanese customers, they don't want to talk to locals. They are very biased; they just want to speak to the Japanese manager; and if the Japanese manager is not around, they will make so much noise at us.

An assistant manager complained that Japanese customers often do not accept what local staff tell them, "but when the Japanese manager comes out and tells them exactly the same thing, they'll accept it."

Because the Japanese customers want to complain to the Japanese manager, it becomes the Japanese manager who settles most of the problems. The local employees, in turn, are not receptive to how the Japanese managers treat the Japanese customers. A Singaporean assistant manager explained,

> We have arguments, like we have different ways of thinking; they always think that the customers are always right. But we say that sometimes it depends on each case.

A store manager said that "even if the customer is wrong, the Japanese manager will say, 'It's OK, you're right, you're right.' This is something the locals cannot take at all. Many staff feel that the Japanese staff are treating the Japanese customers too well." And a store manager said that for the Japanese, "customers are like their heavenly kings." Inevitably and unconsciously, the Japanese managers at the store will always take responsibility for handling the Japanese customers without feeling a need to discuss the problems with the local staff or the local manager.

These problems are exacerbated by language difficulties. Most of the local staff complained that the Japanese customers expect them to understand what they want, even though they are speaking Japanese. We were told time and again that Japanese customers (especially the male salarymen), although able to speak English, sometimes want to communicate only in Japanese and to the Japanese managers. Moreover, as some housewives cannot speak English the problem is aggravated further. In such cases the Japanese staff become little more than translators. Indeed, it is not surprising that some customers grow irritable, given that Yomita-kunai continually advertises itself as providing service by people proficient in Japanese. A local employee who has worked with the company for almost seven years recounted

The Japanese customers expect everyone of us to understand what they want. They can be very impatient at times. Previously, when we only had one cash counter, we had long queues. But our cashiers were trying their best to be fast, but the Japanese customer just threw the book at us and walked off.

On another occasion, a Japanese lady kicked up a fuss when the staff did not understand that all she wanted was a book cover for the book she had bought. In this way, more often than not, the Japanese manager will yield to the demands of the customers as part of company policy is to grant customers the best form of service.

How does this situation relate to the management of the company? The fact that at the store level the Japanese manager often decides what should be done with the Japanese customers despite his formal subordination to the Singaporean store manager implies a continual undermining of the latter's power and position. In previous sections we showed how the distribution of power in the branches is unclear. The Japanese manager, although he is not the store manager, seems to hold certain power by virtue of his being a Japanese expatriate manager in a Japanese firm. The demands and expectations of the clientele and the reaction of the Japanese managers only add to this problem.

Conclusion

This paper can be read as part of the wider study of the "internationalization" of Japanese business interests (Muramatsu 1992; Yawata 1994). To the study of production facilities and financial firms our contribution adds an examination and documentation of a retail, a service organization. Specifically, we have dealt with two issues related to the 'transplantation' of a Japanese book company to Singapore. The first involved the internal organizational arrangements which include a mixture of Japanese and Singaporean elements. As we have seen, to be effective the company has made some basic adaptations and modifications to suit and fit the Singaporean workplace. But problems of different expectations and communications styles continue to create difficulties for the smooth functioning of the company.

In addition, the persisting perceptions of local employees that there is a "real" division line between them and the Japanese expatriate managers is a social fact that underlies all of the activities of the company. While the company has promoted locals to positions of store managers and they hold a substantial amount of power, the long-term question — like questions about similar Japanese firms (Ben-Ari 1995) — is whether these people will have a chance to be promoted in Japan.

The second issue entailed the effects of the Japanese expatriate clientele on the company. As we showed this presence in effect strengthens the informal power of the Japanese managers. This point bears theoretical import in terms of focusing on the manner by which a company's external environment (the clientele) influences its internal organizational arrangements. As we saw, the clientele is a factor that continues to act as a force impeding the localization of Yomitakunai. The managers of the company have (as of yet) not learnt how to handle its dual status as a standard chain which runs retail outlets and purchases books from around the world, and as a specialist concern which supplies the needs of the Japanese living in this country.

Empirically speaking, our case is related to a wider question about the effects of hundreds of thousands of Japanese expatriates in hundreds of communities around the world on local consumer industries. The sheer size and buying power of these people, like the scale and force of other large expatriate communities like the Americans or British, leads to the creation of specialized industries to serve them. These include real-estate agents, food and beverage services, and leisure oriented firms. As of yet however, these organizations have hardly been studied.

Notes

[1] This branch also plays Japanese music as background music. As the manager noted "We don't want to make it typically Japanese also, after all we are in Singapore. But because the percentage of the customers who come in are mostly Japanese, so we have no choice. So our thinking and our way of serving are also Japanized already; no choice already."

Chapter 6

"Where got Japanese Influence in Singapore!"

Chua Beng Huat

Consumerism has been expanding rapidly in Singapore, a consequence of the relative affluence of the population, after more than three decades of continuous economic growth since mid-1960s. This feeding frenzy has rendered Singaporeans open to the accusation of being 'materialistic' at the expense of other values; this criticism is often heard not only from foreigners but also among Singaporeans themselves. Yet, a very large part of the frenetic rate is the consequence of the releasing of frustrated desires imposed by decades of under-development. Consumption is thus one of the many avenues of catching-up with the modern world, symbolized by the owning of all forms of conceivable household and personal commodities; such as televisions, video tape-decks, refrigerators, telephones, cars and fashionable clothes. All these items are imported from elsewhere in Asia, Europe and America. Like other successful Asian economies, Singapore is driven by exporting as much of its industrial product as possible; however, unlike most of them, Singapore produces little of its own consumption goods.

If, as it is often theorized, consumer goods are highly inscribed by the cultural context of their production, then imported goods are accordingly stamped with the cultures of the locations of their origins, and consumption of such goods carries with it the consumption of the attendant cultures. Such an argument under-girds and make intelligible the idea and the fear of 'cultural imperialism' in consumption and consumerism. It is within this argument that the question of possible Japanese 'influence' in

Singaporean everyday life may be posed because Singaporeans consume a very significant amount of imported Japanese goods. My response to the question is unambiguous: There is no 'Japanization' of Singaporeans, by which I mean that there is no significant 'Japanese-ness' in the Singaporean consumer culture.

Such an uncompromising position obviously requires some qualifications. The central issue here is the idea of 'influence'. It would, of course, be nonsensical to argue that consumption of 'Japanese-ness', i.e. the selective consumption of cultural products because they are not only produced in Japan but also represent the idea of 'being Japanese', is entirely absent. There are small pockets of highly committed consumers of certain Japanese cultural products, like those who stay up late to watch Japanese soap-operas, those who spend substantial amount of money and time to read Japanese *manga* and young primary school female students who collect 'cutesie' Japanese stationaries. If one were to study these groups, one would undoubtedly discover their 'career' as 'Japanophile'.[1] These small but highly committed groups of consumers cannot be justifiably said, in my view, to be 'popular'.

I would like to suggest that the term 'popular' be used to denote, minimally, highly visible phenomena which dominate the imagination, if not the reality. A conceptual clarification is necessary here. In the conventional usage, the term 'popular' can denote two phenomena; first, in the sense that is consumed by a very large number of people and second, although consumed by a relatively smaller number of people, the products and the 'rituals of consumption' are highly visible to any passing audience. For example, it is a common 'worry' among adult Singaporeans that 'Western' fast-food will replace local hawker food for future generations. Such a view trades on a substitution of the high visibility of fast-food outlets for the actual quantum of sales and volume of food consumed. In actuality, there are at any one time more pounds of noodles of different flavours and cooking style consumed by Singaporeans than 'Big Macs', 'Whoppers' and various 'American' style fried chicken combined and there is no fear of the former being replaced completely. Such instances of presuming the 'highly visible' to be the actual consumption, accord to the former a sense of being 'popularity'. I would suggest that both senses of the 'popular' be deployed in the analysis of consumer culture, rather than dismissing the 'highly visible' as 'falsely' popular.

With the above caveat and the adoption of two senses of the 'popular', I will reiterate my conclusion that there is no 'Japanization' of Singaporeans; a conclusion that the rest of this chapter will attempt to substantiate.

Some Immediate Impressions

First, a young Japanese anthropologist/sociologist who had spent one whole month in Singapore researching consumerism, declared in my office that 'Singaporeans are very immature in their fashion!', quite unaware that this may be a statement of affront to a Singaporean. In the course of the conversation, the unsaid part of his declaration emerged. To him, Singaporeans' fashion sense appears immature, 'in comparison with Japanese fashion practices'. The difference is indicative of the absence of influence of the latter in the practices of Singaporean dress codes.

Second, a visitor reading through the advertisements in the daily newspaper will be impressed by the presence of Japanese departmental stores in Singapore; Takashimaya, Isetan, Daimaru, Tokyu, Seibu/Parco and Sogo. These department stores are the biggest in the country, with no local or other foreign competitors of similar scale. Their prominence in the city-scape is unchallenged in the retail sector. Yet, if one should go to any of these stores in search of Japanese goods, one would be greatly disappointed. Certainly, there would be spaces allocated for Japanese consumer products, but these are distinctively confined to Japanese goods 'corners', particularly food. This has not always been so. In the early 1970s, when the first of these stores, Yaohan, made its entrance, Japanese goods had been rather extensive. They have since then been diminishing and Yaohan has gone out of business in 1997, due to financial difficulties. Now, in the words of a Japanese Ph.D candidate in Cultural Studies at an Australian university, 'Isetan in Singapore is not a Japanese store, nor is Takashimaya'.

Third, Singapore is culturally a rather defensive space, constantly vigilant against 'polluting' influences from the 'constitutive' outside. This vigilance is raised generally against the 'West/US', against 'Westernization/Americanization', but there is no equivalent anxiety regarding 'Japanization'. Ironically, there is not a single big American department store in Singapore; the one which was a joint venture between local enterprise, Metro, and American chain, 'K-mart' folded after about three years of operation. Indeed, Metro had up to four big stores in the prime tourist-shopping belt of Orchard Road, but it had been progressively edged out of business in this district by the earlier mentioned Japanese stores.

In spite of these impressions, there is no doubt that Japan, via its transnational corporations, has massive economic presence in the Singaporean consumer sector. Japanese products are ubiquitous; witness the cars on the road, the electrical appliances in the homes, the personal electronic gadgets on strolling bodies along Singaporean streets. Furthermore, in both these sectors, Japanese products are preferred over products from other, particularly Asian, nations; for example, Japanese cars and televisions are preferred over Korean ones. The superior technology of Japanese products is readily recognized. However, technological superiority is embedded in culturally 'neutral' commodities, or what Koichi Iwabuchi called 'no smell' Japanese products (personal communication).

The general observation that can be drawn here is that the cultural 'influence' of Japan or the Japanese on Singaporeans, via consumerism, is far less than the economic power would suggest. In the following sections of the essay, I will examine three different areas of popular culture consumption in Singapore to substantiate this. The three areas examined are fashion, food and mass media entertainment.

Fashion

In a city-state where the population is relatively young,[2] and prices of both houses and cars are prohibitive because of limited land and strict legal control, much of the discretionary expenditure of those who are outside the clutches of family responsibilities is spent on self-adornment, on fashion and accessories. Besides, as a successful local designer suggests, in a country where political freedoms are heavily circumscribed, 'the only protest you can make is how you look, short of taking off your clothes. So people make a statement with what they wear' (Teo 1997). This is especially so for teenagers and twenty-somethings who spend freely on diffusion-line designer clothes: casual wear in jeans and t-shirts from European and American designers, such as Armani, Versace, Gaultier, Paul Smith, Dolce and Garbana and Calvin Klein. This market has also be penetrated in more recent years by Australian 'surf wear' companies, like Billabong, Rip Curl and Quicksilver. The jeans and t-shirt ensemble is the common attire of the young, signifying the informality which typifies the Singaporean dress code. The young may buy the same accessories from Japanese sources but will not 'programme' these items on their bodies in the same way as a Japanese youth might; Singaporean youth decidedly do not have Japanese configuration as a model to emulate.

Most of the casual wear designers are marketed through exclusive boutiques that sell no other designers. These are relatively expensive pieces of clothing in their genre, about twice to three times as much as American jeans, such as Levi's and Guess?. However, their affordability has been facilitated by 'discount' houses which sell 'past seasons' fashion at highly reduced prices. The readiness of the young to part with their money for such 'branded' goods has caused much public consternation in the media in Singapore. It has caused mild 'moral panic' and 'teenage bashing' because of the fear, expressed by their elders and the other moral gatekeepers of society including journalists, that the young are not acquiring the habits of frugality and savings, exemplified by the old in a nation where savings rates reach 40 per cent of monthly income.

If at the street level Japanese influence is not present, and often negatively represented as an Other, the possible influence at the high end of the market in formal wear is equally limited; although Kenso, Issey Miyake and Hanae Mori each has their respective boutiques, both in international hotel arcades which are seldom visited by Singaporeans.[3] Here a very interesting and culturally significant development has taken place. It is not the absence of Japanese influence that is significant. It is the observable relative 'disappearance' of 'Western' formal wear in recent years, replaced by 'national' or 'ethnic' clothes. Women's formal wear has undergone a very significant change. It has been 'ethnicized'. The rise of capital in Asia has affected Singapore's cultural terrain, giving Singaporeans a sense of cultural confidence.

This cultural confidence has been ideologically formalized in Singapore into what is now commonly known as 'Asian' values which, it is argued, constitute supposedly the underlying foundation for the rapid capitalist development of the newly developing economies in Asia.[4] This ideologizing has been culturally productive in generating a sense of pride in things 'Asian' among many Singaporeans. This pride is almost 'obligatory' among those who are in the public arena and no where is this more clearly expressed than in the ethnicization of women's dress code at formal, especially televised, gatherings. The 'traditional' (updated in expensive fabric and contemporary tastes) clothes of the three major ethnic groups have made a return on the bodies of women with power or close to power; Indian *sari*, Chinese *cheongsam* and Malay *baju* are now 'power' clothes, their bright colours and floral prints contesting the understated, formal black of Western/modern dress. In this ethnicization, all overt cultural influences from outside have been excluded. Whether this ethnicization will trickle down to the younger generation and trickle out into the mass market remain to be seen.

In the area of fashion, therefore, Japanese influence is not significant. Japanese fashion and fashion designers do not figure significantly among the 'brand' conscious young Singapore consumers. The informality of Singaporean fashion is antithetical to the formality of Japanese fashion code, including street clothes. It is this contrasting informality that had caused the earlier mentioned Japanese urban anthropologist to comment on the 'immaturity' of the Singaporean fashion sense. Against the Japanese practice of strong sense of 'co-ordination', even when (s)he is attired unconventionally in street-wear, the Singaporean practice of seeming randomness of mixing-and-matching is decidedly 'unacceptable', thus 'immature'.

The differences in fashion practices are also noticed by Singaporeans. The dress code of female Japanese tourists seen in the streets of Singapore is itself a code that is so distinct from local practices that it has become a cliché and, sometimes a target of ridicule and derision of Singaporeans. The Japanese dress code is identified in stylised manner as such: very-pale-close-to-white facial make-up, small floral print, lightweight dress in light pastel shades, white nylons or socks, comfortable walking shoes and, although now less frequently spotted, a hat. To the young Singaporeans, this dress code exemplifies the Japanese 'culture of cuteness' (Clammer 1995). In Singapore, 'cute' may be a term of endearment, but 'cuteness' in behaviour and configured appearances – signalling immaturity – is decidedly 'not cool' to Singaporean teenagers. Thus, seen as an unedifying caricature, no Singapore teenager, male or female, will emulate the 'Japanese' code.

Before closing this section, it is opportune to raise a fundamental issue of cultural influence/inscription. In the case of fashion, it must be said that there is by now an 'international' uniformity which has its origin in Western clothes. For men, this consists of different combinations of suit, trousers, shirt and neck-tie. For women, in addition to the same items of clothes as men, there are the dress and skirts. The rate of internationalization in a location depends partly on its contact with global economic and cultural transactions. Generally, the rate is slower for women than men as ethnic codes are usually kept alive by women rather than men, as in the case of Singapore. The Western origin of the internationalized uniform code is almost unremarkable until it is placed in a context, usually in ritual occasions, where the participants revert to their ethnic clothes.

Inserted into the sartorial space of international code are individual designers. A designer may be inspired by either his or her own cultural sources, or borrow from other sources, in creating globally marketable items. To be so marketable, the ethnic/cultural inspiration has to be relaxed and reworked into the international code, thus diluting the cultural inscription on the clothes and its consumers. For the consumer, the identification is with the designer rather than the latter's cultural 'inspirations'. Particular cultural inscriptions are thus refracted through the signature of the designer and the imprint of the international market. Paralleling architecture as a practice, international fashion design is thus a 'star' system rather than a vernacular/cultural system without designers. This is, of course, true of 'Japanese' fashion designers.

Mass Media

Almost all households in Singapore owns a television; indeed, this fact is often used by the ruling political party as an indicator of its success in bringing material richness to the nation, which in turn, legitimatize its right to govern. There are four broadcasting stations, two under the Television Corporation of Singapore (TCS) and two under Television 12 (TV12), all are government owned. One of the TCS channels is dedicated exclusively to English programmes, the other to Mandarin programmes. One of the TV12 station is dedicated to Malay and Tamil/Hindi programmes, the languages of the two minority ethnic groups, Malay and Indians, respectively. The other is the 'arts' channel, which showcases nature/wild life, opera of different languages, art films from around the world and global sports competitions. TCS broadcasts for 24 hours, while TV12 for 12 hours a day.

Only the Chinese channel on TCS broadcasts regular Japanese programmes, dubbed in Mandarin, for up to nine hours per week. None of the programmes are on prime time. The most concentrated broadcast period is on Saturdays; two one-hour drama series, at eleven in the morning and at half-past-five in the afternoon. The rest are half-hour cartoons or animated drama programmes. The scheduling of these programmes are as follows: in the mornings, Mondays at six o'clock; on late week nights at half-past one and at four to five o'clock at dawn. The highest ratings are for the Saturday and Sunday afternoon programmes, six per cent and seven per cent respectively of an estimated audience of approximately three million. The ratings for the other shows range from three per cent to zero per cent.

TV12 has three hours of regular Japanese programmes. All three hours are broadcasts in prime time between ten to half-past-twelve in the evenings. The one-hour documentary on contemporary Japan, *The Japan Hour*, is divided into two halves; the first half is new magazine broadcasts exclusively in Japanese language and the second covers wide ranging cultural practices in Japan – for example, regional cuisine, the fishes consumed by Japanese, where to repair broken home appliances and personal items in cities – and carries English subtitles. (Television sets which have the built-in facilities can receive the programmes in English.) It has an audience rating of three per cent. The other two one-hour programmes are drama series, broadcast in Japanese with English subtitles, both with ratings of two per cent. In addition to these regular programmes, there are occasional programmes of Japanese films and cultural documentaries in the 'foreign language' programmes on the same channel.

The non-prime or 'graveyard' hours of much of the broadcast in the main Chinese channel and the low ratings of prime time programmes on TV12 are indicative of the absence of popular support, signalling the absence of Japanese cultural in-roads into the most popular entertainment for Singaporeans. Indeed, the prime time programmes are there in TV12 only because of very substantial Japanese corporate sponsorship, including Sumitomo.

The last of any popular Japanese drama series was *Oshin*, screened in the 1980s, first in Mandarin and again in English. The 'familialism' of this series had tremendous appeal and most young Singaporeans can still recall their weeping mothers and grandmothers in front of the television; indeed, Oshin has a singular place as the representation of the best of Japanese television drama series or the worst cliché soap opera, depending on the age and gender of the audience in question. I appears that the space for similar genre of 'family' drama in Chinese broadcast has been usurped by a seemingly endless supply of Taiwanese series which dramatize the excesses of Confucian ethics in Chinese families, broadcast on every Saturday and Sunday at early evenings, between six to eight o'clock, with high audience ratings.

Popular music scene in Singapore may be divided into Chinese and English pop, entirely dominated by foreign imports, to the laments of local musicians. The former by Hong Kong and Taiwan artistes and the latter by US and British musicians. Until the mid-1980s, Singapore was a relatively small market for Chinese pop music. The scene was seriously affected by the government's banning of the use of Chinese dialects in the broadcast media of television and radio. This was part of the government's strategy to 'integrate' the Chinese population, which were supposedly 'divided' by their different 'mutually incomprehensible' dialects, through a common language, Mandarin. In the process, the dominant presence of Cantonese pop music, or Canto pop, was replaced by Mandarin songs from Taiwanese singers.

By the late 1980s, saturation of the Hong Kong market and the opening up of the massive mainland China market induced many Canto pop singers to sing in Mandarin. This enabled them to sell their records and to perform on stage in Singapore, which was by then swelling with affluent youth with substantial spending power. Since then, fan clubs of artistes from Hong Kong and Taiwan are formed regularly and the entertainment columns of both Chinese and English newspapers regularly cover the gossip about these singers (Soh 1995). With these developments, Mandarin and Cantonese pop music are now an integrated market of Taiwan, Hong Kong and Singapore, so much so that singers and song-writers co-operate freely across borders; for example, EMI will sign on Singapore song-writers for its stable of singers in Hong Kong and Taiwan (*Straits Times* 1996).

The expansion of Chinese pop music effectively reduced drastically the potential pool of Japanese pop music consumers as it generally draws from the Mandarin-speaking students and young adults. The air-waves of local radio stations are by now almost completely devoid of Japanese popular music. This absence is largely because Japanese is not a common tongue in Singapore;

although those who ply the tourist trade do possess the rudimentary skill necessary for their work. Judging by the small quantum of display in local music shops, Japanese pop is nevertheless consumed by both the expatriate resident Japanese population and, possibly, a small group of Singaporean aficionados. However, there remains one nagging question: To what extent do Singaporeans realize that Taiwanese music is heavily influenced by Japanese and does the fact figure in their appreciation of Taiwanese music? This is a question that must be resolved by further empirical research of the audience.

Any discussion of possible Japanese influences in mass media entertainment will not be complete without mentioning the Fuji Television-TCS co-produced, television talenttime programme, *Asia Bagus* (Asia Good in Malay). The weekly programme showcases contestants from different parts of Singapore, Malaysia, Indonesia, Taiwan and Japan. Winners are awarded with 'minicompo' radio sets from Japanese manufacturers. The show is fronted by a Singaporean DJ/actor/comedian, the zany Najib Ali. He completely dominates the show with his antics. He is assisted by a female Japanese compere and a male Mandarin compere from Singapore or Taiwan. It is staged and taped in Singapore and broadcast locally and in Japan. Contestants sing in any language they choose, from English to their national languages. Those who do not know English do not comprehend each other on the show. The Japanese content is limited to the female compere who plays second string to Najib and contestants from Japan. Rather than conceptualizing this show as an attempt to exert Japanese 'influence' on the rest of Asia, it is more fruitful to think of it as Fuji Television's desire to promote a 'pan-Asianism' and brings it into Japan. However, given that the show is broadcast in Tokyo at one o'clock in the night, its influence on mainstream television audience is likely to be limited, so too its cultural effects.[5]

Food

If there were one area in which 'Japanese-ness' is visibly present in Singapore's public spaces, it is 'Japanese' food. Indeed, counter to trends in other spheres of popular consumption, Japanese food is gaining in popularity, especially *teppanyaki* and *sushi*. There are several reasons for this. First, with the exception of sushi and other raw seafood, other popular Japanese food items bear close proximity to Singaporean Chinese food. For example, *teppanyaki* is similar to Chinese stir-fried cooking, the only difference is that the former is fried on an open flat grill and the latter in a *wok*; *shabu-shabu* is similar to the 'steamboat', where fresh food is cooked in a pot of boiling stock, at the table, by the diners themselves[6]; and finally, *yakitori* is similar to the Malaysian *satay*, where bite-size morsels of meat are skewered on a stick and grilled. Given these similarities, Singaporeans often conceive of such Japanese food items as variations of their familiar palette rather than 'foreign'; an instance of the indigenization of the 'Japanese'. The 'quotient' of consumption of 'Japanese-ness' is not high here although not entirely absent or it would defeat the purpose of eating 'Japanese' food.

Where there is a significant shift in palette is in the consumption of raw food in sushi and sashimi as food, including vegetables, are very seldom eaten raw in Chinese, Malay or Indian practices. Sushi is now sold in convenient see-through plastic boxes in small shoplets, in small stalls at shopping centres and in the most ubiquitous supermarket chain. Quietly and almost suddenly, sushi has become street food, consumed as snacks particularly by the youth and twenty-somethings. These snack stands are owned and operated by Singaporeans and the sushi they sell uses many local seafoods, with a very short shelf-life of a few hours in the tropical heat. Hence, the quality and prices are in sharp contrast to those available at five-star hotel restaurants which use only imported Japanese ingredients, flown daily to Singapore and destroyed daily if not used.

The age of the consumers of what may be called 'street sushi' is significant. It is a generation which spends more time and eats more meals, at irregular intervals and with varied contents, outside than at home. Not surprisingly, in Singapore, as elsewhere globally, the popularization of sushi is part and parcel of the sprouting of Italian pasta outlets, French crosissanterie and restaurants hewed from other Southeast Asian nations, such as Thailand and Vietnam. This expansion signifies the consumption of food as part of the leisure and recreational activities. As these restaurants tend to be informal in character they are conducive to 'hanging out' for the young, which explains their popularity. This is made apparent by the contrast that the formality that is attached to French restaurants where, in Singapore, minimally more than street clothes are required attire. With the exception of selective Thai dishes, internationalized foreign foods have seldom, if at all, been incorporated and domesticated into the family kitchens and dining tables of Singaporeans. At home, the meal remains largely unaffected by internationalization. Only where one or more adult members of the family have spent extensive amounts of time sojourned in another country is there a limited incorporation of food from the familiar country into the daily meal. Here, the incorporation of Japanese food is decidedly rare because Japan has not been a popular destination for either Singapore students or expatriate workers.

In the absence of domestication, consuming Japanese sushi remains the ingestion of the 'exotic'. It is a brief entry 'into an existence far removed from the humdrum of everyday life' where 'a safe but fulfilled return to everyday life' is guaranteed (Cooper 1994:144). Eating sushi and sashimi is thus the briefest experience of an 'exoticized' Japan, particularly for those who have never physically been to Japan. This exoticism is intensified by its rawness, in contrast to Chinese, Indian and Malay foods, particularly the overcooked stews and curries. So exoticized, 'Japan' and 'Japanese-ness', via sushi and sashimi, remain outside the 'cultural-self' of Singaporeans, to be visited at will and when convenient, ever so briefly.

Concepts and Tools

The above instances notwithstanding, the very visible Japanese economic presence in the retail sector and the fact that Singapore is a market for Japanese consumer products must certainly have some influence on Singaporean everyday life. Indeed, there are. However, in such instances Japan provides the concept but not the cultural substance in practice. There are two notable and illustrative examples in the consumption sphere.

First, with the arrival of Japanese supermarkets and department stores, came the concept of 'one-stop' shopping centre; that is, the centre provides services including post-office facilities, a ticketing service for cultural performances and restaurants, cafes and a food court. Until the arrival of the now defunct Yaohan in the early 1970s, the few supermarkets in Singapore, like Cold Storage and the defunct Fitzpatricks, had no facilities for any of these services in their premise or as extensions. Yaohan was the first to establish an extensive cooked-food court in the basement level of its premises in

Orchard Road, Singapore's premier shopping strip. Significantly, this food court initially sold only Japanese food items but slowly and steadily these were replaced by local fast-foods, until there was no trace of Japanese food at all. In turn, food courts are now not only essential service in all new shopping malls but also for large office complexes. Sushi and teppanyaki stalls are commonly found in these new food courts among local foods; they have been recontextualized and embraced by interiorized (brought in doors) Singaporean hawker centres.

Parenthetically, the ability to adjust quickly to the local market conditions and Singaporean tastes is testimony to the Japanese companies' business acumen. The same adjustments to local tastes account for the earlier-noted absence of Japanese contents in large Japanese department stores. Indeed the tastes of Singaporeans have sunk many foreign companies which were over-committed to their own cultural and consumer preferences. These include French companies, *Primptemps* and *Galleries Lafayette*, the up-market Hong Kong department store *Lane Crawford* and the earlier-mentioned down-market American chain *K-Mart*. It appears that for the Japanese companies, as in other successfully internationalized retail businesses, profit is always strategic and essential while selling 'culture' is always tactical and incidental.

Second, perhaps, the Japanese concept with the greatest reach into mass culture of Singapore is the 'karaoke'. It has spawned a range of entertainment outlets from private homes to karaoke lounges and bars and cabarets. As family entertainment, karaoke has become a 'machine' for generating greater family sharing and integration; a family that sings together stays together, perhaps. As commercial recreation, Chinese restaurants provide large open stages for all and sundry to perform to an audience of largely, often unappreciative, strangers. In contrast, karaoke lounges provide private rooms for small parties who prefer to share either the celebration or the embarrassment of their voices or, in other cases, the physical presence of paid 'hostesses' as well. Again, in this case, the Japanese are only to be credited with the concept of singing in 'public' because the karaoke discs and music are almost totally devoid of Japanese songs. Instead, the discs used are often cheaply produced in Taiwan, Thailand and locally and the music ranges from Western pop to those of different Chinese languages, namely, Mandarin, Cantonese and Hokkien. If there were substantive cultural influence, it is the re-emergence of Hokkien music into

Singapore from Taiwan. This dialect, like others, had been suppressed in state-owned broadcast media by the Singapore government in mass entertainment under the campaign to 'encourage' all Chinese to speak Mandarin. Karaoke as 'private' entertainment, even when sung in restaurants, may escape the official sanction. As the proverbial 'forbidden fruit', singing in dialects is popular because it provides the additional pleasure of 'transgression' of government edict.[6]

At the conceptual level, in addition to serving the function of encouraging and assisting individuals to sing, as it does everywhere, karaoke has in a sense extended a common Singaporean street entertainment[7], called colloquially *ge tai* (Singing Stage); troupes of untrained amateur singers perform on a large temporary stage set up for the specific purpose in front of a street audience. Such performances were often a substitute for more traditional street opera and were staged generally during the anniversary celebrations of local deities of particular temples, *in situ*. Formally, the Karaoke is similar to the *ge tai* and its popularity among some Singaporeans is reflected in the fact that individuals would practice specific songs at home until the delivery is polished and then find every opportunity to perform the same tunes in public. The *ge tai*, which was already in its throes of extinction in the 1980s, has been revived in part by the popularity of karaoke, as enjoying others' singing is the other side of performing oneself and in part by the local television artistes as incomes from performing at these events have become attractive enough to entice them to compete with and edge out the amateur singers.

In both instances, the concepts were derived from Japanese cultural practices which are inserted into Singaporean everyday life and in both instances the cultural substances that realize these concepts are non Japanese. This distinction between conceptual and cultural influence is particularly useful in conceptualizing the effects of Japanese technological exports, the 'no smell' Japanese goods, which are readily found in many spheres of Singaporean life. This distinction makes clear the possibility of consuming Japanese goods and concepts without 'consuming cultural Japan' (Ching 1994).

Conclusion

It is apparent that in spite of its very observable presence in the economy of Singapore, not only in manufacturing but also retailing, Japanese cultural influence on Singaporeans is minimal. The cultural 'mainstream' of Singapore is visibly different from that of urban Japan. There is no equivalent of Harajuku in Singapore. There is no green or orange coloured hair among youth, partly because it is proscribed by strict school discipline, while among twenty-somethings, hair is tinted in shades of brown or copper or deep blue close to black. There are few who would dress in layered fashion or the highly individualistic styles of Tokyo youth; on the contrary, 'groupiness' is still the rule in Singapore, especially among lowly-educated Chinese working-class youth, locally known as 'Ah Bengs and Ah Lians', and Mat Rockers, their Malay equivalent; each group has its own fashion sense that is anything but Japanese. While the middle-class youth are on the whole monotonously togged in t-shirts and jeans, if they are not in school uniforms. Both televisual and radio air-waves are dominated by American, British, Hong Kong and Taiwan imports; Japanese soap-operas are broadcast on the minor television station at the worst possible programming hours, from ten o'clock till midnight, weekday evenings, competing with the very popular locally produced Chinese drama series, nightly news and the best American sitcoms and crime series. It is thus little wonder that the Japanese programmes receive very low viewership. In a country where movie going is a very popular entertainment, there are seldom Japanese movies on the screens of all the multiplexes. The only place where consuming 'Japanese-ness' is evident is the popularizing of sushi as fast-food.

There are several possible reasons for the absence of Japanese cultural consumption. First, and most important, is that Japanese is not a common language in Singapore. Some facility may be found among those who are in contact with Japanese tourists and have taken up the language for occupational reasons. Without language facility, the ability of Japanese culture to penetrate the daily life of Singaporeans and the latter's ability to absorb the influence remains very limited.

Second, the absence can be made even more apparent when compared to the success of American cultural influence on Singaporeans, in part facilitated by the ubiquity of English as one of the common languages among Singaporeans. More significantly, however, I believe that the relative success of American influence lies in the very presentation of American culture and products. In general, 'American-ness', whether it is of

New York sophistication, southern California casual or northern Seattle grunge, is sold as a way of life for the 'modern' individual. In this sense, 'American-ness' is ironically unethnically, unexotically and unremakably 'marked' or 'unmarked' because it is the 'universal' modern. In emphasizing the generalized 'modern individual', 'American-ness' is able to interpellate everyone who comes into contact with American cultural products. This ability enables 'American-ness' to be internationalized and American cultural products to form the core of much of life-style consumption around the world. On the other hand, Japanese-ness, like all other consciously 'ethnicized' cultures, can and will be consumed only by non Japanese who explicitly identify with it and thus a desire to be assimilated by it or by others as liminal consumption, as in a theme party for only a brief moment of celebration, with depthless cultural appreciation.

Finally, specific to Singapore, the consumption of Japanese-ness is increasingly reframed into a discourse of Asian-ness. Japan has been mythologically transformed, by the ideological machine of the Singaporean government, into a space that is able to economically and technologically modernize itself without losing its 'traditions'; that is, without being 'Westernized/Americanized'.[8] In this ideological transformation, it is the cultural conservatism of Japan that is being eulogized. This conservatism is re-wrapped in Confucian terms and themes. It is this presumed depth of Japan's cultural resistance to the 'West' and its ability to maintain its cultural 'uniqueness' in the contemporary globalized cultural space that the Singapore government would like Singaporeans to emulate. Ironically, at this level, it is again 'Japan' as a concept that is to be consumed, not the uniqueness of Japanese culture, which by definition cannot cross cultural borders.

In conclusion, as a Singaporean colleague writes, 'Japan remains a foreign and hard-to-understand country in Singapore, and is more so than many Western societies; the historical British colonial connection created an interactive relationship in cultural terms with the West – pre-existing global connections that are now part of the 'local' – that does not exist with Japan' (Wee 1997).

Notes

[1] An example of such focused analysis on Taiwanese youth can be found in Lii and Chen (1998).

2 The possible problems associated with 'ageing' population will not be a concern until about the decade of 2030.

3 Of the three, Issey Miyake has a small but dedicated following. For ethnographic studies of fashion shopping in Singapore, see Chua (1990, 1992).

4 A few Singaporean intellectuals and politicians, notably the Senior Minister Lee Kuan Yew, have been regarded as the appointed speakers at the global level for the promotion of this thesis and its attendant 'values'; they have been dubbed the 'Singapore school'. In view of the economic crisis in Asia since mid-1997, the thesis have been much ridiculed in the mass media. Nevertheless, Lee still maintains the importance of 'Asian values' and blames the debasement of these values on the unscrupulous individual politicians who used the values rhetorically to engage in self-serving practices (*Straits Times*, 23 May, 1998).

5 For a detail discussion of *Asia Bagus*, see Iwabuchi (1994). I have omitted here the popularity in Japan of Singaporean singer and writer of songs and musicals in which he plays the lead roles, Dick Lee. Apparently, his popularity was precisely the appeal to the Japanese of his self-avowed, 'Westernised yet Asian' identity and his use of 'pan Asian' casts in his musicals; see Wee (199–).

6 Along similar idea, the Korean 'steamboat' has become popular with some Singaporeans. In this version, the pot for the boiling stock is made out of copper, hence its surfaces can be used to grill meat, thus combining two modes of cooking in one utensil. Some restaurants now serve both the local and the Korean versions without any additional effort, as the ingredients for cooking are the same.

7 For a similar reason Hokkien films from Taiwan, which are generally shown only during the annual Singapore Film Festivals, are hugely popular. In 1998, a locally produced film, *Money No Enough*, with predominantly Hokkien dialogue, grossed more than $6 million against the production cost of $850,000.

8 It has been suggested that the karaoke's role of abetting individuals to perform is similar to that of the 'geisha', whose task it is not to perform but to provide the excuse for the guests to sing along; hence, the karaoke has been referred to as the 'electric geisha' (Ueda 1994).

9 For detail discussion of Singapore and Malaysian governments' use of Japan as a model of Asian modernization, see (Wee 1997).

Chapter 7

"Not-Precisely-Work": Golf, Entertainment and Imbibement Among Japanese Business Executives in Singapore

Eyal Ben-Ari

Introduction

In this chapter I examine a set of Japanese corporate activities that Allison (1994: 100) terms "not-precisely-work." Specifically, I explore the place of three important activities — dining, drinking, and golf — in the lives of Japanese business expatriates in Singapore. Whereas in my other contribution to this volume I focused on the discursive and cognitive dimensions of the expatriate experience, here I direct my attention to the behavioral level. Dining, drinking and golfing belong to what I have called the "interstices" (Ben-Ari, 1990; 1994) of Japan's organizational life: i.e. to the narrow time-junctures in between "regular" periods of work activity. But they are not residual to, somehow unimportant aspects of, the dynamics of these enterprises. Rather, as a very long line of scholars have shown[1], they are central to such matters as the creation of work-group solidarity, the actualization of managerial control, or the resolution of conflict.

An examination of such "leisure" activities seems especially important in the context of Japanese businesses outside the country. It is important for three interrelated reasons. First, while there are a host of studies of the "transplantation" of Japanese managerial methods abroad, their focus has been almost exclusively on formal aspects of administrative arrangements or production systems (Doner 1991; Fujimoto 1991; Kaplinsky and Posthuma 1994). As of yet, however, apart from scattered reports (Hamada 1992) there has been no systematic effort to explore these "semi-formal" activities that takes place abroad. Yet given the importance of interpersonal relations in any organization, and the Japanese stress on *ningen kankei* (human relations) in particular (Whitehill 1991), one would expect that such activities as partying, entertaining or partaking in sports would be especially important for fostering of group spirit, developing interpersonal ties and inculcating organizational aims.

The second reason derives from current studies of globalization. While earlier versions of such studies naively assumed that various global processes would lead to a homogenization of the world, current approaches are more subtle. Today the stress in much of the literature dealing with various trans-national or global movements is on the emergence of new types and fora for interaction, and the development of multiple identities on the individual and group levels (Kearney 1995). Accordingly, one could envision that it is precisely at those junctures that bring people together in situations where a more "rounded" picture of their selves is uncovered that we would find these new kinds of ties and identities. Thus, we would be able to investigate whether the creation of a "transnational" culture of corporations has led to the emergence of a more international, a new breed of cosmopolitan Japanese (Hannerz 1990).

The third reason for studying these activities is related to the special importance of interpersonal business ties in Asian countries (Redding 1994). Indeed in Singapore itself, Japanese executives are very explicit about the fact that entertaining — drinking, eating, golf, *karaoke*, and occasionally *mah jong* — are used to build human relationships. Many men mentioned that in Asia human relationships are, relatively speaking, more important than in America or Europe. A senior manager from a securities company stated this explicitly when he said that such activities are "less or not appreciated because efficiency and financial technology come first [in America and Europe], whereas in Asia, financial technology and of human relationships go hand-in-hand in doing business." Hence the question here centers on the development of inter-personal ties in the context of Japanese doing business in an Asian society, in Singapore.

Spurred by strong government support, during the last three decades Singapore has become a hub of business headquarters and manufacturing facilities for all of the ASEAN, South-East Asian and, in many cases, South Asian countries (Choy and Yeo 1990). While the large-scale movement of Japanese business interests outside of Japan began in the late 1960s, the shift to Southeast Asia began in the early 1970s (Emmott 1992). At its beginning, this movement comprised mostly production and servicing facilities but in the last decade or so it has increasingly come to include banking, securities and other financial services. Concurrently, while the first moves into the area were carried out by the large firms, in recent years small and medium-sized companies have increasingly come in their wake. In this context, Singapore stands at the forefront of Japan's move into Southeast and South Asia. A plethora of Japanese production facilities, headquarters, and sales and financial centers are now located in this small country (see Ben-Ari, in this volume).

This chapter forms part of my wider study of the Japanese expatriate community in Singapore. I chose that country, because I thought that it would be a suitable venue for examining the social and cultural implications of the "globalization" of Japanese business (Ben-Ari, in this volume). Thus between June 1992 and February 1994, and for a short period in 1995, I carried out my study primarily through interviews and participant observation. Of my 93 interviewees 60 people were related to business (they were overwhelmingly men). These people come from a very large array of sectors such as construction and building, transport and communications, electrical goods and electronics, drugs and chemicals, finance and banks, and trading companies. Reflecting the general patterns of the Japanese presence in Singapore almost all of these people are white-collar organization men who have been posted to the country for a period of between three to five years at the end of which they return to Japan.

Yet theoretically speaking, Singapore seems to offer special advantages for exploring the kinds of issues I have set out. This "little dragon" (Vogel 1991) is marked both by a significant internal diversity — it has three major ethnic groups (Chinese, Malays and Indians) — and by the concentration of a very large number of foreigners (from around the globe) who have come to do business there (Choy and Yeoh 1990). Thus, this island-state would seem to be an "ideal" testing ground for an examination of these issues centering on Japan's "internationalization." In other words, what better place to examine the extent and the character of cross-cultural ties that Japanese business people participate in, for it is in such a setting that they must constantly face, continually be exposed to, a variety of "others."

With their arrival in this city-state, Japanese business people brought with them not only management, production, and service methods but also certain patterns of leisure activities (Manzereitter and Ben-Ari, forthcoming) such as tennis and swimming, concerts and exhibitions, newspapers and books, but above all the pursuits of the "holy trinity" of business-related leisure activities: eating, drinking, and golf. The most important distinction that consistently came up in my interviews in regard to all three activities was between *settai* which refers to entertaining guests and clients, and *tsukiai* which alludes to socializing with colleagues (both Japanese and non-Japanese). Let me briefly sketch out the patterns related to entertaining and socializing and then go on to an exploration of their organizational and personal implications.

Golfing[2]

Three forces have provided impetus for the development of Singapore's golf courses since the 1970s: the growth of an indigenous upper-middle class, the stationing of expatriate business communities (especially the Japanese one) on the island, and the development of golfing tourism (again mainly Japanese) (Ben-Ari 1998). By the 1990s, Singapore had 12 private and 2 small public golf clubs, and 3 more were to be opened in the next few years (*Business Times* 7 May 1992). Given the heavy pressure to join these clubs, total membership is limited and a quota has been set for foreign members. Today, all of the clubs must limit foreign membership to no more than 30 per cent of the total number of affiliations they issue.

This situation has led to the development of two markets for transferable memberships: one for locals and one for foreigners. Given the strength of the mainly Japanese expatriate firms and the power of the new upper-middle class the price of both kinds of membership has steadily increased. For example, in one club that I visited, while local membership may be bought for about US$100,000, a foreign membership can be purchased for about US$170,000. Yet relentless pressure by locals and foreigners for access to golfing facilities has led to the development of new clubs in the country's periphery, mainly the Johor Bahru area of Malaysia (a short drive across the causeway linking the two countries) and Indonesia's Bintan and Batam islands (a brief ferry ride from Singapore harbor) (ibid.). Today, golf clubs in the greater

Singapore area are situated in a hierarchy of prestige: at the top of the hierarchy are the older and larger Singaporean clubs which are located near to the city's center while the lower ends of the status pyramid include newer clubs which are located further away on the island or in neighboring Malaysia and Indonesia.

The popularity of golf in Japan itself owes as much to its pursuit by an aspiring middle-class as to a whole industry of real estate developers, equipment manufacturers, public relations and media representatives, and transport and tourist agents. Yet despite the construction of over 200 courses throughout Japan in the past 20 years, it is still difficult to play regularly: golfers must book rounds months in advance, often drive for several hours to get to courses, pay heavy user fees, and purchase memberships at prices regularly in excess of US$400,000 (*Straits Times* 7 December 1991). It is no surprise then, that given the accessibility, price and proximity of clubs in Singapore that the local Japanese expatriate community, as one person told me, is "*gorufu kureijii*" ("golf crazy").

A few indicators of the patterns of play and participation. While it is difficult to calculate precisely the numbers of active Japanese golfers in the island, the following is a rather conservative estimate. According to professional and journalistic appraisals, there are about 30,000 active golfers in Singapore (a figure which includes foreigners but excludes tourists). Of these golfers, roughly 10 to 15 per cent are Japanese (about half of the foreign members of any given club). Thus by estimates given to me by local club managers there seem to be between 3000 and 4500 Japanese individuals who regularly play golf on the island. These figures imply that about one in every two or three Japanese adults participates habitually in golf. These estimates fit well my findings and impressions. Of the 60 business people that I interviewed 12 did not play golf although 5 of this latter group had tried to play while in Singapore, and another 2 were occasionally invited to play with friends or associates.

In effect, corporate memberships (in principle open to any company registered in Singapore) are the only means by which Japanese individuals secure regular entry into golf clubs. Thus for example, Sumitomo Corporation has corporate memberships in the Sentosa, Singapore Island, Tanamera, and Raffles country clubs in Singapore and in two Malaysian clubs. Similarly, at one of the Sanyo factories on the island, out of 22 Japanese expatriates 10 are members of various clubs. At Nissho-Iwai 10 out of the

21 Japanese managers are members of clubs. The steep prices of membership imply, in turn, that only the bigger companies have affiliation with local clubs, and that the bigger the company the greater the likelihood of belonging to the more prestigious clubs. Conversely, medium sized companies tend to be affiliated with the less prestigious clubs in Singapore, or with golf resorts in Malaysia or Indonesia.

As explained elsewhere in this volume, from a strictly organizational view, the move of any individual Japanese manager to almost any foreign assignment entails a sort of "promotion": people who were department heads in Japan become division heads in Singapore and section heads become department heads. From the perspective of this chapter, such "promotion" has implications for accessibility of golf clubs. Corporate membership is provided both in Japan and in Singapore for individuals who are above a certain level in the organizational hierarchy. At Nissho-Iwai for instance, all heads of departments are eligible for nomination. But because almost everyone is placed at a higher level in Singapore many people who had little or no access to clubs in Japan play regularly in Singapore. An upper level manager of a Japanese furniture manufacturer:

> In Japan I never played because it is so far to travel and very expensive. Anyway in Japan if you are a director or a general manager then you can play; but someone in my position in Japan would never have the chance of playing much. Here it's easier and cheaper to play and so many more Japanese play here than they would in Japan.

Regular golfers reported playing between once or twice a week and once or twice a month. Yet these patterns, I was told, change for individuals according to their personal inclination or the burden of business and family affairs. In contrast to Japan where a golfing excursion usually takes a full day, in Singapore they usually take about half a day. Typically such an outing includes about four of five hours of play and then showers, drinks and food[3]. Some people reported that one primary reason for playing so often was that because outings were relatively short they could frequently be added on to the end of a working day. Finally, my impression is that people who are in general management or in marketing tend to partake in golf to a greater degree than do engineers or production specialists.

I was told on numerous occasions that golfing should be understood along with wider patterns of entertainment including drinking, dining and *karaoke*. A number of men explained that in the context of Singapore, entertainment often also includes conducting guests on sightseeing tours of the island. These activities may be undertaken jointly (as in a whole day affair in which golf is followed by dinner and a visit to a night club) or separately (although golfing occasions invariably include at least a short drink). The choice of which of this array of events to partake of is almost always left to the visitor. A manager at Nissho-Iwai, for example, told me that in Singapore he divided his time entertaining guests and clients between golf and drinks more or less equally. The manager of the furniture making company quoted before, told me:

> It takes a lot of time, what with the 18 holes, the beer afterwards and maybe dinner. It can take a half day of your time, a long part of your working day. But if a client wants to, and especially if it is an important client, for the future of the company then I go with him to play.

Playing golf and going out with guests or clients from outside of Singapore is thus often related to the image and actual facilities that island is perceived to offer for Japanese. For many guests, a business trip to the island — as to many places around the world — is very often combined with a short vacation. Thus a number of people told me that senior managers flying down from Japan for routine meetings will often schedule their visit to include all or part of the weekend so that they can play golf, to catch some of the sights, and to try the variety of cuisines on offer. The implication for the staff located in Singapore is that they often need to plan a schedule for these people.

Patterns of Drinking, Eating and Singing

Patterns of business-related eating and drinking are similar to those found in Japan. Drawing a contrast with Americans, Befu (1986: 111) states that (middle-class) Japanese prefer to entertain business associates at restaurants rather than at home. Similarly in Singapore, although Japanese expatriates live in much larger houses as compared with Japan, they continue to entertain almost exclusively outside the home (also Chiang 1997: 13). Dining, both for *settai* and *tsukiai* is carried out in one of Singapore's hundreds of restaurants although the more important guests are usually taken either to Japanese or to Chinese places. Thus for example, a guidebook for Japanese expatriates (and written in Japanese) lists no less than 84 Japanese and 72 Chinese restaurants excluding hotels (Hello Singapore 1993). The restaurants tend to be concentrated in and around the city's center in Orchard Road, but can also be found dotted around the island or along the sea shore (where many sea-food restaurants are located).

When especially important guests or business clients arrive, they are usually taken to more expensive restaurants in high-class hotels where they are entertained in private rooms. Hosts told me that they do not insist on treating guests to Japanese fare as many visitors are actually interested in trying local foods when they visit Singapore. Indeed, many interviewees suggested that the wide variety of cuisines to be had in Singapore — Chinese, Malay, Indian, Thai or Vietnamese, for instance — was one of the island's drawing points, and offered a contrast to the limited variety at home. There is a large range of prices and meals can cost anywhere between 10 to 20 US dollars to hundreds of dollars for an individual.

After dinner, people often are taken to sing in *karaoke* lounges or to drink in various bars, pubs or nightclubs around the island (although, as will become clear, this activity is usually limited to Japanese groups). While almost all the *karaoke* lounges in Singapore carry Japanese songs along with Chinese and English tunes, there are quite a few specially designed places that cater exclusively to Japanese. While in 1993 there were 35 listed *karaoke* lounges in Singapore (Hello Singapore 1993), these establishments, even more than restaurants, open and close rather rapidly and their number rises and falls due to economic circumstances. In cases where the group is an all-Japanese one (which happens very often), Japanese businessmen prefer to patronize Japanese *karaoke* lounges since they offer more Japanese songs as compared to other establishments. The price of entertainment at Japanese lounges is rather expensive, and a manager from a trading company revealed that a typical night out for five people and including alcohol and "social escorts" would cost about US$1,500.

As in Japan (Rohlen 1974: 103), drinking and eating together tend to be all-male affairs (also Ben-Ari, and Yong, in this volume). Midooka (1990:486) talks of two parts of such occasions: the more formal part and a more informal *nijikai* (second party) where fewer people are present. When women do participate it is usually in the first more formal part of the evening, but later, when people embark to the *nijikai*, the women leave. As in Japan, evenings may last anywhere between two to four hours. While on many occasions a party may stay at one establishment, some men like to bar-hop and spend an hour each at up to three or four bars. A few managers reported occasionally drinking across the causeway in Malaysia in Johor Bahru until four or five in the morning since Singaporean bars close at two o'clock. Yet because of the fatigue that this practice causes it is not done very often.

There are two types of *settai* that the expatriates I studied are involved in: entertaining business clients (either Japanese or non-Japanese); and entertaining superiors and colleagues from Japan. In very general terms, trading and construction companies engage more in the first type of *settai* (aimed at enhancing sales), while all of the companies to which the executives belong tend to be involved in the second type of *settai*. Many of my interviewees — as well as those of Chiang (1997: 9) — noted that, in general, Japanese clients were the more common targets for *settai* as they were more demanding than Americans or Europeans[4]. Yet if the working relationship was unsteady or in its early stages, non-Japanese were also given such treatment.

Within drinking occasions, much stress is placed on commensality: for instance, taking the same dish as clients so that a close "family-like" atmosphere is created. Topics of conversation during *settai* revolve around work-related matters like business conditions and trends in Singapore, rough descriptions and explanations of ongoing projects, and directions for future projects or business. In addition, general topics like personal hobbies and family matters are also brought up. Occasionally, if business dealings have not been completed at the workplace, they may be continued over food and drinks (but never in *karaoke* lounges or golf games).

Many men complained that the service of waiters and waitresses in Singapore was not of the same level as Japan. Yet the greatest complaints centered on the lack of manners of hostesses who are usually expected (in Japan) to provide a "useful 'service' for business encounters between men" (Allison 1994: 15). In Japan, a hostess's skill lies "in keeping the men involved in conversation and her ability to give men a good time. When entertaining, the host wants and needs his guests to be entertained. But this can be a burdensome task, one that the host is only too happy to transfer to a competent hostess" (ibid.). But because hostesses and *mamasan* in Singapore do not speak fluent Japanese, many of the interviewees revealed that they had to make extra efforts in entertaining their guests. They found themselves introducing interesting topics and lighting guests' cigarettes when the local hostesses were not doing their job well.

As mentioned before, *tsukiai* refers to socializing with colleagues from the workplace: Singaporeans, other foreigners and Japanese employees. According to accounts I heard, it is carried out anywhere between twice or three times a week to once or twice a month. In this respect, the smaller the number of Japanese (say below five) in a given company, the more important are the occasions when they go out with locals. While some parties are scheduled and planned ahead of time, on many occasions people simply make off-the-cuff decisions to go out. Most *tsukiai* takes place during lunch or dinner and less frequently in *karaoke* lounges. While *tsukiai* expenses are not formally paid by the company, in effect they are often covered by special budgets and expense accounts. Accordingly, the pattern is for managers to pay for their subordinates and split the payment with colleagues of the same rank.

In general, *tsukiai* is seen as a natural and necessary part of work or of any group effort. An executive in his late forties noted:

Everyone is living in a society, and even the company is a small society, so it is important to keep relationships with everyone. Organizations like the company are made up of people; it is people that organize the company and therefore each one must have some kind of relationship.

Yet such a statement raises more questions than it answers for it tends to gloss over the personal, individual reasons that people participate in *settai* and *tsukiai*.

Careering: Information, Trust and Reputations

How are we to understand the place of drinking, eating and golf in the lives of Japanese business expatriates in Singapore? An answer to this question entails examining these activities not only at one point of time, but more importantly as part of the longer term dynamics of such people's lives. Consequently, if we conceptualize the stint in Singapore (or anywhere abroad) as a stage in individuals' careers then we will be able to understand how people utilize dinners, drinking bouts and golf games as part of their workplace strategies for promotion. As I show elsewhere in this volume, the essence of a career is that it is a predictable sequence of movements, a relay of roles set up to normalize the potentially turbulent flow of persons through an organization. But while from an organizational point of view careers are predictable, from and individual point of view, as Skinner (1983) reminds us, they are uncertain. Given the numerical limits on promotion only some people will be able to advance up the organizational hierarchy.

But what of semi-formal leisure pursuits? My thesis is that golf, drinking and eating represent the main "informal" practices which juniors who are on the managerial track of large Japanese firms use to secure their personal advancement within these firms. A 30-year-old trainee articulated this point in regard to those activities I have defined as "not-precisely-work":

> Socializing in the company is still very important as compared with other societies because in Japan this kind of socializing can help in the promotion system. This is because if the boss asks you to go to socialize, if you don't go or violate his request, this will leave a bad impression and affect promotion.

It is thus in the context of individuals' constant monitoring and maneuvering for organizational advancement that entertaining of clients and guests and socializing with co-workers should be seen. The words of a manager of a Japanese hotel who talked about golfing supports this view:

> I don't think it's all entertainment. I can make all sorts of contacts, to pass information, and if I want to get to someone in a specific field of industry I look for someone who I play golf with and see if he can introduce me.

Building organizational reputations

The most important dimension of this maneuvering involves the creation and maintenance of organizational reputations. Through these "informal" activities white-collar managers strive to create a proper organizational reputation so that they are perceived to have the required qualities for advancement. On a practical level, this implies that Japanese expatriates hosting guests or clients, for example, must make special efforts to make visits to Singapore impressive as possible for the visitors. Almost all of the people I interviewed agreed that in *settai* the bottom line is economic: to increase sales, close a business deal, or establish long-term relationships. I found an indirect indicator of these sentiments, when a number of expatriates some told me that while they would get drunk with their colleagues, they would not do so with clients for fear of saying the wrong things. Indeed, despite the economic downturn of the 1990s, the thousands of dollars that may be spent on any one event are seen as a business investment of serious significance. But the point is that the "economic bottom line" is important in so far as it enhances the reputation of those individuals who have made successful deals or increased sales.

Hosting senior executives from headquarters in Japan should be seen in a similar light. A manager from one of the smaller trading companies told me:

> In Japan you also have opportunities to go out with clients, but here you have them for a few days. It's a special place that they remember when they go back to Tokyo. And then they think back and say, "Ah, that Yamamoto, he is a good guy; he organized a nice visit for me."

As in entertaining clients, there is much room for individual initiative in organizing such activities, but the point is, again, that the reputation of an individual expatriate is often created through establishing a good reputation for the whole subsidiary in Singapore. Talking about the wider importance of hosting managers from Tokyo, a managing director at a construction company told Chiang (1997: 12–3): "it is important to secure good status as an overseas subsidiary. Monetary assistance and staffing policies will be easier if the relationship [between the subsidiary and head office] is good."

Reputations then, are created in and around *settai* and *tsukiai* in both direct and indirect manners. Directly, reputations are created through showing desired characteristics, building trust, or concocting a memorable experience that will be remembered upon a return to Japan. Indirectly, a person can make a name for himself by using informal after-hours activities to lay the ground that will help in clinching deals which themselves will be perceived as part of his reputation. In both cases playing this "not-precisely-work" is part of careering in the sense of making organizational moves aimed at future promotion.

Trust, appraisal and human relations

In a related manner, while executives often seek to build familiarity with their business partners and clients through *settai*, they aspire to create good working relations with their co-workers through *tsukiai*. They seem to work with two similar assumptions in regard to such activities. The first is that clients will choose the company they are most familiar with in order to establish a formal working relationship, and that entertaining is the first step in initiating such a relationship. The second is that it is only on the basis of mutual closeness (but not necessarily friendship) that an efficient and productive working environment can be created. One interviewee, for instance, told Chiang (1997: 20): "It takes a long time to get close to a person, and every encounter of *tsukiai* leads to a development of a different aspect of the relationship. As such, both parties are able to get a different feeling or perception of the opposite party when they return to the office the next day." Other managers mentioned that on the basis of the insights they gained about their subordinates during informal meetings they would be better able to allocate different formal assignments and tasks.

Along these lines, I was told time and again that in both kinds of encounters — *settai* and *tsukiai* — almost nothing is said directly about business dealings, although there are general discussions about such issues as the Singaporean business environment or the conditions of Japan's economy. The emphasis, as many informants told me, is very much on the creation of trust. The director of Sumitomo Bank told me, "when you return to the office the next day it is easier to talk." A lower level administrator in Toyota's trading company said that these are opportunities for "making contact and building relationships; so we tend to talk only about golf and not about actual business because the aim is to create a relationship." The director general of Fujikura reported that he likes to discuss hobbies and music and the social habits of people in Singapore, but only occasionally to converse about company matters. The head of Tomen corporation observed,

> We talk about the economic situation in Japan, the management systems of different companies ... About my home, I come from Okayama, about the quiet there, about the mountains, about the rivers. And about the good and bad

things about Singapore. I have friends who served for example in Indonesia and they compare it to Singapore.

A closely related issue entails how the "character" of clients or co-workers is uncovered during informal meetings. When I asked the manager of a local country club about how golf is related to business transactions, he chuckled and answered that golf is

a real test of character ... So if you want to find out your potential business partner you play golf with him: see whether he is reliable. So that is why a lot of business starts on the golf course. Directly but also indirectly in the sense that if you are not sure of your partnership with this person, you invite him for a game of golf ... You cannot hide in the game of golf: the body language, the way you play the game, the way you react to a bad shot, the way you react to a good shot, this shows up everything. So golf reveals your character.

Similarly, I was told that *settai* activities like dining and drinking were often engaged in to learn more about clients' personalities. In the more relaxed atmosphere, an executive from a heavy machinery company observed, "it is easier to inspect the attitudes and personalities of the people whom you have to work with in the future." Referring to both *settai* and *tsukiai*, a managing director of a real-estate company told Chiang (1997: 10) that when going out to *karaoke* lounges:

We are just watching the personality of the client or new boss. He may be very shy at first and won't sing any songs but after several attempts to encourage him to pick up the microphone, he may finally sing. Then he starts to open up and sing more songs. But for those who do not like to sing, we will know after a few attempts and we will not force them.

The point in such "inspections" is, of course, gauging such characteristics as the openness, gregariousness, poise or ease of new clients, guests or colleagues.

Managing information

A manager at Sumitomo Corporation noted something else. He began by noting that he and his friends often talk about their families and friends, but more significantly (if unsurprisingly) they very often talked about "what happens at the office." Other people noted that when playing or drinking with colleagues or with relatively close friends from Japan, a lot of information about "office politics" is exchanged. Thus it is in regard to *settai* with guests from company headquarters or *tsukiai* with co-workers that the management of information regarding the internal politics of the main offices is most important.

Such information is crucial for a number of reasons. First, information regarding ongoing business projects and trends available in the Singapore office may not be as sufficient and timely as that found in Japan, and thus not indicate the future directions of company work. Thus very often new ventures and projects undertaken by the firm figure as prominent subjects for discussions and debates. Moreover, it seems that it is especially with the economic downturn of the last few years that such information gathered through "informal" entertainment is of special importance. In addition, some senior managers also make use of these events to hear the views of lower level subordinates because they are less directly involved in official meetings or the formation of official policy. A manager at Tokyo Bank:

> I sometimes go out with my Singaporean colleagues but it is for lunch, with the Japanese it for dinner, drinking and sometimes *karaoke*. ... It is very important because then we [the Japanese] can relax and have time for ourselves. We talk about work, about new projects. Each one of us has different projects so we talk to each other about how to establish and handle them. Then we talk about the office, the local staff, about different problems.

Second, and more importantly, the executives in Singapore are especially interested in the personnel and organizational changes that take place in Japan. New promotions, new prospects for overseas assignments, the establishment of new offices and departments, and the successes and failures of certain individuals, are among the concerns people said they gossiped about. A typical example was given by a sales executive at Matsushita:

> We sometimes *tsukiai* with our classmates (*dooki*), such as people who entered Matsushita the same year as me and who I got to know during the company training system. I still keep in touch with them. Japan has a life-long employment system

164

and my colleagues are also my rivals and we need to check our relative position during *tsukiai*. We can speak more frankly and exchange a lot of information. It is very useful for us because we consider some classmates to be our allies. They can help us in difficult situations and provide support. I order to keep this support, I always try to keep this sort of relationship even if they are in a different section.

The flow and management of information is related back to building reputations. Skinner (1983: 65) points out that in any organization with a fairly stable work force, reputations become widely known, and that much of a person's behavior can be attributed to attempts to shape how others view him. Over the long term, the "kind of relationship a person has with any of his co-workers can become the content of gossip which directly affects superiors decisions about reassignments. Any act or statement may become part of the body of information about a given person" (Skinner 1983: 69). For executives who are posted overseas for periods of between three to five years, and who are effectively disconnected from many of the ongoing meetings and exchanges in Japan, the maintenance of organizational reputations is even more important.

Socialization of new organizational members

Another central purpose of *tsukiai* is to socialize recently arrived managers into the mores and business climate of Singapore and into the special circumstances of the local subsidiary. As Japanese expatriates are regularly rotated every few years, many executives make a conscious effort to welcome newcomers, get close to them, and help them adjust to the new working environment (which can be quite stressful at the beginning). It is especially in the informal atmosphere of entertaining, as I was told numerous times, that new colleagues are familiarized with the local goings-on and start building relationships with their fellow colleagues. Referring to these issues, the secretary of the Japan Chamber of Commerce told me that *tsukiai* was used to "facilitate familiarity" (he used English):

> It's a way to talk about common problems like job-hopping among Singaporeans; like helping newcomers and welcoming

them by telling them how to set up a company, how to determine wage policy, how to recruit employees, how to pay salaries and so on.

Many interviewees agreed with this assessment and told me of the opportunities such engagements offered for the exchange of information and for the "education" of newly arrived executives. For managers who had just arrived in Singapore then, golfing occasions and going out for food and imbibement often provide good chances for "learning the ropes."

Creating solidarity and managing conflict

From the managerial perspective — and this view fits well with the Japanese corporate ideology of "firm-as-family" (Fruin 1980; 1983) — *tsukiai* carried out in small work-groups helps to create unity and solidarity among employees. A general manager from a large Japanese department store noted:

> For a sales group made up of eight people, for example, when we go out together, we feel part of the group, even like a family. We talk about things like my sick father in Japan or how successful my daughter is at school. As the atmosphere in the office is serious, we need another more relaxed atmosphere. Especially to the more senior managers, if a job needs to be carried out by a group, it can be done more effectively through gatherings in a group. That is, you get to know more about one another during non-office hours.

Similarly, a director from a construction company noted that such occasions were used: "to bring up dissatisfactions to subordinates after a meal, or to give praise for present performance and sometimes suggestions for improvement." Later, he referred to the teaching role of *tsukiai*: my "subordinates will appreciate and even accept my objective suggestions and thus improve the working relationship between them." Another manager in his early thirties noted: "The boss has to manage not only the job but also the staff; to nurture (*sodateru*) the staff ... The manager has to know about the subordinate's situation and company *tsukiai* is a place where he does it."

As in Japan, a complementary aspect of such occasions entails their importance for releasing tensions and managing conflict (Ben-

Ari 1994: 12–15). Hence, it is especially during drinks (after meals or a game of golf) that Japanese expatriates often take the opportunity to voice complaints regarding staff and management, topics which are not discussed in the office. When I asked the chief of a Japanese press agency what he did to release stress, his unequivocal answer was "drinking and *karaoke.*" An executive from one of the Japanese airlines said that the going out for drinks "allows you to express all sorts of things, to relax." A young executive explained: "Company *tsukiai* with colleagues is good for recovering from frustration ... I can complain with my colleagues and this is enjoyable."

But this release of tension seems to be limited to the Japanese employees. Indeed, one of the managers interviewed by Chiang (1997: 37) said that he was very surprised when he heard local employees talking about bonuses and comparing salaries during office hours. He could not understand such behaviour, since Japanese usually voice their grievances "after hours." Drawing a contrast between the patterns found among the Japanese and Singaporean employees, a number of men explained that as Singaporeans can (and do) resign they feel less need to vent their feelings with colleagues. Thus, they inadvertently linked the expression of grievances by Japanese managers during bouts of imbibement to their lack of exit options from the companies in which they were employed.

The price of entertainment

Yet despite my stress on how drinks, food and sports figure in people's career moves, a word of caution should be sounded at this juncture. We must be wary of attributing too a steady, coherent, or fully conscious motivation to informal "after hours" behavior. The whole attitude towards *settai* and *tsukiai* encounters is permeated by fluctuations and ambivalence. Just as the workplace is sometimes marked by periods of disquiet, fatigue, or strain so it is with such occasions. The deputy manager of a Japanese business hotel mentioned that while he enjoyed playing golf and socializing, he often felt that it "is hard, just like work." A deputy manager at Komatsu said that at times he felt that he just could not decline to join drinking occasions because they were part of his job. This kind of attitude may explain some of the complaints that I heard (especially from executives in trading companies) that continuous nights of *settai* were physically and mentally tiring when combined with the demands of normal working days, and that excessive drinking diminished the pleasures of *settai*. The general manager of Fujikura rather candidly registered his feelings: "I am only human and sometimes I don't feel like going to play golf but would rather stay at home and rest. But I feel that I have to go because golf is part of work."

It is precisely because these activities are important to individuals' careers that such attitudes are sounded. The general manager of a department store usually attends about two thirds of *tsukiai* activities (with the Japanese employees of his firm) to which he is invited, but admitted "it is not enjoyable to socialize purposely with colleagues from the office, and if the others do not care, I would rather not go." Another man talked of feeling obligated (*giri*) to attend parties and golf games, and observed that as for *karaoke*,

> with colleagues that one chooses, it is fun and enjoyable, but usually not in a big group with the managing director, manager, and assistant manager. In this case, it becomes a duty, so everyone feels obliged and no one will say one does not like it.

Finally, there is an attitude that I encountered very rarely during research. I was discussing the term "*shinjinrui*" (lit. new human being) (Linhart 1988: 288) which is used to characterize younger people in Japan, when a junior Marubeni manager said that such a term does characterize him: "Take my boss here in Singapore, if you ask him then he doesn't know whether playing golf is business or something private. I don't like this in-between feeling, of not knowing what it is that I am doing." Yet these kinds of expressions are very much the exception. Because of the self- and organizational selection of managers who are assigned to overseas postings one finds very few dissenting voices.

For the vast majority of Japanese business people in Singapore then, the master script connecting golf, entertainment and work involves quite clear career moves. My emphasis on careering does not imply that individuals do not enjoy golfing or eating and drinking together or that they participate in such activities only for utilitarian ends. Almost all of the men I interviewed emphasized how much they relish the opportunities Singapore offers them to play golf, or the enjoyment they feel from simply fraternizing with other people. What I do want to emphasize is that such enjoyment takes place within organizationally defined careers in which individuals are heavily invested.

The "Internationalization" of Japanese Corporations?

Yet a final question remains. Given that these "after hours" activities occur in Singapore — that is, in a venue outside of Japan — in what way (if at all) do they contribute to the breakdown of boundaries between Japanese and non-Japanese employees, and to the inculcation of a "cosmopolitan" outlook among the Japanese business expatriates? When I began fieldwork in Singapore I was heavily influenced by various academic and popular arguments about the increasing "internationalization" of Japan. Accordingly, I assumed that it would be especially activities defined as "not-precisely-work" that would provide such opportunities for the Japanese expatriates because of the direct interaction they afford with members of other cultures. As became clear during my fieldwork, however, my expectations were confounded. Let me begin with golf.

In the vast majority of cases the Japanese tend to play among themselves. For example, 10 people said that 90 per cent of the time they play with other Japanese, and all of the others stated that in the majority of cases they play with their co-nationals. What I did find, however, was that while the expatriates were not crossing international boundaries through golf, they consistently spanned inter-firm borders. I discovered that these business people tended — much more than in Japan — to play with members of other (and very often competing) firms.

In general, Japanese expatriates play within a number of social and organizational circles beyond their own company. The first circle comprises partners and friends from "families" of corporations (sometimes but not always *keiretsu*). For instance, a manager from Nomura Securities explained that he played with a group of people from his company, the Nomura Research Institute, a Nomura related insurance company and the Daiwa Bank. Individuals of the Mitusi group play in what is called the *Sanyukai* (the friendly association of the three), while members of Sony's six Singapore companies also tend to gather for golf (and other types of entertainment). These corporate "families" play either in ad-hoc groups or in the framework of more formal tournaments.

The second circle involves two very active organizations: the Japan Chamber of Commerce and the Japanese Association. The Chamber (or, more often, one of its constituent committees) for instance, regularly organizes tournaments in which representatives of companies in a certain industry or sector (travel, construction, or electronics, for example) participate. The third circle is made up of graduates of a certain number of universities (*daigaku no atsumari*). Over the years graduates of such establishments as Tokyo, Keio and Waseda universities have organized associations (in Singapore) which provide occasional opportunities for dining or golfing together. Expatriates participate in one or another of such circles as often as every month or as little as once a year. The director of the Sumitomo bank noted that apart from regular games with his colleagues, "I play in three tournaments every year: one with the Sumitomo companies in the Seiyu-kai; once with all of the Japanese bankers in Singapore; and once in a tournament organized by the Chamber of Commerce for the Japanese banks and general trading companies."

Patterns of eating and drinking are roughly similar. While much of *settai* entertaining is devoted to hosting non-Japanese clients, the most important occasions involve visitors or guests from Japan (most commonly from company headquarters). While there is some variation between firms, in general, socializing with locals very frequently takes the form of joint lunches or very formal parties (such as Christmas galas). In the overwhelming majority of cases, informal socializing — *tsukiai* — involves only the Japanese members of a given company. Here again the Japanese custom of eating and drinking in the framework of two parties is of importance. As with women, so too the locals usually participate in the more formal occasion which almost invariably includes food. But later when the Japanese embark to the second party (the *nijikai*) local employees tend to leave or are simply not invited along for "another drink."

Why do the Japanese limit their contact to co-nationals? Most interviewees linked the limited language abilities of Japanese people to the lack of comfortableness of playing or socializing with members of other cultures. The secretary of the Japan Chamber of Commerce:

> The Japanese are not so good in foreign languages. That is why it easier for many Japanese businessmen to speak

Japanese and then it becomes easier to meet other Japanese businessmen. In this way it becomes easier to exchange information.

Others mentioned that they felt less "on guard" when playing with other Japanese people or that they could relax in their own language. One perceptive individual, a sports coordinator at a local Singapore country club, noted the following when I asked about the tendency of the Japanese to play golf among themselves.

> The other foreigners tend to speak English but the Japanese want to feel at home among themselves. They are relaxing because of the words they use, the language they use and the punchline is different. They probably feel more relaxed when they play among themselves. And when they play with someone else they have to pretend to be someone else, use a language that they are not comfortable with.

It is especially in regard to *tsukiai* that this theme came up. I was told numerous times that while Japanese do not feel really relaxed during eating or drinking with other nationals because of difference in food habits, that underlying everything was lack of comfortableness in another language and especially the non-verbal parts of interaction. The director of Fuji Xerox in Singapore told me that drinking with non-Japanese is difficult

> because in Japan we have *nomi-communication* [lit. drinking communication] which only Japanese can understand. Overall, if we include others [non-Japanese] we cannot enjoy ourselves 100 per cent because through drinking we will have frank communication which is the most important thing, the Japanese style of communication. Usually after we finish at the office we go out, everybody, drinking and to do some talking. Sometimes we talk about difficult things and if local people join in, then it is difficult to relax ... For example if someone comes in then we have to switch to talking English and then suddenly people become quiet. Maybe only those who are good at English will talk with the new person and the rest are quiet.

Accordingly, parties with locals are often pared down to the minimum seen as necessary for maintaining smooth working relations. A Matsushita executive said that he went out with his

Singaporean colleagues twice or three times a year (for end of the year or New Year's parties) which he saw as "compulsory."

A related reason for the lack of interaction between Japanese managers and their Singaporean employees entails Singaporean attitudes (Ng and Ben-Ari in the volume). In Singapore's local working culture, it is perfectly acceptable to decline an invitation from colleagues or superiors to join them for dinner or drinks. One manager in his forties noted, "Singaporeans will not go even if we force them to go. Singaporeans usually put their priority first. [Japanese] bosses are afraid to suggest going out nowadays because later nobody wants to go." Another man noted that Singaporeans tend to stress family life and do not want to socialize after work. A third man noted that the locals did not look for the development of long-term relations at work and thus ties with co-workers were rather shallow.

As noted however, informal events served to initiate and cement inter-firm ties between Japanese managers belonging to different companies. Indeed, it is precisely because the expatriates hold more senior positions than in Japan that they can create ties outside their firm. But the future-oriented ties that these business people create and maintain with members of other corporations appear to differ from the kinds of relations that Americans cultivate. While Americans may use such ties later on in their careers in their personal movement between firms, all of my Japanese interviewees stated that they did not intend to leave their companies in the near future. Rather, they saw cross-firm ties in terms of opening possibilities for future business relations with other firms. Take the words of a deputy director at Komatsu:

> Listen, in Japan it's really hard to get to know senior people from other business firms. Here in the Japanese community [in Singapore] you play golf with someone, and when you get back to Japan you can just pick up the phone and say "hey, we played golf together back in Singapore." It's very important.

Another manager observed that he interacts with members of other firms "in order to broaden my way of thinking."

From a behavioral point of view these are far from unimportant points. All of these occasions — eating, drinking and golfing — are validating mechanisms for the social and cultural order of the workplace and for the dividing line between Japanese and non-

Japanese. Such events validate this order and this dividing line because participating in them implies (at least in part) an acceptance of a set of relationships that define someone's right to arrange a party, to specify time and location, or for inviting others to a "second party." While "opposed" to normal working experiences, these situations are always subordinated to — i.e. governed by the logic of — the everyday relations of the workplace.

Conclusion

In this chapter my argument has been that activities categorized as "not-precisely-work" like golfing or drinking among Japanese business expatriates in Singapore should be understood in terms of their place in people's management of their careers. To reiterate a point made earlier, I do not dismiss the contention that the people enter these occasions for enjoyment and relaxation. But to overemphasize their "diversionary" dimension is to lose sight of how these activities figure as a means to build one's organizational reputation and enhance opportunities for promotion.

According to my analysis then, golfing occasions, bouts of imbibement or company dinners seem to lead to very little "internationalization": neither in the sense of creating and maintaining contact with locals or other foreigners nor in the sense of a greater awareness of the cultures of "others." In an interesting manner, being posted overseas does not so much represent a process of "going international" as one of "going national" (Ben-Ari in this volume). During their period of service in Singapore, business expatriates tend both to create and maintain ties with Japanese from other geographical areas and workplaces in Japan, and to be much more aware of their national identity and the cultural assumptions and practices that they share. Paradoxically, despite being posted abroad, the vast majority of these people are still (whether drinking or golfing), "playing ball" in the Japanese ballpark.

Notes

*Thanks are due to Lise Skov, Brian Moeran and Boas Shamir for comments on earlier versions of parts of this paper.

[1] See Allison 1994; Atsumi 1979; Befu 1986; Cole 1971; Dore, 1973: 205; Linhart 1986; Midooka 1990; Moeran 1986; Rohlen, 1974; Takada 1983; and Toren 1995.

[2] This section draws heavily on Ben-Ari (1998).

[3] As in Thailand (Cohen 1995), the move has been from a form of private members' clubs to integrated leisure complexes which include golf courses, tennis courts and swimming pools, meeting and convention facilities, business centers and dining and drinking sites.

[4] Chiang (1997: 31) was told that sometimes attempts were made to lose money to clients during *mah-jong* games, and I was told that women escorts were occasionally arranged for clients. According to my impression, however, these practices were undertaken only in a minority of cases.

Chapter 8

The Happiness-Making Machine: Soka Gakkai and Japanese Cultural Presence in Singapore

John Clammer

Introduction

Throughout history religion has been one of the most formative influences on the cultures of Southeast Asia. In successive waves, religious ideas originating outside the region have transformed indigenous perceptions of self, cosmos, kinship and political and social order, have created new patterns of ethics and aesthetics, have imposed new cuisines and fashions and have, in ways both obvious and subtle, irrevocably altered the spiritual landscape and religious geography of a whole sub-continent. Hinduism's immense influence on Cambodia, Java and Bali, Therevada Buddhism's transformation of Thai and Burmese society, the impact of Islam from southern Thailand east as far as the Philippines have been amongst the most important factors in the formation of world views, economies and political systems. The subsequent appearance of Christianity, which especially in its Catholic variant has had a profound impact on Southeast Asian societies as diverse as Vietnam and the Philippines, and the coming of Mahayana Buddhism with Chinese migrants have woven yet further threads into the religious tapestry in an area which has both been the recipient of influences from the east and the west and the transformer of those influences into distinct local patterns – Javanese mysticism, Philippine folk Catholicism, or the Vietnamese Cao Dai movement for example.

Since these deeply formative cultural periods, many newer varieties of religious doctrine, practice and experience have implanted themselves throughout Southeast Asia – Protestant Christianity and it's so-called 'charismatic' or Pentecostal expression and the neo-Hindu Sai Baba movement are examples – quite apart from indigenous sectarian movements such as the plethora of healing, divination and spirit medium cults amongst Chinese religionists (Clammer 1983). The latest wave of influence, in a process that shows every sign of upsetting or transforming the conventional theory of secularization, has come once again from the east, but this time from Japan, in the form of the spread overseas of the so-called Japanese 'new religions' (*shin-shukyo*).

The category of 'new religions', or even their more recent manifestation the 'new new religions' (*shin-shin shukyo*) comprises a very large number of religious movements some of which date from pre-war and many from more recent years and which, despite the alleged non-religiosity of Japan, have attracted large numbers of adherents, have in some cases built large religious complexes and even universities, and which collectively have redrawn the religious portrait of contemporary Japan (Reader 1991). Many of these religions have their roots in the indigenous Shinto tradition of Japan (for example Tenrikyo), others in Buddhism (for example Rissho Kosei-kai). Almost all are syncretic, some even having Christian or Jewish elements despite the very minority status of the first and the almost total absence of the second tradition in Japan (the Iesu no Mitama Kyokai or the Makuya movement being major examples), some are largely regional in nature, such as Kurozumi-kyo which is concentrated in the Okayama prefecture of western Japan (Hardacre 1988), and many of the larger ones are now nation-wide. Some have now begun to spread overseas initially amongst Japanese expatriate communities and Japanese permanently settled abroad, in Hawaii, California and Brazil for instance, and from there to the native populations (Clarke and Somers 1994).

This chapter will examine one example of this last category – the Soka Gakkai, a Buddhist-based 'new religion' which, having established a formidable presence in Japan with several million members, extensive property, a publishing house, a university and an affiliated political party with substantial representation in the Diet (the Japanese parliament), has begun to spread abroad to North America, Europe, South America (where there is a large community of Japanese origin) and most recently to Southeast Asia. The influence of Soka Gakkai is being felt throughout the region, especially amongst its ethnic Chinese minorities, but here its position and implications of its spread will be traced in the one society in Southeast Asia which has a Chinese majority – Singapore – in which the movement is reckoned by some commentators to be the fastest growing religion in a society which already boasts a veritable supermarket of faiths.

The choice of Singapore as the case study is not fortuitous for other reasons too. It is a small but ethnically very diverse society with a population of three million with Chinese, Malay, Indian, Arab, Eurasian, European, Japanese and Southeast Asian communities, economically dynamic, and politically highly controlled. It is a society that has long prided itself on being a crossroads of east and west and it is religiously complex with almost all the major and many of the minor faiths of Asia represented. It is also heavily influenced by Japan: there is a large Japanese expatriate business community, the city-state abounds with Japanese departmental stores, restaurants, karaoke lounges, language schools and bookstores selling translations of Japanese literary, scientific and managerial works as well as their Japanese language originals. Japanese-made television programmes are common and there is a weekly hour-long broadcast on one of the state-run television channels, one half being about some aspect of Japan in English, the other half being news in Japanese. A large number of Singaporeans walking the streets are, unwittingly or not, wearing Japanese fashions and most who drive are certainly behind the wheels of Japanese cars.

Singapore is then, if not a microcosm of the rest of Southeast Asia (its high level of urbanization, Chinese ethnic and political dominance and political system and culture make it unrepresentative) is nevertheless an ideal laboratory for both the study of religious change and of Japanese cultural influence (and of the links between the two). Very clearly in this case – that of the introduction, spread, assimilation and impact of Soka Gakkai – these factors meet, illustrating not only some of the qualities of Singapore society, but also very revealingly, deeper levels of Japanese cultural influence and penetration than can be uncovered by such more surface level phenomena as fashion behaviour or by simply studying the by now more familiar economic impact of Japan, important as these levels are. They are all in any case connected and interpenetrate, and a theoretical sub-theme of this chapter will be to explore the connections, in a non-Weberian way, between religion, culture and economic activity as well as to deepen the understanding of the connections between religion and political culture in Southeast Asia.

Origins and Spread of the Movement

The Singapore Nichiren Shoshu Buddhist association was formally registered in the country as a religious entity in 1972. Aspects of its influence had already been felt in a rather indirect way as a small percentage of the rapidly growing Japanese expatriate community in Singapore were members of the home organization of laity in Japan and brought their religious practices with them when they were posted to Singapore. The percentage was small largely because in their recruitment of staff large Japanese corporations of the kind that had a presence in Southeast Asia tend to avoid selection of known members of the new religions for fear that their involvement in an alternative organization will dilute commitment to the company, the primary focus of loyalty and social identity for many Japanese workers (Rohlen 1979). Early interest in Singapore as a missionary field was initially restricted to these somewhat resistant Japanese. By the beginning of the 1970s however this was changing as an increasing number of native Singaporeans were showing signs of interest in Japanese Buddhism, especially its more accessible kinds, as Japanese economic and cultural influence in Southeast Asia grew with Japan's industrial expansion and growing postwar confidence. So in 1972 the Singapore Nichiren Shoshu Buddhist Association (NSS) was registered with the Registrar of Societies and by 1975 had already begun to participate in the National Day celebrations that mark Singapore's independence each August. By the 1980s the NSS was very visible at this politically important occasion, supplying in 1987 2000 volunteers to take place in the torch-light grand finale of the National Day display and a further 200 marshals to help in the training and organization of participants in other displays (*Straits Times* 1987). This signalled that the group had come a long way from the tiny group that used to meet in private homes in the 1960s under the influence of a Japanese expatriate and even from 1972 when the group with less than 100 members registered themselves as an association of lay believers in Nichiren Daishomin's brand of Buddhism (Chan 1988: 10).

Nichiren (1222–1282), a former priest of the Tendai sect of Japanese Buddhism, was the founder of a reformed Buddhism based on the supremacy of devotion to the Lotus Sutra. His reforms, though widely challenged, drew much of their legitimacy from the widespread belief at the time that the last era of the decline of Buddhism was in progress and Nichiren was believed by his followers to be a reincarnation of the original Buddha returned to save mankind from its troubles.

After Nichiren's death the movement fragmented into a number of sects, one of which by way of the teachings transmitted through Nikko, founder of Taiseki-ji Temple near Mount Fuji, is now largely recognized as the orthodox one. Soka Gakkai, founded in 1930 as the Soka Kyoiku Gakkai or 'Value-Creating Educational Society' was created as the organization of lay followers of Nichiren Shoshu – the 'orthodox sect of Nichiren'. The founder, Makiguchi Tsunesaburo, was a school teacher who attempted to merge Nichiren's Buddhism with his own theory of value creation. Under its second president, Toda Josei, the word '*kyoiku*' (education) was dropped from the title of the organization and the association was reorganized stressing on the one hand its links with the Taiseki-ji and on the other vigorous proselytization, especially through the creation of Young Men's and Young Women's divisions. Under its third and current president, Ikeda Daisaku, Soka Gakkai has cultivated a new and less aggressive public image, has stressed cultural and even intellectual activities, Ikeda for example having published a book containing a dialogue with Arnold Toynbee (Toynbee and Ikeda 1989). Mainstream and conservative political activities have also been stepped up and the Soka Gakkai affiliated political party (Komeito or 'Clean Government Party') has become a small but significant force in parliament. In 1975 Soka Gakkai International was formed to promote peace, culture and international understanding based on Nichiren's principles. Soka Gakkai has since spread world-wide and has become a major participant in the carnival of religions that now fills the post-secular world (Saunders 1972; Thomsen 1963).

In Singapore the NSS exists to promote Nichiren Buddhism and recognizes Taiseki-ji as the head temple the priests of which are uniquely qualified to transmit the Gohonzon, the miniature copy of the Daigohonzon, a large wooden tablet bequeathed to Taiseki-ji by Nichiren and believed to contain universal power. It also recognizes Soka Gakkai International as the parent organization and members when possible make pilgrimages to Japan to visit Taiseki-ji, but is otherwise independent in its day-to-day running and organization. This situation has since been complicated by a feud between the priests of Taiseki-ji and Soka Gakkai creating problems about the transmission of gohonzon to members. Four 'centres', so called rather than 'temples' now exist in Singapore and the organization is financed through the contributions of its own local members.

Exact figures of membership are impossible to obtain, but estimations range from 6000 to 10,000 families (membership being computed by family rather than by individual adherence). Organization is very hierarchical stretching from headquarters down through chapters, districts and groups on the vertical axis and including units based on age, gender and special interests on the horizontal axis (Chan 1988). The four main divisions are Men's, Women's, Young Men's and Young Women's and the members of each local group are horizontally organized into the appropriate division. Sub-groups for students, teachers, medical workers, a dance troupe, Chinese orchestra, choir and a band form the daily points of contact between members and the organization. The individual is tightly integrated into this intersecting network of vertical and horizontal ties. Full members (those who have received the *gohonzon*) are admitted after regular attendance at *gongyo* (recitation of the Lotus Sutra) and other meetings of the NSS, interviews and a conversion rite. After admission members enshrine their *gohonzon* in a *butsudan* or wooden chest in their homes as the focus of their personal religious devotions. Numerous activities – daily *gongyo* in the home, *daimokukai* or group chanting sessions, discussion groups, division meetings, special interest group meetings, study groups and the taking of examinations to proceed up the hierarchy, pilgrimages to Japan, social work activities such as visits to homes for the aged and participation in public events such as the National Day celebrations provide a full and busy religious life for every member (and one can see why Japanese companies discourage membership!)

What we then see in the NSS is the successful transplanting of a Japanese religious movement – both its theology and its social organization – to Southeast Asian soil, where it has taken root, grown rapidly and attained substantial public visibility through its National Day performances, its glossy publications such as its magazine *Eternal Aurora* published in a bilingual Chinese/English format and its social work activities. Organizationally it is fairly tightly controlled and requires substantial commitment of time, energy and money from its members. In a country noted for its pragmatism and materialism the question naturally arises of what accounts for this phenomenon? What has caused its growth, how does it connect to Japanese cultural presence in the region and what are its wider implications for the development of Singapore society and culture?

Interpreting the NSS

Twenty-five years ago Joseph Tamney made the prediction that Buddhism was undergoing irreversible decline in Singapore (Tamney n.d.: 261–264) on the ground that Buddhism was peripheral to the lives of most Chinese Singaporeans and as such it had never undergone a reform movement amongst the laity. Tamney's prediction seems to have been falsified on several counts – a revival of Therevada Buddhism has taken place, there have been protestant-like movements amongst Buddhists generally, partly because of the challenge of Christianity, another relatively successful religion in Singapore (Clammer 1991), and Japanese forms of Buddhism have spread in Singapore. Buddhism in Singapore in fact has undergone extensive modernization in the last decade, and the popularity of Nichiren Buddhism is a major part of this process, both as an expression of activist Buddhism and as a threat to some of the more established forms and potentially even to non-Buddhist religions such as Christianity.

The question naturally arises of how this popularity is to be explained. The answer falls essentially into two parts. The first relates to the cultural impact of Japan in Southeast Asia, especially in those places – like Singapore – where there is a substantial Chinese population. Japan is of some interest to most Singaporeans, but especially to Chinese for a number of reasons. For Malays and Indians there is little cultural affinity with Japan – no linguistic or historical links, no commonalities of religion and not all that much interest in the organization of business life. But for Singaporean Chinese there are many points of contact: Japan is part of the 'Kanji area'- its language is written using the Chinese characters, there have been many points of historical contact both between Japan and China and between Japan and Singapore, there is intense interest in Japan's post-war economic success, technology and management techniques and there are affinities in religion, both communities sharing the Mahayana Buddhist tradition, albeit in rather different forms. Interest, cultural links and proximity (Tokyo is less than six hours away by air from Singapore) predispose many Chinese Singaporeans to considerable sympathy for both the material and non-material products of Japanese civilization.

And then there are the specific characteristics of Soka Gakkai itself and of its social organization as a religious movement. The emphasis on study for examinations in doctrine and the rewarding of success in these with diplomas appeals very much to the Singaporean love of educational advancement and constant (verifiable) self improvement. Most NSS members in Singapore are enrolled in study meetings designed to prepare them for the hierarchy of examinations stretching from the entrance examination to the advanced levels. Although in no way formally defined as such Soka Gakkai is clearly seen as an ethnic religion – almost all its members in Singapore are Chinese – and in some ways as a class one. This latter point needs some explanation. The membership of NSS includes representatives of most social classes including professionals, but appears to be weighted towards middle and lower middle class Chinese. Its main rival in Singapore is seen as Christianity which is widely perceived as an upper/upper-middle class religion. And indeed empirically Christianity has been relatively unsuccessful in attracting working/lower-middle class adherents. Part of the appeal of NSS is that it is seen either as classless (something like a Chinese equivalent of Islam) or as a religion which is open to those of less education and less social status than Christianity. Conversion is thus seen as being intra-ethnic, from one form of Buddhism to another rather than into an alien religious tradition, and into a religion which is less cerebral than Christianity and which offers an attractive package of practical activities, an 'Asian' identity, clear lines of advancement, a less class-biased social pattern and a comfortable ethics which identifies the good not with self denial, but with what one desires.

NSS in Singapore also has some interesting sociological features which increase its attractiveness. It has an almost equal male/female membership profile, uses Chinese language to a greater extent than Christianity (Clammer 1991), has female leadership in the Women's and Young Women's divisions, and has links to the political leadership as evidenced by its high profile participation in National Day events, the very high level reception given to Soka Gakkai president Ikeda when he visited Singapore in 1988 which gives it substantial legitimacy. Other forms of revised Buddhism, especially the Therevada tradition, appeal (like Christianity) primarily to the English-educated middle class and are seen in any case as multi-ethnic religions (many Therevada followers are of Sri Lankan origin for instance, or are Peranakan Chinese who speak Malay). Soka Gakkai also has, like its rival Christianity but unlike Mahayana Buddhism or the various forms of Chinese religion, a clear-cut set of doctrines and practices. Its endorsement of earthly desires, absence of a puritanical moral code and its evangelistic and group-oriented character make it attractive to pragmatic, materialistic Singaporeans who nevertheless desire support and fellowship in a highly urbanized and in many ways alienated society.

NSS and Japanese Cultural Diffusion

At the Singapore end of the Japan–Singapore nexus then the success of NSS at a time when the growth of the parent organization is widely believed to have peaked is an extremely interesting phenomenon related to a wide range of factors including ethnic patterns, the politics of religion in a highly plural society, the desire to find a religion linguistically, ethically and socially compatible with lower-middle-class Chinese norms and also one which is not too different from Chinese religious and cosmological expectations. An analysis in these terms would be of interest mainly as an exercise in the internal sociology of religion in Singapore. But there are questions beyond these and in this context especially the interpretation of Japanese cultural presence in the region. NSS represents the successful localization of what is becoming a fairly universal movement – an achievement that Bryan Wilson sees as being a major factor in the expansion of sect-like new religious movements (Wilson 1982:179). The universal movement in this case is interesting precisely because it is of Japanese origin and itself reflects a synthesis of Buddhism and aspects of Japanese culture. Does the overseas expansion of Soka Gakkai represent the genuine internationalization of Japanese religious culture – its taking on a world role comparable to Christianity, Islam or even other forms of Buddhism – or the expansion of Japanese hegemony by other means than the purely economic (political expansion having failed dismally in the past and being in today's political climate in Japan domestically unacceptable)? What does it say about the future expansion of Japanese cultural influence in Southeast Asia and beyond?

Much of the impact of the new religions can be seen along two axes: the influence that they have exerted over the religious scene in the countries where they have taken root – on other religions, on social organization and on attitudes towards things such as healing – and their power of influencing attitudes towards Japan. A number of the new religions, and most especially the new new religions have, despite their very distinctively Japanese roots, rapidly taken on an internationalist and even universal character. Soka Gakkai is a major exemplar of this trend, but there are other examples such as Kofuku no Kagaku, Mahikari, and the Seicho no Ie which have expanded internationally and which have an international department at their headquarters in Japan and which publish material in a number of languages. Interestingly in most cases this expansion has been facilitated by the religions in question playing down their Japanese origins and stressing their commitment to universalist programmes of world peace, intercultural communication and friendship between peoples, the promotion of culture and charitable, relief or development activities. The way in which their Japaneseness appears in these contexts is not as culture, but rather on the basis of Japan being somehow uniquely qualified to teach the world having been a 'victim' (presumably of the atomic bombings of Hiroshima and Nagasaki) and having become a peace-loving country, the only one amongst the major industrialized countries to have a constitution that specifically renounces war. The expansion of the new religions overseas is in no small way related to the post-war rehabilitation of the image of Japan. This is especially true in Southeast Asia: Singapore for example was occupied by the Japanese during the last world war and suffered substantially.

There is also some evidence to suggest that the overseas expansion of the new religions follows the same rules as the expansion of capitalism: when the domestic market is saturated, go overseas. There is some suggestion that membership growth amongst some of the major new religions in Japan, including Soka Gakkai, has peaked – the field is crowded, new entrants keep appearing and the crisis in early 1995 surrounding the new new religion Aum Shinrikyo and its link to terrorist activities has made many Japanese suspicious of the claims of all of these faiths. The economic success of Japan has also meant the availability of funds and the openness of Southeast Asian (and other) governments to Japanese investment and the perception of Japan as no real political threat means that there are no real ideological barriers to the acceptance of cultural influences from Japan, many of which – fashions, departmental stores, television programmes for example – have come anyway via the normal channels of international trade.

Almost certainly, too, the success outside Japan of the new religions needs to be related to the international appearance of new religious movements. The Japanese new religions are well placed to exploit this trend: they already have efficient organizational infrastructures in place, possess coherent theologies, have the strong yen behind them, can associate themselves with other aspects of Japanese culture which have proved attractive to the rest of the world and they are beneficiaries of the extensive international interest in eastern spiritualities. For reasons totally unconnected to Japanese influence, Singapore has seen a revival of interest in religion across a wide spectrum for at least the last 20 years and which still shows no signs of abating. Since the 1970s the local Christian population has expanded substantially and has achieved high social visibility, the Muslim community has been heavily influenced by missionary movements within Islam such as the Dakwah movement, the Hindus have been stimulated by the appearance of groups such as the neo-Hindu Sai Baba movement and there has been substantial modernization and revival within Buddhism, including the growing attractiveness amongst English educated middle class Chinese of Therevada Buddhism and the almost frantic building of new Mahayana temples and the refurbishing of old ones.

This supermarket of revived expressions of religion has been however by no means simply a return to the past forms. Revival has taken place in the context of a rapidly modernizing and almost totally urbanized city state. This has brought with it demands for more coherence in doctrine and for more simplicity in practice – a kind of protestantization of religion in general – at the same time as there is an opening by way of what is sometimes broadly called 'new age' influences to ideas of spiritual healing and reincarnation. The Japanese new religions almost invariably contain these elements, but can present them, unlike the amorphous new age movement, as parts of a tradition. In relation to the spread of Japanese new religions in the west, two commentators suggest that

The modern garb in which they present Japanese core values such as the importance of the pacification of the ancestors and the spirits of the dead, notions of spiritual causality of illness, the emphasis on this-worldly success and happiness, also attracts many (Clarke and Somers 1994: 7).

This combination of spirituality eastern-style and pragmatism is a potent brew, which also explains why Japanese 'old religions' have not spread like the new ones. Zen Buddhism for instance, despite the huge amount of publicity that it has received outside Japan, has very few adherents in the west and almost none in Singapore. Its simplicity, discipline and self-denying ethics have not recommended it at all to the modern Singaporean.

What on the other hand has attracted Singaporeans has been the pragmatism, organization and world-affirming ethics of Soka Gakkai together with the fact that NSS is not a temple-based organization. Temples tend to express traditional Japanese culture, whereas the NSS worship centres allow a more selective filtering of Japanese influences, something that has also happened elsewhere, such as in the United States (Melton and Jones 1994:42–43). This ability to turn Nichiren Buddhism in to a successful lay movement has likewise given Soka Gakkai the edge over other Nichiren-based new religions such as Reiyukai and its own offshoot Risshokosei-kai, and has enabled both the parent organization in Japan and its branches overseas to survive the controversy and subsequent split with the Nichiren Shoshu temples in Japan without too much damage, the main problem being the provision of funeral and ancestral rites and the conferring of the gohozon on new members. The effect of the 1991 'excommunication' of all the members of Soka Gakkai both in Japan and abroad by the high priest of Nichiren Shoshu is likely to speed up the 'protestantization' of Soka Gakkai in Japan and to confirm such tendencies amongst its overseas branches, especially those with a high degree of autonomy such as the one in Singapore. In this respect the separation may actually reduce the degree of Japanese influence on Soka Gakkai in Singapore, something that Brian Bocking predicts for Britain, where there is also a well established movement (Bocking 1994: 120–122).

This question also raises a deeper level issue for analysis. On the surface the spread of any new religion seems to contradict the theory of secularization, and to suggest, on the contrary that a re-sacralization of the world is taking place. If membership, attendance at worship or construction or usage of religious buildings are taken as the criteria of secularization then NSS would seem to be an anti-secularization movement. But if the content of NSS is examined closely, and indeed seen as parallel to many other Japanese new religions with their this-worldly and success oriented ethics, another point of view emerges. In commenting on the spread of Japanese religions in Brazil (a country of high religiosity and a large ethnic Japanese community), Peter Clarke proposes the following idea in relation to one of the major internationalist new religions, the Seicho-no-Ie:

> For its members, Seicho-no-Ie ideas seem to have consider-able explanatory power where the changing world of Brazil is concerned. Moreover, they are seen to empower individuals to take control over their own destiny in a world where all forms of authority and power seem to have failed. This enabling notion of the self as divine and in control of one's own destiny and all that affects it would seem to be one of the movement's chief attractions. These ideas however tend to relativize and marginalize faith in and reliance on the supernatural order and in this respect Seicho-no-Ie can be said to facilitate a move away from a faith in divine intervention from above, in an external source of super-natural power upon which humans depend for salvation and from faith in the miraculous, to belief in the enabling, energising, dynamic power of the god within. It also suggests that Seicho-no-Ie in facilitating the change from belief in divine intervention in human affairs towards a faith in the idea of 'self' as god or divine and totally responsible for all that happens acts as a 'secularising' agency and is similar in this respect to other 'Self-Religions'. (Clarke 1994:160–161)

Implicit in this comment, despite the author's own ill-concealed religious assumptions, is an interesting theory of secularization as it applies to the case of the Japanese new religions, It suggests that, far from being a re-secularization or re-enchantment of the world, the new religions, while undoubtedly meeting many very real human needs for order, healing, meaning and empowerment, actually accelerate secularization rather than retard it. In which case they should be seen as new cultural or social movements rather than as religions. The fact that NSS in Singapore does actually present itself in this guise then becomes doubly interesting.

It also says something interesting about Southeast Asian perceptions of Japan. Japan is seen in the region as, compared with say the Philippines or Thailand, a 'non-religious' society. In fact, as any Japanologist will know, levels of interest in and often practice of religion are actually high (the new religions themselves being evidence of this). What is actually in contention here is not the presence, but the form, of Japanese religion. In Japan religion is frequently seen as part of everyday life, rather than apart from it. Formal religious institutions have played little role in public life since the post-war disestablishment of State Shinto. If it is not a contradiction in terms, it would be almost true to say that, to generalize, the Japanese practise a 'secular religion' and that this deep religio-secularity stems from sources quite fundamental to Japanese culture and which do not stem from the same causes as secularization in the west.

If this is true it puts the question of Japanese cultural influence in Southeast Asia in a new light. It suggests that this influence not only takes more obvious forms (e.g. fashion), but also changes conceptions of the self and of human nature and as such not only subtly reconstructs many aspects of Chinese culture in Singapore, but also undermines the legitimacy of the existing religious traditions not by attacking them as systems of doctrine (the famous Soka Gakkai evangelistic technique of 'shakubuku' or 'bend and flatten' or 'break and subdue' or coercive persuasion being given very little attention in the Singapore movement for instance), but by undermining their cosmology and offering as an alternative one that appears to be 'Buddhist', but which also contains large doses of Japanese concepts of the self as person, as body and as actor-in-the-world (for discussion of which see Kasulis, Ames and Dissanayake 1993 and Ames, Dissanayake and Kasulis 1994).

This argument also parallels that of two Southeast Asian scholars who, in a book that otherwise surprisingly does not even mention Japanese new religions, develop a similar theory of secularization in relation to non-Muslim religious movements in Singapore's immediate neighbour, Malaysia (Ackerman and Lee 1990). In this work the authors suggest that 'As a social process, secularization individualizes participation in religious activities. The new religious movements reflect this process in the sense that they attract followers on a voluntaristic basis, offering concrete methods both of problem-solving and of meeting personal needs in everyday life' (ibid.:163). In this view participation in religious activities is not the issue: the central question is the movement towards individualization of religious expression. And paradoxically it may be the case that religious movements that seem to be communal in orientation like NSS may, despite their high level of organization, actually promote pragmatism and individualization at a more fundamental level.

As in Malaysia, ethnicity and religion are central to the definitions of social identity employed by Singaporeans. But whereas 'The conjunction of ethnicity and religion in Malaysia dichotomizes the religious arena into a Muslim and non-Muslim field' (Ackerman and Lee 1990: 4), in Singapore it separates people into primarily a Chinese/non-Chinese division, and secondarily into Chinese who have converted to a 'non-Chinese' religion (mainly Christianity) and those who retain their allegiance to a 'traditional' religion. But in the context of rapidly modernizing Singapore close association with a traditional religion has until recently at least implied some kind of backwardness. With the reforms within Buddhism and with the appearance in Singapore of Nichiren Buddhism, this equation no longer holds: it is now possible to be Chinese, Buddhist and modern at the same time through membership in a reformed branch of Buddhism, and especially through membership in the NSS with its positively progressive and desirable Japanese features reinforced by the government's 'look East' policies. Ethnicity and religion can be brought together in an attractive package that now separates the progressive and modern Chinese from the traditional ones.

The NSS alternative also has other attractive features. It shares many of the organizational characteristics of Christianity without sacrificing a Buddhist content; it is similarly a high commitment religion in which, unlike many Chinese sectarian movements membership, is incompatible with multiple religious affiliations. Its ethical pragmatism, high level political connections, hierarchical structures and education- (even exam-) oriented approach make it both attractive in itself to many Singaporeans and an attractive alternative to Christianity, its main rival. The ethnic dynamics of Singapore, government fear of the over-expansion of Christianity and the constant search in post-colonial Singapore for a set of 'Asian values' which will provide a basic ideology for the whole society while being based if possible on Chinese Confucian/ Buddhist principles (Clammer 1993) provide a tailor-made environment for the expansion of Nichiren Buddhism in Singapore. This is not to say that the movement has been without its critics. It has been attacked quite naturally by Christians who, given the very evangelical nature of local Christianity, see it as a major threat; by those still suspicious of Japan's real intentions and interests in Southeast Asia; and, perhaps most significantly by local Buddhists of non-Nichiren persuasions. This latter group also quite naturally see the NSS as a threat to their own specific doctrinal positions and as drawing away membership and revenues from the longer established denominations. This opposition to the NSS has provoked a literature of critique which sees the Nichirenists as attempting to displace the centrality of Shakyamuni Buddha's position as the source of true Buddhism, as materialistic and intellectualistic, as copying the Christians with their emphasis on evangelism, as being exclusivist, aggressive and sectarian, as being doctrinally selective, and as being based too closely on inappropriate characteristics of the Japanese. In one anti-Nichiren text these last are interestingly described as dependence, anomie, regimentation, materialism and ignorance of true Buddhism (Piyasilo 1988:119–122).

This very negative evaluation of NSS from a practitioner of (presumably) Therevada Buddhism of course represents a position which, to someone outside of Buddhism altogether, appears merely as sectarian squabbling of a kind very familiar to anyone who has studied the development of Christianity for example. But it is also of sociological significance, not only because it indicates that the NSS is operating on contested terrain, but also because of its very unflattering depiction of Japanese society. In Piyasilo's book, while it might of course be argued that he has misunderstood and caricatured Japan, the position that the Japanese have joined Soka Gakkai in such large numbers mainly because of social problems in their own society represents a real counter-trend to the Japan flatterers. Representations of Japan in Southeast Asia are themselves contested, partly because of old memories of war and occupation, partly because of the perception of contemporary Japan as pursuing imperialism by economic and now cultural means rather than by military ones, and partly because readings of the nature of Japanese society are not uniform. To many Singaporeans Japan, despite its technological achievements, is seen as far too group oriented to be attractive. On other grounds the same Japan that produces elegant fashions and state-of-the-art computer games is also largely responsible for the rape of the Southeast Asian rain forests because of its insatiable demand for timber. Many Singaporeans have by now visited Japan as tourists or for working purposes, and many bring back mixed reviews.

If at the everyday level the images of Japan shared by Singaporeans are mixed ones, so they are also by intellectuals and professional interpreters of Japan. Again while some of these are negative evaluations of past history or of present society, others are attempts to evaluate the specific role of religion in accounting for Japan's economic success. The question of Japan's achievements and what might be learned about the mechanisms underlying this and discovering what might be applied to Southeast Asian societies has become something of a local industry. Perceptions of the NSS naturally fit into this discourse, which is certainly not restricted to Singapore, but has also occurred in those societies in the region such as Thailand which are largely Buddhist in religion and which are also undergoing rapid modernization. In this light Japanese Buddhism has been evaluated, contrary to Piyasilo's view, in a very positive light as being highly functional to effective development through its virtues of compassion, honesty, endurance, diligence, tolerance, simplicity, purity and high regard for aesthetic values (Pensri 1989:14–27) which have exercised decisive influence over the development of Japanese politics, nationalism and social welfare policies. This reading too can be criticized for its essentialism, simplicity and lack of detailed understanding of Japanese history and the complex role of religion within it, but it does also indicate a desire in Southeast Asian scholarly discourse to understand the linkages of religion and economic development.

The introduction of Nichiren Buddhism into Singapore and its subsequent expansion and consolidation makes a fascinating case study of several social processes: of religious change, of religion and ethnicity, of the secularization process. In this context it is also, or is primarily, an illustration of the expansion of Japanese cultural influence. Following the growth of a Japanese economic presence in Southeast Asia has come the spread of fashion, cuisine and media. Religion is rarely one of the early things to spread in societies where missionary zeal is lacking. While in the past Japan has certainly tried to export its economic and political influence, it has not been a society that has attempted to export its religions.

And nor for the most part could it be, as Japan has either been the recipient of continental religious influences (Buddhism and Confucianism) or has been the possessor of an indigenous tradition (Shinto) which has been too national in character – or even quite literally nationalistic – to make an export product. Nichiren Buddhism, however, has reversed this tendency by evolving a form of Buddhism evangelistic and potentially universalistic in character. By the 1960s this became linked with the widespread desire in Japan to begin to put the past behind and to play a positive role in promoting world peace and harmony. Given Japan's political history and past record, this would be difficult to do by political means, and the rise of the new religions and their own desire to internationalize at exactly this point in time provided the mechanism through which a benign cultural influence, riding on the skirts of economic influence, could begin its spread.

The question remains of finally interpreting this phenomenon. At one level the spread of the new religions can be seen as a positive thing – as Japan genuinely putting a new face on its relationships with the rest of the world, as a symptom of internationalization within Japanese society, as part of a world-wide resurgence of interest in religion and as part of a pattern of non-political influence in the world on the part of its second biggest economy. Quite apart from its role in the internal dynamics of Singapore society, the spread of Nichiren Buddhism in Southeast Asia can be read in this way.

On the other hand the same evidence can also be seen in a different light. In all of the new and new new religions, despite their universalist pretensions, Japan has a clear role as the promised land and as the centre of the world. This centrality may now indeed be seen in spiritual rather than in political terms, but centrality it remains. This vision as Japan as the centre is naturally played down in material that the new religions produce for international consumption – rather the message is of Japan as victim and peace-loving carrier of eastern spirituality – but it is very much present in material in Japanese designed for internal consumption at home. In almost all cases what is stressed is the spirituality, not the underlying Japanese social organization that accompanies in practice full incorporation into the world view and organization of the new religions. It is still an open question of the extent to which these aspects will spread – something very much dependent on the extent to which overseas branches of the new religions begin to assert their autonomy, become themselves more 'protestant' and follow the logic of their parent bodies in breaking free of a Japan centred 'papal' system of centralization. This is indeed likely to happen unless and until Japanese society itself becomes more international and incorporates into itself influences flowing from Southeast Asia and elsewhere, including religious ones, rather than seeing itself as the new and exclusive fountainhead of culture in Asia. The case of Soka Gakkai in Singapore, whose central mandala and object of worship, the gohonzon, was once described by Toda Josei, the second president of the parent organization, as 'the happiness making machine', demonstrates very centrally the attractiveness of Japanese cultural influences in Southeast Asia, but also the ways in which these are adapted, incorporated into local ethnic stratification patterns and political cultures, and of the ways in which these influences can become the basis of a critique of Japanese society itself. Japanese cultural influence in Singapore is extensive, but it is not unitary or uncontested, and it is to a great extent in the field of religion that its eventual role in Southeast Asia is being worked out and which will determine the extent to which Japanese patterns of thought and social organization can ever be expected to take root.

Chapter 9

Tenrikyo in Singapore: Rerepresenting the Japanese Presence

Tina Hamrin

By February 1942 the Japanese occupation of Singapore was an accomplished fact, and for the subsequent three years the island was under the rigorous control of the Japanese imperial authorities. Although in historical terms this was a brief period of time, many local commentators have suggested that it nevertheless moulded the contemporary "distinctive Singaporean character" (Murray and Perera 1996: 16). As one survivor of the occupation N.I. Low, orphaned at the age of nine when both his parents died of cholera, puts it

> To British law we in Malaya had owed the inestimable blessing of having some firm ground in the quagmire of life. If we did this or this, we rendered ourselves liable to the pains and penalties of the law; if we did not we were safe. Within the confines of the law therefore, the incalculable did not play so devastatingly with our peace of mind. The Japanese did away with all that. As one shopkeeper put it, one's head might be on one's shoulders in the morning and by the evening the two might have parted company (Low 1995: 119).

During my fieldwork in Singapore in 1997 a consistent comment from older Chinese citizens when asked about the occupation years was that "The Japanese were awful! We will never forget what they did here!" Yet the Japanese are back in large numbers, especially in the fields of business and manufacturing and as tourists. Although they keep a low social profile, often as a result of lack of language ability in English or one of the local languages, their presence is visible in the streets, in the rental housing market, in the expanding number of Japanese restaurants, departmental stores and book-stores and in local places of leisure. The ethnic diversity of Singapore with its communities of Chinese, Malays, Indians, Eurasians, Sinhalese, Arabs, Jews, Filipinos, Europeans and other smaller groups has, like it or not, been yet further enriched and diversified by the addition of this large if mostly transient group of Japanese. This ethnic diversity is reflected in the religious composition of the country where approximately 53 per cent of the inhabitants belong to some kind of Chinese religion (including Mahayana Buddhism), 17 per cent are Muslims, a little over 10 per cent are Christians (3 per cent Roman Catholic) and the remainder are spread amongst Hinduism and a number of small minority religions (Beskow 1995: 461). Among this latter group, approximately 250 are affiliated with Tenrikyo.

The environment in which the Singaporean branch of Tenrikyo now flourishes — a highly urbanized commercial and industrial city state — is very different from the setting in which this prominent example of the Japanese "new religions" was established. The foundress, Nakayama Miki, was born in 1798 into a farming family and subsequently married one Nakayama Zembei, a landowner who farmed near Nara, the ancient capital of Japan before the migration of the political center to Kyoto, Kamakura and eventually Edo (Tokyo) and then and still a major site of religious activity. When Miki (subsequently called Oyasama by her followers) was 40 her son Shuji began to suffer from serious and incapacitating leg pains and Miki consulted a prominent healer in the area, one Nakano Ichibei around whom a healing cult had formed and of which Miki became a devotee. During a healing ritual in 1838 Miki who was supposed to be assisting the *yamabushi*, the healer, herself slipped into a trance. For three days she remained in a state of possession and when she emerged she explained that she had been possessed by the only true and original God whom she called Tenri-O-no-Mikoto: God the Parent. During her possession she claimed that she had been commissioned as the "Shrine of God" whose mission was to build a divine kingdom for all human beings, a perfect world in which everyone would have a joyous life in unity with God.

According to subsequent Tenrikyo doctrine on the last day of her trancelike state the religion was born, at the moment when the Creator came to earth and became one with Oyasama. But the new religion remained very much an individual revelation since it did not have any members until 1862. In 1863 a turning point was reached when a carpenter, Iburi Izo (1833–1907) became a member and a small shrine was built. Master Iburi had a profound influence on almost everything that Miki herself wrote, material that became the doctrinal basis of the developing religion, and was himself the author of a prominent body of canonical texts. Iburi became Miki's successor when she died in 1887 and in his *Osashizu* or divine revelations composed between 1897 and the year of his own death wrote himself securely into that succession, stating for example that "Now I will start the construction of roads all over the world to pave the way for *Tenrikyo*. Divine wisdom which the Foundress has kept locked in Her alone shall henceforth be given through Master Iburi" (Offner and van Straelen 1963: 57). Iburi was also astute in public relations and in 1888, the year following Miki's death the religion was recognized by the authorities under the name of Shinto Tenri Kyokai although assigned to the category of Shinto Honkyokai as one of the Shinto sects (*kyoha shinto*) embracing miscellaneous religious groups (Shimazono 1991: 61). Nakayama Shin'nosuke (1866–1944), a son of Miki's third daughter meanwhile became leader of Tenrikyo's secular relations and thanks to his lobbying Tenrikyo was one of the thirteen Shinto sects recognized as legitimate by the ultra-nationalist government in 1942. During the intermediate period it had continued to grow in Japan and even had mission outposts overseas in places where there were Japanese communities, including Singapore where some Tenrikyo members established a small and then unrecognized church in 1922. Between then and the 1960s occasional members came and went, engaging in peaceful activities such as flower arrangement and ceramic art design as well as religious observances with the motive of not only practising their own faith, but also of pitching a camp in a place where the scars of Japanese wartime presence were not yet healed.

In 1969 Rev. Chihara Terumi was assigned to come to Singapore to prepare for the establishment of a mission post and in February of the same year Miyamoto Yutaka arrived in Singapore as a student, dispatched by the Tenrikyo Young Men's Association. On May 5 1971 the Tenrikyo Mission Centre in Singapore was registered at the Registry of Societies under the name "Singapore Tenrikyo Headquarters." On the 16 November of the same year Rev. Inoue Akio was assigned to come to Singapore and almost five months later on April 18 1972 the Mission Centre was inaugurated.

With the Rev. Inoue as its director the mission moved from the Katong district in eastern Singapore to the more central and prestigious Namley Avenue and again in July 1974 to 40 Watten Estate Road where it was renamed the Tenrikyo Centre of Southeast Asia. Through voluntary labour called *hinokishin* the membership erected a worship hall, the first Tenrikyo place of worship ever in Singapore, and this was formally dedicated on 9 November 1975 by the Rev. Nakayama Yoshikatzu, the Director-in-Chief of Administrative Affairs of Tenrikyo. Less than a year later the Tenrikyo Cultural Center in Southeast Asia was established in the very central Hong Leong Building "for the purpose of using this as the focal point of missionary work through cultural activities" (Tenrikyo 1981: 117). To promote an extra curricular activities center a music instructor was employed in 1977 and in the same year Rev. Tsuji Toyoo became the second director of the Tenrikyo Mission centre. The Overseas Mission at the Tenri University sent a voluntary group to Singapore in February 1978 and from Singapore seven members of the center made a pilgrimage to Jiba in Tenri City. A year later another six members went to the headquarters in Japan as pilgrims and in August 1980 the first conference of representatives of the mission posts in Southeast Asia was held.

The 10th anniversary of the Tenrikyo Mission Center in Singapore was celebrated in May 1982 at the time when the Rev. Shimizu Kunio, the then Director of Administrative Affairs, visited Singapore. During these years pilgrimages to Japan became an important activity of members of the Singapore centre, an activity stimulated still further by the third director of the Mission Center, the Rev. Umetani Tadaaki who was appointed in 1986. By this time the need for a mouthpiece for the growing movement was felt very strongly and in 1988 the *Regional Reports of Mission Posts in Southeast Asia* was published. In the summer of 1988 the Yobuku Association of Tenri University started sending "summer missionaries" and in the autumn of that year a property at 38 Watten Estate Road was purchased by the Mission Center. In 1990 the Tenrikyo Towa Fellowship was established and a year later the Culture Section was moved to the International Plaza and a second hall of devotion was dedicated. In 1992 the Shinbashira, the highest leader at the Japanese headquarters, visited Singapore to officiate at the 20th anniversary of the establishment of the mission.

To make it the center of a spider's web of activities in Southeast Asia, the Tenrikyo headquarters has grand plans for Singapore. The mission in Singapore since the 1980s has been seen as being poised to "take advantage of Singapore's unique blend of various cultures, races and languages and will study ways and means of solving many problems of missionary work in overseas countries" (Tenrikyo 1981: 117) as through its religious teachings and cultural activities it seeks the realization of what are taken to be the universal teachings of Tenrikyo. These teachings must for members be expressed through *hinokishin* or the "daily donation of physical action," whether this takes the form of labour for the mission directly (such as building work) or social service to the wider community. The story of Tenrikyo in Singapore can be read to a great extent as the manifestation of a very serious attempt to clean away bad karma: as a kind of catharsis for all Japanese who ever did anything wrong in the area. According to members of Tenrikyo, who are well aware of the history of Japanese involvement in Singapore, especially during the war years, the movement is all about *innen* (karma). As one publication puts it:

> Needless to say, seeds do not always sprout soon after they have been sown. So it is with causality. In some cases the seeds sprout in one's lifetime. In other cases the seed sprouts only after many generations have passed. One can, upon quiet reflection, discern the reasons for the appearance of causality if it is the result of one's own conduct. In the case of causality from a previous life or lives, however, one must first reflect on one's own past and then on the lives of one's forebears (Tenrikyo 1993b: 55–56).

It is through *hinokishin* that bad can be turned into good and it is *hinokishin* that will make Singapore a better place for Japanese expatriates since it is the "dust" that has accumulated on the souls of the Japanese in Singapore since 1942 that prevents the Highest Almighty from fulfilling his divine plan. But to the extent that the members of Tenrikyo bring their minds and hearts into line with the cosmic blueprint, they will help to create a world without sickness, so believers maintain.

The location of Tenrikyo within the spectrum of religions in Singapore must thus be seen both in terms of its specific doctrines and the ways in which these are expressed in Singapore, and in terms of the social and historical context in which they find themselves today, and in particular the perception of other ethnic groups of the behaviour of the Japanese and their relationship to their host society. To understand this location more comprehensively, a short description of Tenrikyo doctrine will be attempted, and I will then focus on *hinokishin* and its specific role in a country where the mental attitude of the Japanese has been attacked by most other ethnic groups, and especially on Tenrikyo's groundbreaking work through *hinokishin* amongst handicapped people.

Tenrikyo emphasizes a way of thinking that is based on a form of individual psychology, not so dissimilar to that advocated by Alfred Adler when he broke away from Sigmund Freud and repudiated psychoanalysis in 1911. In Tenrikyo stress is laid on social "driving forces" seen as the propelling power behind actions and which constitute the motive force of human creativity. Social intercourse makes people conscious of their own motives and goals and a group like Tenrikyo provides a certain lifestyle that frames and gives shape to the personalities of its members. According to Adler the human being is born with a social interest even stronger than sexual motivation and a wish to be in contact with other beings. This process begins with the relationship between mother and baby, and is thereafter extended to wider social relations, group identification and the ability to live the part of another thanks to the power of insight and empathy. In this context, Tenrikyo's theories about "compensation" are of interest.

The Japanese in Singapore have all been told, in one way or another, that they are expected to be ruthless, either because such a quality is coded into their genes or because of socialization. The moral situation of quite a few Japanese in Singapore is that they are a kind of living score-board, unfortunately with ancestors who failed to score. In some cases they have been able to repair what their parents did thanks to their collected karmic plus points, and some have themselves compensated for their own former mistakes. A lot of money is brought into the country by Japanese who possess enormous economic power without having of course any formal political role. But there are many Japanese expatriates, mostly company workers and managers, who have not been able to buy any letters of indulgence. For some of them Tenrikyo and its method of *hinokishin* is of utmost importance, for to be able to cancel the defects of one's own or another's performance is of profound significance. This itself needs setting in a wider theological context.

According to Tenrikyo doctrine, the religion came into being because God the Parent (*Tenri-O-no-Mikoto*) who created this world and all mankind, revealed himself through the foundress,

Nakayama Miki (later as we have seen termed *Oyasama*) whom God took as his shrine so that His will to save all mankind might be realized through this revelation. Briefly, the goal of salvation is to realize the joyous life in this world by accepting God's omnipotent providence. Once this has been universally done, the world will change into a truly peaceful place of cheerfulness and brightness. To fulfil the will of God the Parent we should cleanse our minds by trying to purify them. We will then discover the central theme of reality — a life of faith. While the body is a "thing lent" by God, from the human standpoint it is a "thing borrowed," so we should use it properly in accordance with the intentions of the lender. We are permitted the free use of our minds, so their misuse appears as the clouding of God's protection. Such misuse is compared to dust settling on a mirror. Originally there were no evil persons, but dust settling on their "original minds" brought about false perceptions and accordingly distorted actions. If on the other hand we work to sweep this dust away we can rid ourselves of it and as we begin this process a positive desire to cleanse ourselves will develop. Tenrikyo teachings deny the existence of original sin. But selfishness blinds us and a person who is selfish thinks that everything resolves around herself, so the initial problem is to become aware of the "dust." God the Parent teaches us that illness and troubles are given to us for the sake of promoting urgent self-reflection. But unfortunately, many people, unaware of this, allow themselves to be overwhelmed by their suffering which results in envy of others, cursing heaven and becoming weary of life.

However, if one truly understands parental love, through this alone the appearance of the world and its perception will be completely changed. Through the merciful guidance of God the Parent we will see that our problems originate in the accumulation of "dust" and so we will work to clean it away, a continuous process in this life as although dust comes off easily, more piles up again without our being aware of it. But this life is not the only reality and Oyasama taught that what we usually call death is really a passing away for rebirth. When the time comes for us to pass away we return our bodies to the Lender and we will come back again into this world with new bodies lent by Him. It is much like taking off old clothes to put on new ones. We shall reappear in this world by borrowing new bodies appropriate to our previous lives. Although we must return our bodies our souls alone remain eternally ours. Robert Kisala shows that Tenrikyo members believe in three distinctions when it comes to the human person: mind, body and soul and suggests that

> The mind, encompassing the psychological functions of awareness, will, etc., ceases to function at death; the body, being "a thing lent" by God, is returned to God at death; but the soul, through the process of *denaoshi*, which literally means to make a fresh start, takes on a newly lent body and is reborn into this world (Kisala 1994: 77).

The mental "dust" which we carry over from our previous lives is called bad *innen*. Again according to Kisala, "the term "karma" is avoided in favor of the transliteration of the Japanese term *innen*, presumably to emphasize Tenrikyo's distinctive understanding of this belief" (Kisala 1994: 77).

It is *innen* which results in all physical phenomena. Bad *innen* is expressed in the various kinds of problems which arise in our daily lives. Rather than struggle against these problems we should voluntarily try to change our mental direction. Whatever befalls us is a manifestation of heavenly reason and is for our enlightenment. Understanding this we can rely wholly on God's parental love and desire for our salvation. This leads us from suffering to joy, to *tanno*. *Tanno* is a form of mind that is purified to a state of true sincerity. It is not mere resignation, but indicates a state of satisfaction as it is the means to settle the mind through changing *innen*. The blessings of God the Parent will pervade the whole being of one in whom the state of *tanno* is perfected, and such a person will know that it is God who constantly sustains him. The happiness and deep emotions that arise from the state of being will appear naturally in resulting physical actions. This action is *hinokishin* ("acts done for others"). Tenrikyo teaches that "forgetting greed we work in *hinokishin*" and that in the joy of *hinokishin* there is no "I", since the ego and all forms of human thought are set aside. And without greed and without "I" there is only one side to the human mind — sincerity, an overflowing of purity, cleanliness and brightness. The heart of God the Parent is hastening only to save all His children and He teaches us explicitly that the mind that desires to save others is based on true sincerity and that it is by saving others that one is also saved. Oyasama is herself regarded as the embodiment of this teaching and Tenrikyo is the encapsulation of the revelation given to her which enables those who follow it to experience the joyous life and to move towards the goal of salvation.

These self-proclaimed Tenrikyo teachings suggests that *hino-kishin* is equivalent to the state of *muga* sought by many Japanese Buddhists and in other examples of the Japanese "New Religions." In one of these, the Tensho-kotai-jingu-kyo, the ego is also put aside, but in this case during ecstatic dancing (the *muga-no-nai*) and the description made by members of this "Dancing Religion" have much in common with the explanations that explicate egolessness during *hinokishin* among Tenrokyo members (Hamrin 1996: 232). There is consequently an intimate connection between *hinokishin* and *innen*. As Kisala puts it

> Original *innen* is proclaimed as the ontological basis of mankind, which according to Tenrikyo doctrine, was created by God the Parent that it might enjoy the "Joyous Life", the Tenrikyo expression for the salvific state. Furthermore, it is believed that this salvific state will encompass all of humanity ... thus the concept of original *innen* has a teleological element, being the gradual unfolding of that which was ordained at the beginning of time (Kisala 1994: 77).

In the Singapore context, as a former Japanese colony, *innen* demands compensation. The members are told first to reflect on their own past and then on the lives of their parents and other Japanese predecessors. The outcome of this self-confessionalism should be *hinokishin*, since such actions have a healing effect on the past as well as the present, an attitude embodied in the activities of the foundress Oyasama herself who, in one of her songs (Mikagura-uta III: 8) wrote "There is nothing so trying as illness. So from now on, I, too, will devote myself to *hinokishin*."

Salvation — the joyous life (*yokigurashi*) — is achieved here on earth not in some future state. The means to this — the clearing of bad *innen* — devolves naturally on volunteer activities in the spirit of *hinokishin*. In a Singapore largely devoid of obvious social movements, in which non-citizens are excluded from political activity and where there are few NGOs or glaring "development" problems, but in which the State, ever eager to privatize areas of social concern, encourages charities to take on activities that elsewhere would be the responsibility of government, this not surprisingly takes the form of social service. As early as 1976, the year that the Tenrikyo Cultural Center was established, the then director wrote in the Tenrikyo journal

I think that before speaking about *innen* we should, first of all, help each other. The more we consider the doctrine of "*kashimono, karimono*" (a thing lent, a thing borrowed), I think that it is our obligation to actively express the endless energy stemming from joy and gratitude of good health. We should, without setting a price, cheerfully devote ourselves to *hinokishin* (Tanaka 1976: 5).

This attitude has continued to be a central part of Tenrikyo thinking in Singapore, supported as it is by teachings from the Japanese headquarters that "*Hinokishin* is performed by followers of the Path day after day whereby their joy at being alive is expressed through their actions" (Tenrikyo 1993a: 1). In Singapore *hinokishin* is not only a matter of rough and heavy work. When the spadework has been got through, home help is done, for example by visiting the Tampines Home to cut hair, help with meal feeding and to take wheelchair-bound patients out for walks. Among the hundred active members of Tenrikyo in Singapore many are Chinese-Singaporeans for whom *hinokishin* is not done for anything (obvious at least) done by their ancestors, but which still has the effect of offsetting the accumulation of bad *innen* which is almost inevitable even in leading an ordinary life. There are two mission stations in Singapore that alternate when it comes to holding services and the Mission Center holds services on the third Sunday of the month. Associated with such services seen as worship in a conventional religious sense, there is also *hinokishin*, which for Japanese members includes cleaning the area of the Japanese cemetary and visiting isolated members in Johor (in Malaysia across the causeway from Singapore) to do monthly service in their homes. But all members regardless of ethnicity are expected to take part in regular social welfare work, interpreted in Tenrikyo teachings in an interestingly individualistic way.

Social welfare refers to each individual's "well-being" in a "society", not the welfare of a society as a whole at the expense of some individuals. It does not disregard the sufferings, if any, of individual persons, on condition that the society is rich and affluent. Social welfare does not refer to the aggregate of welfare in a society but aims at the realization of each individual's welfare in it (Okubo 1982: 1).

In the context of Singapore society and of its complex religious geography Tenrikyo teaching about the necessity, practicality and karmic qualities of *hinokishin* are located at a theologically and sociologically interesting juncture. The individualism of the Tenrikyo interpretation of social welfare fits very well with the general ideology of the Singapore State — its push towards privatization of welfare, its belief in the necessity for every individual rather than society as a whole to take responsibility for health-care and old-age provision, and its "pragmatism" (Clammer 1985). This practical individualism is intensified by the underlying theoretical or theological individualism of Tenrikyo which marries a universalism in the sense of a desire to spread the message of the religion everywhere with an underlying psychology of individualistic essentialism which accords very well with many of the ideas found in Chinese religions in Singapore and also in local varieties of Protestant Christianity (Clammer 1991) although it adds its own nuances to these.

The pragmatism of Tenrikyo and its accompanying ethical system has indeed been specifically contrasted by Tenrikyo apologists with "Western" religions. The Tenrikyo scholar Okubo Akinori for example, who is a leading exponent of the idea that social welfare is an endeavor to improve the conditions of society so that each individual can lead a happy life, has also made something of a career out of criticizing non-Japanese interpretations of Tenrikyo. In his *Gaikokujin no mita Tenrikyo* ("Tenrikyo as Seen by Foreigners") he has criticized foreign interpretations of the religion for their "inevitable tendency to make the faith a historically-conditioned scheme of salvation and an institution rather than a religion whose real essence is a subtle and shifting relation of believers to God" (Ellwood 1982: 60). In a post-colonial society this provides not only a religion freed from the organizational and ontological burdens of the "colonial religions," but also provides a new generation of Chinese-Singaporeans, increasingly imbued with individualism and the attributes of the new middle classes in Southeast Asia — including consumerism (Robison and Goodman 1996) with a religion that is flexible, adaptable and which stresses happiness now rather than sin or future salvation (see also Clammer on Soka Gakkai in this volume).

For the Japanese members Tenrikyo possesses these advantages too and at the same time allows both the assertion of ethnic identity (it is after all very much a Japanese religion despite its hopes to universalize itself) and provides the mechanism of compensation. That is to say *hinokishin* as a remedy against bad *innen,* both that which has been accumulated by ancestors (racially defined, not necessarily personal ones) and that which might be generated by the individual in the course of living everyday life. The Japanese community in Singapore finds itself caught in a highly ambiguous situation. Respected to some extent or even feared for their economic power in the present, they are also distrusted or even despised for their behaviour in the past. Local shopkeepers and hoteliers are only too happy to milk the droves of Japanese tourists and the language is widely studied locally too, but not out of love for Japanese culture, but for economic expediency. To be needed and not trusted, to be seen as the technological giant but the moral pygmy of Asia, is not a comfortable location. The Japanese are brought up to care about what other people think about them and their actions. To do good in an explicit way is itself very good: it is good to show others how good you are. But Japanese in Singapore have also had to learn that it is also necessary to suppress significant aspects of their egos — such as the sense of belonging to a special race. But repudiated aspects of the self continue to exist and are connected to ideas of personal identity, which may become a problem if these shadow aspects are associated with guilt and aspects of the past that are unworthy or shameful. Shadowlike aspects bring in their train apprehensions about the risk of being an outcast of society, or at least of being kept out and rejected if those shadow parts are detected and exposed. For Japanese living in Singapore under the constant pressure of these ambiguities, *hinokishin,* as the means to overcome bad *innen,* becomes more than simply good works, it is both the route to the joyous life through the apprehension of one's true nature, and the means to rebuild identity by finally banishing the shadows. Compensation overcomes guilt and with it establishes the possibility for a new set of social relations to be established with the members of the host society.

The notion of *innen* then points both to the core of Tenrikyo teachings and to the contextualization of those teachings in a situation where there are very specific and historically justified feelings of guilt. As one Tenrikyo scholar puts it

> In the teaching of Tenrikyo, the word *innen* while including the general meanings with which the term has been associated, involves a deeper meaning as a principle which reveals the ontology of human beings, that is the basis of

human existence. The basis of human existence consists of an individual basis and a universal basis shared by all mankind (Hashimoto 1979: 31).

In the West, we call something similar to the latter "archetypes," and, in fact, Tenrikyo scholars have been influenced by C.G. Jung. Hashimoto Taketo, among others, thinks that the idea of the collective unconscious may afford a clue to the understanding of *innen* in people's previous lives. *Innen* explains *hinokishin* and Hashimoto continues "Original *innen* is the fundamental principle which clarifies the purpose of creation by God the Parent and the structure and function of His providence, and consequently explains the intrinsic, essential or ideal mode of human existence" (Hashimoto 1979: 32). It is the teleological principle of *innen* and the teleological principle of *hinokishin* that plays the crucial role in the practice of Tenrikyo members in Singapore, starting with the Japanese members and from them spreading to the Chinese–Singaporean ones, both being liable to bad *innen* although for different historical and personal reasons. The result of good practice is furthermore not only the cleansing of one's own personal *innen*: it also promotes the only genuine basis for human community:

> Man is intrinsically a social being having been created to lead the joyous life ... the individual comes to be only because there are other individuals. To put it in another way, the self exists only because there is non-self. The individual who leads the joyous life transcends the distinction between the self and others. To extend the self and to identify with non-self, that is one of the essentials of personal maturity and is the intrinsic existence of man (Hashimoto 1979: 33).

Tenrikyo, at the present moment at least, is a tiny minority religion in Singapore, shunned even by most of the large Japanese expatriate community. As such it is but one movement in a complex religious mosaic constantly undergoing shifts, realignments, changes of allegiance and revivals (Kuo *et al.* 1988). But interestingly, however small, it is a religious movement with Shinto roots existing in an environment dominated principally by Buddhism. This fact both suggests parallels with its situation in Japan, where Shinto and Buddhism have long coexisted in a complex relationship of sometimes rivalry and sometimes toleration. Today for example in Japan, a small Shinto shrine can be found within the precincts of most Buddhist temples. And Shinto is to some extent shunned even in Japan because of its association with Emperor worship and the excesses of militarization in pre-war and wartime. In Southeast Asia its association is likely to be even more keenly remembered. Tenrikyo's management of its relationship to the historical associations of Shinto we will return to shortly. But here, in the context of the religious geography of Singapore, it is useful to first comment on its doctrinal relationship to Buddhism.

Buddhist interpretations of karma are usually "based on the supposition that those who find themselves in disadvantaged situations are responsible for their own fate" (Kisala 1994: 79). In Tenrikyo on the other hand, working for others through *hinokishin* avoids fatalistic and discriminatory explanations of *innen*. Instead karmic effects are directed toward the establishment of the joyful state that means salvation. *Hinokishin* is a reciprocal process of action and the enhancement of joy and gratitude. Speaking of its individual members a Tenrikyo publication explains that, for example, "amid the rising tide of environmental issues throughout the world they can be made instrumental in helping people to awaken to the truth that we live in the body of God, that we are part of the body of God, by offering them an opportunity to work closely upon their environment" (Tenrikyo 1990: 1). The teleological element of original *innen* is thus applied to *hinokishin* which becomes the mechanism of action and purpose for both repairing the world of the present and future, and also in some sense the past.

This activity is not surprisingly, like many spiritual endeavours, fraught with its own dangers. Japanese Tenrikyo members doing voluntary work in homes for the aged or handicapped in Singapore are motivated by the longing for salvation and the joyous life. They so much want "credit" for themselves and to compensate for wrongs done by their ancestors that they sometimes overdo it, and paradoxically their very niceness, their smiling faces and eager helpfulness, can trigger feelings of resentment and prejudice in others. The very actions intended to sweep away the accumulated *innen* may as a result end up in more being unintentionally acquired. The motive is to be nice, but the behaviour may be very trying: the dreams and action embodied in *hinokishin* may not in fact produce the "right" result and the teleological hopes invested in right-action may not necessarily be fulfilled.

Many of the Japanese membership are aware of this paradox — of their very location in Singapore actually exacerbating the karmic problem that they are labouring so diligently to solve. Recognition of this has something of a revolutionary effect on the thinking of many of them, since it forces upon them the perception of the fact that if *hinokishin* is seen simply as an action motivated by its outcome, then the relationship between the actor and the one acted upon becomes purely instrumental. This of course violates the true nature of the relationship between self and other and for this not to happen fulfillment must reside in the encounter itself, not in its putative outcome. When for example handicapped people are treated as equals, and not as if they are in some way polluted (as is often the case in Japan) a positive dialogue develops and the satisfaction is here and now and the joyous life is present not future. *Hinokishin* then is the joyous life *per se*.

Although today in the standard classifications of Japanese "New Religions" Tenrikyo is usually grouped with those whose origins lie in Shinto, this understanding of *hinokishin* is clearly shaped by the Buddhist Pure Land tradition. Nakayama Miki was herself brought up in a Jodo Shinshu setting in which the compassion of Amida Buddha was of the greatest importance. In the Tenrikyo doctrine of *hinokishin* we have the *bodhisattva* ideal modified to fit a Shinto frame. In Mayayana Buddhism the "mind of enlightenment" or "awakening mind" is called *bodhicitta*. "This *bodhicitta* results from deep compassion for the suffering of others" (Williams 1989: 198). To those who believe in Amida Buddha, at the time of death the compassionate Buddha will appear "to conduct his followers, who have awakened *bodhicitta* and practiced merit, wishing to be reborn in the Pure Land, to Sukhavati" (Williams 1989; 253). In Singapore the Tenrikyo members "practice merit" through *hino-kishin*, especially through taking care of ill and handicapped people as this is the ideal and most selfless expression of compassion.

The idea of *hinokishin* is thus intimately linked with the *bodhisattva* concept. Essentially a *bodhisattva* is one who refuses ultimate salvation while any others as yet remain unsaved and who returns to earth through successive reincarnations to assist others on the path to enlightenment. As the Japanese scholar Nakamura Hajime puts it "The career of the *bodhisattva* is traditionally held to begin when the devotee first conceives the aspiration for enlightenment (*bodhicitta*) and formulates a vow to become a Buddha and work for the weal of all beings" (Nakamura 1987: 267). To Tenrikyo members, like early Mahayana *bodhisattvas*, life is a matter of endeavoring to save others and to freely transfer merit to others. As the Singapore Tenrikyo Center secretary explicitly puts it "*hinokishin* can also be seen as 'merit-transfer'." The practitioner on the *bodhisattva* path is expected to perfect six (in later traditions expanded to ten) virtues — *dana* or giving, *sila* — "morality" or the observation of the Buddhist precepts, *ksanti* or patience and forbearance, *virya* or effort, *dhyana* or contemplation and *prajna* or "transcendental insight" (Nakamura 1987: 268).

These virtues and their later elaborations can easily be traced in Tenrikyo ideals where, shaped in a Japanese form and under the mantle of Shinto, the *bodhisattva* project is stated in more modern form. The *bodhisattva* personifies compassion, and that is both an emotional state and an ethical norm that the Foundress carried with her from Jodo Shinshu. The one who acts only for him/herself has ignored the will of the Parental God, but through *hinokishin* and through living a life in accordance with Nakayama Miki's ritual regulations, this life and the next will be joyous. The reincarnation implied by this doctrine is another Buddhist feature in this Shinto-stamped religion. This "internal syncretism" which is a feature of Tenrikyo is important both for its political position in Southeast Asia and for its appeal to potential converts. Older people remember only too well the State Shinto that provided the ideological underpinning of the militarist order under which Singapore suffered so much. And younger ones are not likely to be attracted to a religion which embodies a world view so alien to most Chinese Singaporeans who provide effectively the only source of locally-born converts.

According to members interviewed in Singapore, both Japanese and Singaporean, Tenrikyo does indeed have Shinto roots, but should not be called Shinto itself. The current director of the Tenrikyo Mission Center in the International Plaza in Singapore was himself born into a Tenrikyo family, but local members were not. Some of the local mission staff had been members for as long as 18 years (the current secretary for 10). In every case it was friends who had brought them to Tenrikyo and according to none of the interviewees were any existential crises predominant in their decision to convert. Most were just curious and Tenrikyo as a religious choice struck them as being very attractive. Most also were from what in Singapore is often called "Taoism" — in practice an amalgam of Taoism, Mahayana Buddhism, spirit mediumship and Confucianism (Clammer 1983), but could now, as fully-fledged members, describe in detail their understanding of *hinokishin* as the core of their religious practice — as "healing through meeting."

It is not altogether surprising given this doctrinal basis that the focus of Tenrikyo work in both Japan and Singapore should be on work with the handicapped. In both societies, but most especially in Japan, the objective of "full participation and equality" for the handicapped is far from realized. There are of course in Singapore a range of residential homes and facilities for the handicapped and in particular for crippled children, for the blind, deaf and mute and for the mentally disabled, and also for the aged sick who cannot be cared for at home. There are additionally disabled persons who live relatively independently out in the community, but who need assistance with daily care, cleaning or shopping. While there are welfare professionals, in general the burden of care, especially for the non-institutionalized handicapped, falls on family members. Where there are none, or where they themselves are aged or sick, Tenrikyo has found a major role to play in addition to providing help and visitation services mainly at the Tampines Home. Members visit the bedridden aged to provide friendship and practical assistance, help with mentally handicapped children and provide entertainment and visitation at the residential homes especially on national holidays and other occasions when inmates feel especially lonely and neglected by the busy society outside. Apart from its very practical impact on the lives and self-esteem of those assisted, this work has profound religious significance for Tenrikyo members.

According to Rev. Omukai of the Singapore Tenrikyo Mission Center, the theoretical description of Tenrikyo attitudes to social welfare as described by movement scholars such as Okubo (1982: 1–30) is actualized in the practice of *hinokishin* among handicapped persons in Singapore. Helping the handicapped is in general a bit odd amongst the Japanese, so by Japanese standards Tenrikyo is doing monumental work, although at the cost to members of quite deliberately making themselves "different," the one thing Japanese generally do not like to do. To the members interviewed at the Singapore Tenrikyo Mission, the practicality of *hinokishin* was to walk the Bodhisattva path: to transfer merits certainly, but primarily in this world of phenomena, to promote "healing through meeting." Speaking of the normal "facts" of social psychology, Maurice Friedman notes that "In human life together, it is a fact that we set the other at a distance and make the other independent that allows us to enter into relation, as an individual self, with those like ourselves" (Friedman 1992: 167). Among the Japanese however, disabled people have not been "like ourselves," but have been regarded with contempt and suspicion. But in Tenrikyo all real living is meeting and existential and relational trust stand at the heart of life. According to Friedman, a psychologist deeply influenced by dialogical psychotherapy,

> Through this "interhuman" relation we confirm each other, becoming a self with the other. The inmost growth of the self is not induced by one's relation to oneself, but by the confirmation in which one person knows him- or herself to be "made present" in his or her uniqueness by the other. Self-realization and self-actualization are not the goal but the by-product. The goal is completing distance by relation, and relation here means cooperation, genuine dialogue, and mutual confirmation (Friedman 1992: 168).

During interviews with Tenrikyo members in Singapore it became apparent that, without any studies of dialogical psychotherapy on their part, they had realized what mutual confirmation could be like. One altruistic follower of Nakayama Miki assured me that in *hinokishin* the Tenrikyo member does not treat the other as an object to be simply known and used, and that in this deep but practical religiosity, based on compassion and expressed through care-taking, there is a quality that is hard to find in secular welfare. In principle then, the Tenrikyo members have learned through their doctrine to make other people "present" and to confirm handicapped people who are in many ways marginalized in society. Thanks to the member who has polished his/her own soul, a kind of healing takes place and merits are transferred. Through being with disabled people at the Tampines home and through the "dialogue" that takes place there, mission-work becomes therapy in more than one sense. In Singapore, amongst Tenrikyo members, disabled persons become "pure": they are both presented with the "joyous life" and become the means for its attainment. Tenrikyo in Singapore consequently has a double mission. One, like the other *shin shukyo* (Japanese New Religions) is to spread what it believes to be the truth of its own religious message. The other, and here Tenrikyo goes somewhat beyond its rivals, is, through the medium of welfare work, to rebuild both the present reputation and karmic status of the formerly despised Japanese community in Southeast Asia.

Thanks to Tenrikyo, an ethnic group that has been held in contempt by many Chinese Singaporeans since February 1942 has recovered much of its reputation through social welfare activities done in the name of Oyasama by what is actually a very small group of people. The members of Tenrikyo believe in fact that Japan, in many ways, is actually needed in Singapore. Naturally there is the economic dimension and Singaporean petroleum, pharmaceutical and electronic products need to find outlets in the Japanese market (Lim 1995: 47). At the same time the residual bad feelings against Japan, stemming from the war years, cannot be eradicated simply by trade and economic relationships (which could, given the balance of payments in favour of Japan indeed exacerbate them). Cultural exchanges as well are needed, and this is something expressed in Tenrikyo doctrine and practice, both through *hinokishin* and through more obviously cultural activities.

Tenrikyo, despite its obviously Japanese roots and characteristics, is in principle a universal religion. It is moreover as we have seen, one in which social welfare activities are worship and where taking care of the other is salvation. Compared with other Japanese religious groups that have recently been in the news, such as Aum Shinrikyo with its belief that the surrounding world is hostile and is something that should be destroyed, Tenrikyo clearly has a highly constructive relationship to its cultural surroundings. The form of worship has strong psychological and social functions. *Hinokishin* is partly turned towards Oyasama as a kind of thanksgiving service, and is partly an action that gives the individual satisfaction since it is "edifying." So although the cult action is primarily objective, i.e. to thank the Parental God in an explicit way, it also has strongly felt subjective effects and this in turn promotes a feeling of solidarity with other members and promotes a spirit of community with the larger society surrounding them.

One way in which this is very conspicuously expressed is through the teaching of the Japanese language. At the Tenrikyo Cultural Center approximately 250 people took Japanese language lessons during 1996. Teaching Japanese has (paradoxically) been a very important mission in this universalistic religion. The members interviewed will not call Tenrikyo a Japanese religion, but a universal one. Even in the 1960s the language had a high priority for proselytizing reasons. The question of teaching the Japanese language was extensively discussed for example when the Southeast Asia Seminar Group organized by the headquarters of the Tenrikyo Young Men's Association visited Singapore on its 50th anniversary on 28 April 1968. Teaching the language, explaining Japan to outsiders and promoting interest in Japanese culture and generally promoting friendship between the Japanese and the peoples of Southeast Asia, is consequently seen as an important part of the mission of Tenrikyo.

Interestingly however Tenrikyo distinguishes itself from many other of the *shin shukyo* in that it does not ascribe any specialness to the language in any spiritual sense. There is a widespread belief in Japan that, in the words of Peter Dale (1995: 86), "words and things are linked by an inner spiritual force, *tama* (soul, spirit), which was held to embue the thing/word (*koto*) with a resident *mana*-like power (=*kotodama*). The ritual invocation of this power was called *kotoage* (lifting up words/things)." In many of the so-called New Religions in Japan this "power of words" is an important concept and in several of them it is believed that Japanese words have esoteric messages coded into them.

> When a devotee uses a chant, blessing, curse or myth in ritual way, the power that arises ... does not come from personal desire or hope, but from its sacredness. In turn the sacred word has the power to structure existence, organize human life, and recreate everyday events in terms of the eternal. divine model. When speech is used as a ritual act and possesses transcendent force, the words the devotee uses become extremely important (Streng 1991: 54).

But for Tenrikyo members in Singapore, this use of "magical words" has been transcended in that action has become more important than words and the most special of these actions is *hinokishin*. In fact *hinokishin* is both an action and a symbol standing for something beyond itself and social welfare activities while instrumental in one dimension, have symbolic meaning in another.

Tenrikyo remains one of the very smallest religions in Singapore. It has not succeeded in expanding much through the attractiveness of its doctrines in the veritable supermarket of religions that is contemporary Southeast Asia. Its social welfare activities, charitable and benevolent though they are, have done little to contribute to its visibility or influence in Singapore. Tenrikyo has not established the close political connections with the government that its sister Japanese *shin-shukyo* Soka Gakkai has very successfully done (see Clammer's chapter in this volume). It has no influential internationally known leader and it does not talk about peace as loudly as Soka Gakkai does either. So far the teachings of Tenrikyo have been meaningless to the average Singaporean and as a result have remained as a marginal phenomenon on the edges of mainstream Singapore society. Its Shinto roots do not benefit it much here either, but if anything intensify its isolation and marginality.

Soka Gakkai, as is apparent by its activities and organization in Singapore and elsewhere internationally, moves with the secularized society and has constantly adapted itself to shifts in thinking and behaviour. It knows whom to turn to and when. It is in short a highly pragmatic religion. Its leader Ikeda Daisaku uses Western logic and categories when discussing events and philosophy with prominent foreign intellectuals (e.g. Toynbee and Ikeda 1989) while Tenrikyo leaders continue to speak a specifically Buddhist/Shinto language of faith. In the highly urbanized and commercial setting of Singapore, people are on the whole more concerned with economic rather than spiritual advancement. Faith, in its Tenrikyo frame, does not reach far outside of a small circle because it is "too Japanese." Its teachings are in other words too much a vehicle of Japanese history, and its mythical dimension, which places Japan at the center of its cosmology, understandably grates on many people's feelings in Singapore. Its possible status as an agent, witting or unwitting, of new forms of Japanese cultural imperialism are all too apparent, and its Shinto roots deepen this suspicion amongst those old enough to remember the war.

At the same time Soka Gakkai, Tenrikyo's main "rival" in Singapore has a clearer Buddhist identity, and Buddhism in some form is the religion of the majority of Singaporeans. In Soka Gakkai International, the overseas arm of the home religion, the religious teaching is in any case often thrown into the shade by peace-talk. The focus is on the hot issues that are more likely to engage idealistic people such as environmental questions and conflict resolution. In this fast moving world of religious one-upmanship, Tenrikyo has not successfully competed and so appears as a "departed glory," a times-long-past phenomena in this part of Southeast Asia which its social welfare activities seem to do little to reverse. It has not updated or indigenized its religious message sufficiently to appeal to enough people in the secularized setting of Singapore: social welfare is good, but is not enough of a pull to attract newcomers in any numbers.

In conclusion two comments can be made. Firstly, that its formal cycle of growth has been quite like that of Soka Gakkai: a modest beginning amongst the Japanese expatriate community in Singapore expanding, largely through attractive cultural activities (language classes, music, etc.) to the Singaporean Chinese community. But there the parallels end. Soka Gakkai has successfully massified itself through a complex island-wide organizational structure, through active missionary outreach and attractive publications in English and Chinese and very much through high-level political contacts and visible and publicity attracting philanthropic activities (see Clammer above). By stressing international peace and development efforts it has furthermore succeeded in representing Japan as a land of peace and the center of a new order in Asia, and thus defusing the fears of new forms of Japanese imperialism in Southeast Asia — not only economic domination, but also religious domination too. Tenrikyo on the other hand has kept a much lower profile in Singapore and has restricted itself in its attempts to rehabilitate the Japanese image largely to social welfare activities of a very practical and less visible (although arguably more valuable) character. This signals the variations in the presence of the Japanese New Religions in Southeast Asia which certainly do not constitute a unitary phenomenon.

Secondly, it is not only the sociological patterns which are interesting, but the specifically religious ones too. Soka Gakkai, as itself a form of reformist and "Protestant" Buddhism, fits more obviously into the religious landscape of Singapore, where its militant and iconoclastic elements have been played down. Tenrikyo on the other hands, with its distinctive Shinto roots, has no organic place in the religious economy of Singapore — it is a "foreign body" cosmologically and sociologically. But yet, despite its small size and its little power, it sees itself engaged in a spiritually significant task, one being carried out by no one else — that of repairing karma and as such undoing the negative effects of the past, creating a better future and recovering the image and moral status of the Japanese in Singapore. In all the debates about cultural flows and the Japanese cultural role in Southeast Asia expressed through fashion, media and consumer goods, this aspect of religious influence is usually overlooked. The story of Tenrikyo in Singapore may appear as a small footnote to an intellectual discourse dominated by the economic and the political, but it represents nevertheless an important dimension of the Japanese presence: beyond golf and business a profound humanitarianism, and beyond the humanitarianism an attempt to transform the spiritual heritage of Shinto from something narrow and nationalistic into something universal and life enhancing.

References

Chapter 1

Appadurai, Arjun 1986 "Theory in anthropology: centre and periphery," *Comparative Studies in History and Society*, 29, pp. 356–361.

Appadurai, Arjun 1990 "Disjuncture and difference in the global cultural economy," *Theory, Culture and Society*, 7, pp. 295–310.

Ben-Ari, Eyal 1998 "Golf, Organization and 'Body Projects': Japanese Business Expatriates in Singapore," in Sepp Linhart and Sabine Fruhstuck (eds) *The Culture of Japan as Seen Through its Leisure*, Albany: State University of New York Press.

Benedict, Ruth 1946 *The Chrysanthemum and the Sword: Patterns of Japanese Culture*, Boston: Houghton Mifflin.

Brannen, Mary Yoko 1992 " 'Bwana Mickey': constructing cultural consumption at Tokyo Disneyland," in J.J. Tobin (ed.) *Remade in Japan: Everyday Life and Consumer Taste in a Changing Society*, New Haven: Yale University Press.

Chan, David 1993 "The big bad West," *Commentary* (Singapore), 11, 1, pp. 105–113.

Chong Li Choy and Caroline Yeo 1990 "Multinational Business and Singapore Society," in Chong Li Choy *et al.* (eds) *Business, Society and Development in Singapore*, Times Academic Press, pp. 102–106.

Cohen, Erik n.d. *Golf in Thailand: From Sport to Business*, Jerusalem: Department of Sociology and Anthropology, Hebrew University of Jerusalem.

Clammer, John 1997 *Contemporary Urban Japan: A Sociology of Consumption*, Oxford: Blackwell.

Creighton, Millie R. 1991 "Maintaining cultural boundaries in retailing: how Japanese departmental stores domesticate 'things foreign'," *Modern Asian Studies*, 25, 4, pp. 675–709.

216

Cronin, Richard P. 1992 *Japan, the United States and Prospects for the Asia Pacific Century*, Singapore: Institute of Southeast Asian Studies.

Dale, Peter N. 1995 *The Myth of Japanese Uniqueness*, London: Routledge.

Dobson, Wendy 1993 *Japan in East Asia: Trading and Investment Strategies*, Singapore: Institute of Southeast Asian Studies.

Ensign, Margee M. 1992 *Doing Good or Doing Well? Japan's Foreign Aid Program*, New York: Columbia University Press.

Fardon, Richard (ed.) 1990 *Localizing Strategies: Regional Traditions of Ethnographic Writing*, Edinburgh: Scottish Universities Press.

Fungtammasan, Artorn 1990 "Japanese literature in Thailand," in Kunio Yoshihara (ed.) *Japan in Thailand*, Kyoto: Kyoto University Center for Southeast Asian Studies.

Geertz, Clifford 1968 *Islam Observed: Religious Development in Morocco and Indonesia*, Chicago: University of Chicago Press.

Goodman, Roger 1993 *Japan's "International Youth": The Emergence of a New Class of Schoolchildren*, Oxford: Clarendon Press.

Gong, Gerrit W. 1984 *The Standard of 'Civilization' in International Society*, Oxford: Clarendon Press.

Hannerz, Ulf 1990 "Cosmopolitans and locals in world culture," in Mike Featherstone (ed.) *Global Culture*, London: Sage.

Hook, Glenn 1989 "Internationalization of contemporary Japan," *The Japan Foundation Newsletter*, 17, 1, pp. 13–16.

Honda, A. 1990 *Gaikokujin Rodosha no Jinkin* [Human Rights of Foreign Workers], Tokyo: Nikkan Kogyo Shimbunsha.

Iriye, Akira (ed.) 1975 *Mutual Images: Essays in American-Japanese Relations*, Cambridge, Mass.: Harvard University Press.

Iwasaki, Ikuo (ed.) 1983 *Japan and Southeast Asia: A Bibliography of Historical, Economic and Political Relations*, Tokyo: Institute of Developing Economies.

Juwana, Hikmahanto 1993 "Japan's defence conception and its implications for Southeast Asia," *The Indonesian Quarterly*, 21, 4, pp. 483–494.

Koike, Kazuo and Takenori Aoki (eds) 1987 *Skill Formation in Japan and Southeast Asia*, Tokyo: Tokyo University Press.

Krongkaew, Medhi 1989 "The Japanese economy according to Thai economists," in Kunio Yoshihara (ed.) *Thai Perceptions of Japanese Modernization*, Kyoto: Kyoto University Center for Southeast Asian Studies.

Lash, Scott and John Urry 1994 *Economies of Signs and Space*, London: Sage.

Mahatir, Mohamad and Ishihara, Shintaro 1994 *'No' to ieru Ajia* [The Asia That Can Say 'No'], Tokyo: Kobunsha.

Matsumoto, K. 1991 *The Rise of the Japanese Corporate System*, London: Kegan Paul International.

Mimura, Yohei 1987 "The internationalization of Japanese business," *IHJ* (*International House of Japan Bulletin*), 7, 3, pp. 1–6.

Miyoshi, Masao (ed.) 1991 *Off Center; Power and Culture Relations Between Japan and the United States*, Cambridge, Mass.: Harvard University Press.

217

Morris-Suzuki, Tessa 1984 "The south seas empire of Ishihara Hirochiro; a case study of Japan's economic relations with Southeast Asia 1914–41," in Alan Rix and Ross Mouer (eds) *Japan's Impact on the World*, Melbourne: Japanese Studies Association of Australia.

Mouer, Ross and Yoshio Sugimoto 1986 *Images of Japanese Society*, London: Kegan Paul International.

Nitta, F. 1992 "Shopping for souvenirs in Hawaii," in J.J. Tobin (ed.) *Remade in Japan: Everyday Life and Consumer Taste in a Changing Society*, New Haven: Yale University Press.

Oe, Kenzaburo 1982 "The center and the periphery," in Guy Amirthanayagan (ed.) *Writers in East-West Encounters: New Cultural Bearings*, New York: Macmillan.

Otabe, Yuji 1990 "Japanese occupation policy in Singapore 1942–45," in Peter Lowe and Herman Mosehart (eds) *Western Interactions with Japan: Expansion,the Armed Forces and Readjustment 1895–1956*, Folkstone: Japan Library.

Parkin, David 1978 *The Cultural Definition of Political Response*, London: Academic Press.

Robertson, Roland 1992 *Globalization: Social Theory and Global Culture*, London: Sage.

Robison, Richard and David S.G. Goodman (eds) 1996 *The New Rich in Asia: Mobile Phones, McDonald's and Middle Class Revolution*, London: Routledge.

Scolinos, Elaine 1988 "Japan: coming to terms with internationalization," *Asian Affairs*, 15, 2, pp. 91–104.

Shafie, Tan Sri Mohammed Ghazalie 1990 "Japan in Asia: in search of purpose and direction," *Speaking of Japan*, 11, 117, pp. 10–12.

Sinlarat, Paitoon 1989 "Thai perceptions of Japanese modernization: education," in Kunio Yoshihara (ed.) *Thai Perceptions of Japanese Modernization*, Kyoto: Kyoto University Center for Southeast Asian Studies.

Soderberg, Marie 1993 "Japanese development aid: trendiness versus reality," *Japan Forum*, 5, 2, pp. 217–219.

Taira, Koji 1993 "Multinational human resource management: a case study," *East Asia*, 6, pp. 43–61.

Tanaka, Yuji 1984 "Japan and the Pacific: the banana trade with the Philippines," in Alan Rix and Ross Mouer (eds) *Japan's Impact on the World*, Melbourne: Japanese Studies Association of Australia.

Toyota Foundation 1993 *Occasional Report*, No. 17, Tokyo.

Vella, Walter F. 1968 *The Indianized States of Southeast Asia*, Honolulu: University of Hawaii Press.

Ventura, Ray 1992 *Underground in Japan*, London: Jonathan Cape.

Vishwanathan, Savitri 1975 "Paradox of Japan's nationalism: relations with Asia," in Toyomasa Fuse (ed.) *Modernization and Stress in Japan*, Leiden: E.J. Brill.

Vishwanathan, Savitri 1992 "Indian approaches to Japanese studies," in Harumi Befu and Josef Kreiner (eds) *Othernesses of Japan: Historical and Cultural Influences on Japanese Studies in Ten Countries*, Monographien aus dem Deutschen Institut fur Japanstudien der Philip-Franz-von-Siebold-Stiftung.

Yoshihara, Kunio (ed.) 1989 *Thai Perceptions of Japanese Modernization*, Kyoto University: Center for Southeast Asian Studies.

Yoshihara, Kunio (ed.) 1990 *Japan in Thailand*, Kyoto: Kyoto University Center for Southeast Asian Studies.

Chapter 2

Aldrich, Howard 1979 *Organizations and Environments*, Englewood Cliffs: Prentice-Hall.

Aldrich, Howard and Diane Herker 1977 "Boundary Spanning Roles and Organizational Structure," *Academy of Management Review* 2, pp. 217–230.

Appadurai, Arjun 1996 *Modernity at Large: Cultural Dimensions of Globalization*, Minneapolis: University of Minnesota Press.

Bartelett, Charles A and Sumantra Ghoshal 1995 *Transnational Management: Texts, Cases and Readings in Cross-Border Management*, Chicago: Irwin.

Befu, Harumi and Kazufumi Manabe 1991 "Ninonjinron: The Discursive Manifestation of Cultural Nationalism," *Kwansei Gakuin University – Annual Studies* 15, pp. 101–115.

Befu, Harumi and Nancy Stalker 1996 "Globalization of Japan: and Cosmopolitanization or Spread of the Japanese Village?" in Harume Befu (ed.) *Japan Engaging the World: A Century of International Encounter*, pp. 101–120. Publication Number 1, Center for Japanese Studies, Teikyo Loretto Heights University.

Ben-Ari, Eyal 2000 "Globalization, 'Folk Models' of the World Order and National Identity: Japanese Business Expatriates in Singapore," in Marie Soderberg and Ian Reader (eds) *Japanese Influences and Presences in Asia*, London: Curzon Press.

Brannen, Mary Yoko 1992 "'Bwana Mickey': Constructing cultural consumption at Tokyo Disneyland," in J.J. Tobin (ed.) *Re-made in Japan*, pp. 216–334, New Haven: Yale University Press.

Chan, David 1993 "The Big Bad West," *Commentary* (Singapore) 11 (1), pp. 105–113.

Choy Chong Li and Caroline Yeo 1990 "Multinational Business and Singapore Society" in Chong Li Choy *et al.* (eds) *Business, Society and Development in Singapore*, pp. 102–106. Singapore: Times Academic Press.

Cohen, Anthony P. 1994 *Self-Consciousness: An Alternative Anthropology of Identity*, London: Routledge.

Cohen, Erik 1977 "Expatriate Communities," *Current Sociology* 24(3).

Cohen, Robin 1997 *Global Diasporas: An Introduction*, Seattle: University of Washington Press.

Creighton, Millie R. 1991 "Maintaining cultural boundaries in retailing: How Japanese department stores domesticate 'Things Foreign'," *Modern Asian Studies* 25(4) pp. 675–709.

Cronin, Richard P. 1992 *Japan, The United States and Prospects for the Asia Pacific Century*, Singapore: Institute of Southeast Asian Studies.

219

Dale, Peter N. 1986 *The Myth of Japanese Uniqueness*, London: Croom Helm.

D'Andrade, Roy G. 1992 "Schemas and Motivation" in Roy G. D'Andrade and Claudia Strauss (eds) *Human Motives and Cultural Models*, pp. 23–44. Cambridge: Cambridge University Press.

Dikotter, Frank 1990 "Group Definition and the Idea of 'Race' in Modern China (1793–1949)," *Ethnic and Racial Studies* 13(3), pp. 420–432.

Dore, Ronald 1987 *Taking Japan Seriously*, Stanford: Stanford University Press.

Gong, Gerrit W. 1984 *The Standard of 'Civilization' in International Society*, Oxford: Clarendon.

Goodman, Roger 1991 *Japan's International Youth: The Emergence of a New Class of Schoolchildren*, Oxford: Clarendon.

Goodman, Roger 1998 "A Model for All Seasons? East Asian Education and the Problem of Drawing Lessons from Other Societies, in Yishay Yafeh, Ehud Harari and Eyal Ben-Ari (eds) *Lessons from East Asia for the Development of the Middle East in the Era of Peace*, The Hebrew University: The Harry S. Truman Institute for the Advancement of Peace.

Gupta, Akhil and James Furgeson 1992 "Beyond 'Culture': Space, Identity and the Politics of Difference," *Cultural Anthropology* 7(1) pp. 6–23.

Hamada, Tomoko 1992 "Under the Silk Banner: The Japanese Company and Its Overseas Managers," in Takie S. Lebra (ed.) *Japanese Social Organization*, pp. 135–164, Honolulu: University of Hawaii Press.

Hannerz, Ulf 1992 *Cultural Complexity: Studies in the Social Organization of Meaning*, New York: Columbia University Press.

Inmaura, Hiroshi 1982 *Nihonjin no Kaigai Futekio*, Tokyo: NHK Books.

Katzenstein, Peter J. 1996 *Cultural Norms and National Security: Police and Military in Postwar Japan*, Ithaca: Cornell University Press.

Kearney, M. 1995 "The Local and the Global: The Anthropolgy of Globalization and Transnationalism," *Annual Review of Anthropology* 24, pp. 547–65.

Kobayashi, Tetsuya 1978 "Japan's policy on returning students," *International Education and Cultural Exchange*, 13(4) pp. 15–16 and 47.

Kotkin, Joel 1993 *Tribes: How Race, Religion and Identity Determine Success in the New Global Economy*, New York: Random House.

Kunda, Gideon 1992 *Engineering Culture: Control and Commitment in a High-Tech Corporation*. Philadelphia: Temple University Press.

Manabe, Kazufumi 1992 "Japanese Cultural Identity: Old Tradition, New Technology," *Sociology Department Studies* (*Kwansei Gakuin University*), No. 66., pp. 119–122.

Manabe, Kazufumi and Harumi Befu 1992 "Japanese Cultural Identity: An Empirical Invstigation of *Nihonjinron*," *Japanstudien: Jahrbuch des Deutschen Institutes fur Japanstudien der Philip-Franz-von-Siebold-Siftung*, 4, pp. 89–102.

Mouer, Ross and Yoshio Sugimoto 1986 *Images of Japanese Society*, Kegan Paul International.

Nakane, Chie 1974 The Social Background of the Japanese in Southeast Asia, *The Developing Economies*, 10(2) pp. 115–125.

220

Ortner, Sherry B. 1973 "On Key Symbols," *American Anthropologist*, 75, pp. 1338–1346.

Parkin, David 1987 *The Cultural Definition of Political Response*, London: Unwin.

Plath, David 1983 "Life Is Not Just a Job Resume?" in David W. Plath (ed.) *Work and the Lifecourse in Japan*, pp. 1–13. Albany: State University of New York Press.

Raz, Jacob and Aviad E. Raz 1996 "'America' Meets 'Japan': A Journey for Real Between Two Imaginaries," *Theory, Culture and Society* 13(3), pp. 153–192.

Robertson, Roland 1992 *Globalization: Social Theory and Global Culture*, London: Sage.

Rohlen, Thomas P. 1992 "Learning: The Mobilization of Knowledge in the Japanese Political Economy," in Shumpei Kumon and Henry Rosovsky (eds) *The Political Economy of Japan – Volume 3: Cultural and Social Dyanamics*, pp. 292–320. Stanford: Stanford University Press.

Samuels, Richard J. 1994 *"Rich Nation – Strong Army": National Security and the Technological Transformation of Japan*, Ithaca: Cornell University Press.

Sender, Harry 1995 "Focus Japan: Offshore Attractions," *Far Eastern Economic Review*, June 15.

Shafie, Tan Sri Mohammed Ghazalie 1990 "Japan in Asia: In Search of Purpose and Direction," *Speaking of Japan* 11 (117), pp. 10–12.

Shiraki, Matsuhide 1998 "Personnel Practices and their Implications for Globalized Japanese Companies in Southeast Asian Countries," in Yishay Yafeh, Ehud Harari and Eyal Ben-Ari (eds) *Lessons from East Asia for the Development of the Middle East in the Era of Peace*. The Hebrew University: The Harry S. Truman Institute for the Advancement of Peace.

Skinner, Kenneth A. 1983 "Aborted Careers in a Public Corporation," in David W. Plath (ed.) *Work and the Lifecourse in Japan*, pp. 50–73, Albany: State University of New York Press.

Soderberg, Marie 2000 "Asia as Seen from the Perspective of the Japanese General Trading Companies," in Marie Soderberg and Ian Reader (eds) *Japanese Influences and Presences in Asia*, London: Curzon.

Spencer, Paul (ed.) 1990 *Anthropology and the Riddle of the Sphinx: Paradoxes of Change in the Life Course*, London: Routledge.

Stanley, Thomas A. 1988 "Japan as a Model for Economic Development: The Example of Singapore," in Gail Lee Bernstein and Haruhiro Fukui (eds) *Japan and the World*, pp. 232–244, London: Macmillan.

Sugerman, Leonie 1986 *Life-Span Development: Concepts, Theories and Interventions*, London: Methuen.

Vishwanathan, Savitri 1992 "Indian Approaches to Japanese Studies," in Harumi Befu and Josef Kreiner (eds) *Othernesses of Japan: Historical and Cultural Influences on Japanese Studies in Ten Countries*, pp. 281–293. Monographien aus dem Deutschen Institut fur Japan-studien der Philip-Franz-von-Siebold-Stiftung.

Wallerstein, Immanuel 1991 *Geopolitics and Geoculture: Essays on the Changing World System*, Cambridge: Cambridge University Press.

Wee, C.J.W.-L. 1996 "The 'Clash' of Civilizations? Or an Emerging 'East Asian Modernity'?," *Sojourn* 11(2) pp. 211–230.

White, Merry 1988 *The Japanese Overseas: Can They Go Home Again?* Princeton: Princeton University Press.

Yoshino, Kosaku 1992 *Cultural Nationalism in Contemporary Japan: A Sociological Inquiry*, London: Routledge.

Yoshino, Michael Y. and Thomas B. Lifson 1988 *The Invisible Link: Japan's Sogo Shosha and the Organization of Trade*, Cambridge, Mass.: MIT Press.

Chapter 3

Asiaweek 1981, 16 January, p. 16
—— 1981b, 30 October, p. 19
—— 1982, 10 December, pp. 41–42
—— 1983a, 18 February, p. 49
—— 1983b, 9 September, p. 33
—— 1983c, 16 September, p. 33
—— 1983d, 23 September, p. 22
—— 1984a, 24 February, p. 62
—— 1984b, 6 July, p. 23
—— 1984c, 7 September, p. 31
Far Eastern Economic Review 1980a, 15 February, p. 26
—— 1980b, 1 August, p. 54
—— 1981a, 15 May, pp. 34–36
—— 1981b, 20 February, p. 60
—— 1982, 25 June, p. 58
—— 1983a, 28 April, pp. 14–16
—— 1983b, 11 August, p. 17
—— 1983c, 8 September, pp. 23–24
—— 1984a, 22 March, pp. 10, 23, 26
—— 1984b, 2 February, p. 8ff.
—— 1984c, 18 October, p. 46
—— 1986, 3 April, pp. 44, 50–51
—— 1987, 19 March, pp. 44–45
—— 1989a, 9 March, p. 24
—— 1989b, 18 May, p. 36
—— 1990a, 6 September, p. 25
—— 1990b, 8 November, p. 22
—— 1998, 1 October, pp. 86–87
Hall, Ivan P. 1973 *Mori Arionori*, Cambridge, MA: Harvard University Press, pp. 185–186, 250–251.
International Herald Tribune 1995 "Singapore Way of Satellites," July 12, p. 13
Marshall, Bryon K. 1967 *Capitalism and Nationalism in Prewar Japan: The Ideology of the Business Elite 1868–1941*, Stanford, CA: Stanford University Press.
South China Morning Post 1998, 9 December, p. 16

Straits Times 1979, 3 January, p. 7
—— 1985, 7 March, p. 12
Wang Gungwu 1995, "Asia to turn Japanese," *The Times Higher Education Supplement*, June 9, p. 16

Chapter 4

Atsumi, Reiko 1979 "*Tsukiai* – Obligatory Personal Relationships of Japanese White-Collar Company Employees," *Human Organization* 38(1), pp. 63–70.

Ben-Ari, Eyal 1993 *Sake and "Spare Time": Management and Imbibement in Japanese Business Firms*. Papers in Japanese Studies No. 18. National University of Singapore: Department of Japanese Studies.

Brinton, Mary 1993 *Women and the Japanese Miracle: Gender and Work in Postwar Japan*, Berkeley: University of California Press.

Carter, Rose and Lois Dilatush 1976 "Office Ladies," in Joyce Lebra, Joy Paulson, and Elizabeth Powers (eds): *Women in Changing Japan*, pp. 75–88, Stanford: Stanford University Press.

Cohen, Erik 1977 "Expatriate Communities," *Current Sociology* 24(3).

Edwards, Walter 1989 *Modern Japan Through its Weddings: Gender, Person and Society in Ritual Portrayal*, Stanford: Stanford University Press.

Goodman, Roger 1990 *Japan's Intentional Youth: The Emergence of a New Class of Schoolchildren*, Oxford: Clarendon.

Hamada, Tomoko 1989 "Cultural Dynamics, Gender, and Meaning of Task in a Japanese High Tech Firm in the United States," in Tomoko Hamada and Ann Jordan (eds) *Cross Cultural Management and Organizational Culture*, pp. 115–132. Studies in Third World Societies Number Forty-Two.

Iwao, Sumiko 1993 *The Japanese Woman: Traditional Image and Changing Reality*, Cambridge, Mass.: Harvard University Press.

Kawashima, Yoko 1995 "Female Workers:An Overview of Past and Current Trends," in Kumiko Fujimura-Fanselow and Atsuko Kameda (eds): *Japanese Women: New Feminist Perspectives on the Past, Present and Future*, pp. 271–293, New York: Feminist Press.

Lam, Alice 1993 "Equal Employment Opportunities for Japanese Women: Changing Company Practice," in Janet Hunter (eds) *Japanese Women Working*, pp. 197–223, London: Routledge.

Lo, Jeannie 1990 *Office Ladies, Factory Women: Life and Work at a Japanese Company*, Armonk: M.E. Sharpe.

McLendon, James 1983 "The Office: Way Station or Blind Alley?" in David W. Plath (ed.) *Work and Lifecourse in Japan*, pp. 156–182. Albany: State University of New York Press.

Nakano, Yumiko 1995 *The Experience of Japanese Expatriate Housewives in Hong Kong: The Reproduction of a Conservative Social Pattern*, M.A. Thesis, Department of History: University of Hong Kong.

Pharr, Susan 1981 *Political Women in Japan: The Search for a Place in Political Life*, Berkeley: University of California Press.

223

Pharr, Susan 1984 "Status Conflict: The Rebellion of the Tea Pourers," in Ellis S. Krauss, Thomas P. Rohlen and Patricia Steinhoff (eds) *Conflict in Japan*, pp. 214–240, Honolulu: University of Hawaii Press.

Quah, Jon S.T. and Stella R. Quah 1990 "The Limits of Government Intervention," in Kernial Singh Sandhu and Paul Wheatly (eds) *Management for Success: The Moulding of Modern Singapore*, pp. 102–127, Singapore: Institute of Southeast Asian Studies.

Rohlen, Thomas P. 1974 *For Harmony and Strength: Japanese White-Collar Organization in Anthropological Perspective*, Berkeley: University of California Press.

White, Merry 1988 *The Japanese Overseas: Can They Go Home Again*, Princeton: Princeton University Press.

Whitehill, Arthur M. 1991 *Japanese Management: Tradition and Transition*, London: Routledge.

Chapter 5

Abegglen, James C. 1984 *The Strategy of Japanese Business*, Cambridge, Mass.: Ballinger.

Ben-Ari, E. 1990 "Ritual strikes, ceremonial slowdowns: Some thoughts on the management of conflict in large Japanese enterprises," in S.N. Eisenstadt and Eyal Ben-Ari (eds), *Japanese Models of Conflict Resolution*, pp. 94–124, London: Kegan Paul International.

Ben-Ari, Eyal 1993 *Sake and "Spare Time": Management and Imbibement in Japanese Business Firms*, Papers in Japanese Studies No. 18. Department of Japanese Studies, National University of Singapore.

Ben-Ari, Eyal 1995 "Japanese Enterprises Abroad and Images of the Global Order: Japanese Executives in Singapore", *Management Japan* 28(2), pp. 25–32.

Blumenthal, Tuvia (ed.) 1987 *Japanese Mangement at Home and Abroad*, Beer-Sheva: Ben-Gurion University of the Negev Press.

Choy Chong Li and Caroline Yeo 1990 "Multinational Business and Singapore Society," in Chong Li Choy *et.al.* (eds) *Business, Society and Development in Singapore*, pp. 102–106. Singapore: Times Academic Press.

Clark, Rodney 1979 *The Japanese Company*, New Haven: Yale University Press.

Cole, Robert E. 1979 *Work, Mobility and Participation*, Berkeley: University of California Press.

Cronin, Richard P. 1992 *Japan, The United States and Prospects for the Asia Pacific Century*, Singapore: Institute of Souteast Asian Studies.

De Vos, George A. 1975 "Apprenticeship and paternalism," in E.F. Vogel (ed.), *Modern Japanese Organization and Decision Making*, pp. 210–217, Tokyo: Tuttle.

Dore, Ronald 1973 *British factory, Japanese factory: The Origins of National Diversity in Industrial Relations*, London: George Allen.

Dore, Ronald 1984 "Introduction," in S. Kamata, *Japan in the Passing Lane*, London: Unwin.

224

Fruin, W. Mark 1980 "The family as a firm and the firm as a family in Japan: The case of Kikkoman Shoyu Company Limited," *Journal of Family History*, 5, pp. 432–449.

Fruin, W. Mark 1983 *Kikkoman: Company, clan and community*, Cambridge, MA: Harvard University Press.

Griffin, Ricky W. 1993 *Management*, New York: Houghton-Mifflin.

Hamabata, Matthews M. 1990 *Crested Kimono: Power and Love in the Japanese Business Family*, Ithaca: Cornell University Press.

Hamada, Tomoko 1992 "Under the Silk Banner: The Japanese Company and Its Overseas Managers," in Takie S. Lebra (ed.) *Japanese Social Organization*, pp. 135–164. Honolulu: University of Hawaii Press.

Hanami, Tadashi 1979 *Labor Relations in Japan Today*, Tokyo: Kodansha.

Hayashi, Kichiro 1986 "Crosscultural Interface Management: The Case of Japanese Firms Abroad," *Japanese Economic Studies* 15(1), pp. 3–41.

Hazama, Hiroshi 1978 "Characteristics of Japanese Style Management," *Japanese Economic Studies* 6(3–4), pp. 110–173.

Higashi, Chikara and Peter G. Lauter 1987 *The Internationalization of the Japanese Economy*, Boston: Kluwer.

Kennedy, Margaret M. 1979 "Generalizing from Single Case Studies," *Evaluation Quarterly* 3(4) pp. 661–678.

Kiefer, Christie W. 1980 "Loneliness and Japanese social structure," in J. Hartog et al. (eds) *The Anatomy of Loneliness*, pp. 425–450, New York: International Universities Press.

Komai, Hiroshi 1989 *Japanese Management Overseas: Experiences of the United States and Thailand*, Tokyo: Asia Productivity Board.

Muramatsu, Shinobu 1992 "International Joint Ventures of Japanese Firms in Asian and Pacific Countries," in Sung-Jo Park (ed.): *Managerial Efficiency in Competition and Cooperation*. pp. 149–175, Frankfurt: Campus Verlag.

Rohlen, Thomas P. 1974 *For Harmony and Strength: Japanese White-Collar Organization in Anthropological Perspective*, Berkeley: University of California Press.

Sethi, Sethi, Nobukai Namiki and Carl L. Swanson 1984 *The False Promise of the Japanese Miracle: Illusions and Realities of the Japanese Management System*, New York: Pitman.

Van Wolferen, Karel 1989 *The Enigma of Japanese Power: People and Politics in a Stateless Nation*, New York: Papermac.

Yawata, Yasusada 1994 "Socio-cultural Background of Competitive Management and Technology in the Western Pacific Rim," in Helmut Schutte (ed.): *The Global Competitiveness of the Asian Firm*, pp. 3–21, New York: St. Martin's Press.

Yoshikawa, Akihiro 1991 "Globalization and restructuring the Japanese economy," in Harry H. Kendall and Clara Joewono (eds): *Japan, ASEAN and the United States*, pp. 31–46, University of California, Berkeley: Institute of East Asian Studies.

Yoshino, Michael Y. and Thomas B. Lifson 1988 *The Invisible Link: Japan's Sogo Shosha and the Organization of Trade*, Cambridge, Mass.: MIT Press.

Chapter 6

Ching, Leo 1994 "Imaginings in the Empire of the Sun: Japanese mass culture in Asia," *boundary 2*, 21, pp. 198–219.

Chua, Beng-Huat 1990, "Steps to becoming a fashion consumer in Singapore," *Asia Pacific Journal of Management* 7, pp. 31–47.

Chua, Beng-Huat 1992, "Shopping for women"s fashion in Singapore," in Rob Shields (ed.) *Lifestyle Shopping: The Subject of Consumption*, London: Routledge.

Clammer, John 1995 *Difference and Modernity: Social Theory and Contemporary Japanese Society.* London: Kegan Paul International.

Cooper, Dave 1994 "Portraits of paradise: themes and images of the tourist industry," *Southeast Asian Journal of Social Science*, theme issue: Cultural Studies in the Asia Pacific, 22, pp. 144–160.

Iwabuachi Koichi 1994, "Return to Asia? Japan in the global audio-visual market," *Sojourn*, theme issue: Mass media: local and global positions, 9, pp. 226–245.

Lii, Ding-Tzann and Chen Zhao-Yong 1966 "Satellite TV and national imaginary: Japanese melodrama on Star TV as an example," *Mass Communication Research* 56, pp. 9–34 (Taiwan in Chinese).

Soh Seok Hoon 1995 *Fandom in Singapore.* Paper lodged with Department of Sociology, National University of Singapore.

Teo, Peter 1997 *The Straits Times*, 8 June, pp. 24

The Straits Times, 1996, 10 February, pp. 4

Ueda, Atsushi 1994 *The Electric Geisha: Exploring Japan"s Popular Culture*, Translated by Miriam Eguchi, New York: Kodansha International.

Wee, C.J.Wan-Ling 1996 "Staging the 'new' East Asia: Singapore"s Dick Lee, pop music and a counter-modernity," *Public Culture* 8, pp. 489–510.

Wee, C.J. Wan-Ling 1997 "Buying Japan: Singapore, Japan and an 'East Asian' modernity," *The Journal of Pacific Asia* 4, pp. 21–46.

Chapter 7

Allison, Anne 1994 *Nightwork: Sexuality, PLeasure and Corporate Masculinity in a Tokyo Hostess Bar*, Chicago: Chicago University Press.

Atsumi, R. 1979 "Tsukiai-Obligatory personal relationships of Japanese white-collar company employees," *Human Organization*, 8, pp. 63–70.

Befu, Harumi 1986 "An Ethnography of Dinner Entertainment in Japan," in Takie S. Lebra (ed.) *Japanese Culture and Behavior*, pp. 108–120, Honolulu: University of Hawaii Press.

Ben-Ari, Eyal 1990 "At the Interstices: Drinking, Management and Temporary Groups in a Local Japanese Organization," *Social Analysis* 26, pp. 46–64.

Ben-Ari, Eyal 1994 "Sake and 'Spare Time': Management and Imbibement in Japanese Business Firms," *Papers in Japanese Studies* No. 18., Department of Japanese Studies: National University of Singapore.

Ben-Ari, Eyal 1998 "Golf, Organization, and Body Project: Japanese Business Expatriates in Singapore," in Sepp Linhart and Sabine Fruehstueck (eds) The Culture of Japan as Seen Through its Leisure, pp. 139–161, Albany: State University of New York Press.

Chiang, Liling Denise 1997 After Hours Entertaining and Socializing Among Japanese Expatriates in Singapore. Honors Thesis, Department of Japanese Studies. National University of Singapore.

Choy, Chong Li and Caroline Yeo 1990 "Multinational Business and Singapore Society," in Chong Li Choy et.al. (eds) Business, Society and Development in Singapore, pp. 102–106, Singapore: Times Academic Press.

Cohen, Erik 1977 "Expatriate Communities," Current Sociology 24(3), pp. 5–133.

Cohen, Erik 1995 "Golf in Thailand: From Sport to Business," Southeast Asian Journal of Social Science 23(2), pp. 1–17.

Cole, R.E. 1971 Japanese blue collar: The changing tradition, Berkeley: University of California Press.

Doner, Richard F. 1991 Driving a Bargain: Automobile Industrialization and Japanese Firms in Southeast Asia, Berkeley: University of California Press.

Dore, R. 1973 British factory, Japanese factory. The origins of national diversity in industrial relations, London: George Allen.

Emmott, Bill 1992 Japan's Global Reach: The Influences, Strategies and Weaknesses of Japan's Multinational Companies, London: Arrow.

Fruin, W.M. 1980 "The family as a firm and the firm as a family in Japan: The case of Kikkoman Shoyu Company Limited," Journal of Family History 5, pp. 432–449.

Fruin, W.M. 1983 Kikkoman: Company, clan and community, Cambridge, MA: Harvard University Press.

Fujimoto, Toyoharu 1991 Management Challenge: The Japanese Management System in an International Environment, Singapore: McGraw-Hill.

Hamada, Tomoko 1992 "Under the Silk Banner: The Japanese Company and Its Overseas Managers," in Takie S. Lebra (ed.) Japanese Social Organization, pp. 135–164. Honolulu: University of Hawaii Press.

Hannerz, Ulf 1990 "Cosmopolitans and locals in world culture," in Mike Featherstone (ed.) Global Culture, pp. 237–252, London: Sage.

Hello Singapore 1993 Hello Singapore, Singapore: Crown Enterprise.

Kaplinsky, Raphael with Anne Posthuma 1994 Easternization: The Spread of Japanese Management Techniques to Developing Countries, London: Frank Cass.

Kearney, M. 1995 "The Local and the Global: The Anthropolgy of Globalization and Transnationalism," Annual Review of Anthropology 24, pp. 547–565.

Linhart, S. 1986 "Sakariba: Zone of 'evaporation' between work and home?" in Joy Hendry and Jonathan Webber (eds) Interpreting Japanese society: Anthropological approaches, pp. 198–210, Oxford: JASO Occasional Papers No. 5.

Linhart, Sepp 1988 "From Industrial to Post Industrial Society: Changes in Japanese Leisure-Related Values and Behavior," Journal of Japanese Studies 14(2), pp. 271–307.

Manzereiter, Wolfram and Eyal Ben-Ari forthcoming "Leisure and Consumer Culture in Postwar Japan," in Josef Kreiner, Hans-Dieter Vulschleger and Ulrich Mohwald (eds) *Modern Japanese Society: A Handbook*, Leiden: Brill.

Midooka, Kiyoshi 1990 Characteristics of Japanese-style communication, *Media, Culture and Society* 12 pp. 477–489.

Moeran, B. 1986 "One over the seven: Sake drinking in a Japanese pottery community," in Joy Hendry and Jonathan Webber (eds), *Interpreting Japanese society: Anthropological approaches*, pp. 226–242, Oxford: JASO Occasional Papers No. 5.

Redding, S.G. 1994 "Determinants of the Competitive Power of Small Business Networking: The Overseas Chinese Case," in Hellmut Shutte (ed.) *The Global Competitiveness of the Asian Firm*, pp. 101–120, New York: St. Martin's.

Rohlen, T.P. 1974 *For Harmony and Strength: Japanese White-Collar Organization in Anthropological Perspective*, Berkeley: University of California Press.

Skinner, Kenneth A. 1983 "Aborted Careers in a Public Corporation," in David W. Plath (ed.) *Work and the Lifecourse in Japan*, pp. 50–73, Albany: State University of New York Press.

Takada, M. 1983 *Sakariba no Shakaigaku*, Tokyo: PHP.

Toren, Christina L. 1995 *Japanese Workers in Protest: An Ethnography of Consciousness and Experience*, Berkeley: University of California Press.

Vogel, Ezra F. 1991 *The Four Little Dragons: The Spread of Industrialization in East Asia*, Cambridge, Mass.: Harvard University Press.

Whitehill, Arthur M. 1991 *Japanese Management: Tradition and Transition*, London: Routledge.

Chapter 8

Ackerman, S.E. and Raymond L.M. Lee 1990 *Heaven in Transition:Non-Muslim Religious Innovation and Ethnic Identity in Malaysia*, Kuala Lumpur: Forum.

Ames, R.T., W. Dissanayake and T.P. Kasulis (eds) 1994 *Self as Person in Asian Theory and Practice*, Albany: State University of New York Press.

Bocking, B. 1994 "Of Priests, Protests and Protestant Buddhists: The Case of Soka Gakkai International," in Clarke, P.B. and J. Somers, (eds) *Japanese New Religions in the West*, Folkestone: Japan Library.

Brown, D. 1993 "The corporatist management of ethnicity in contemporary Singapore," in G. Rodan (ed.) *Singapore Changes Guard: Social, Political and Economic Changes in the 1990s*, Melbourne: Longman Cheshire; New York: St. Martin's Press.

Chan, S.Y. 1988 *A Study of Nichiren Shoshu in Singapore*, Unpublished Academic Exercise. Department of Sociology, National University of Singapore.

Clammer, J. (ed.) 1983 *Studies in Chinese Folk Religion in Singapore and Malaysia*, Singapore: Contributions to Southeast Asian Ethnography 2.

Clammer, J. 1988 "Singapore's Buddhists Chant a Modern Mantra," *Far Eastern Economic Review*, 29 December, pp. 26–28.

Clammer, J. 1991 *The Sociology of Singapore Religion*, Singapore: Chopmen Publishers.

Clammer, J. 1993 " Deconstructing Values: The establishment of a national ideology and its implications for Singapore's political future," in G. Rodan (ed.) *Singapore Changes Guard: Social, Political and Economic Directions in the 1990s*. Melbourne: Longman Cheshire; New York: St.Martin's Press, pp. 34–51.

Clarke, P.B. 1994 "Japanese 'Old', 'New' and 'New New' religious movements in Brazil," in Clarke and Somers, (eds) pp. 150–161.

Clarke, P.B. and J. Somers (eds) 1994 *Japanese New Religions in the West*, Folkestone: Japan Library.

Hardacre, H. 1988 *Kurozumiko and the New Religions of Japan*, Princeton: Princeton University Press.

Kasulis, T.P., R.T. Ames and W. Dissanayake (eds) 1993 *Self as Body in Asian Theory and Practice*, Albany: State University of New York Press.

Melton, J.G. 1994 "New Japanese Religions in the United States," in Clarke and Somers (eds) *Japanese New Religions in the West*, Folkestone: Japan Library, pp. 33–53.

Pensri Kanchanomai 1989 "Religions and Japanese Modernization," in Kunio Yoshihara (ed.) *Thai Perceptions of Japanese Modernization*, Kuala Lumpur: Falcon Press and Kyoto: Centre for Southeast Asian Studies.

Piyasilo, Ven. 1988 *Nichiren: The New Buddhism of Modern Japan*, Petaling Jaya: The Friends of Buddhism Malaysia.

Reader, I. 1991 *Religion in Contemporary Japan*, Honolulu: University of Hawaii Press.

Rohlen, T.P. 1979 *For Harmony and Strength: Japanese White Collar Organization in Anthropological Perspective*, Berkeley: University of California Press.

Saunders, E.D. 1972 *Buddhism in Japan*, Rutland, Vt., Tuttle.

Straits Times (Singapore) 1987 August 8.

Tamney, J.B. (n.d.) "An analysis of the decline of allegiance to Chinese religion." In Riaz Hassan and J.B. Tamney, (eds) *Analysis of an Asian Society-Singapore. Singapore*, Department of Sociology, University of Singapore.

Thomsen, H. 1963 *The New Religions of Japan*, Tokyo: Charles E. Tuttle.

Toynbee, A. and D. Ikeda 1989 *Choose Life: A Dialogue*, Oxford: Oxford University Press.

Wilson, B. 1982 *Religion in Sociological Perspective*, New York: Oxford University Press.

Chapter 9

Beskow, Per "Religion: Singapore," In *Nationalencyklpedin*. Hoganas: Bokforlaget Bra Bocker AB, pp. 461–462.

Clammer, John (ed) 1983 *Studies in Chinese Folk Religion in Singapore and Malaysia*, Singapore: Contributions to Southeast Asian Ethnography, No.2

Clammer, John 1985 *Singapore: Ideology, Society and Culture*, Singapore: Chopmen.

Clammer, John 1991 *The Sociology of Singapore Religion: Studies in Christianity and Chinese Religion*, Singapore: Chopmen.

Dale, Peter, N. 1995 *The Myth of Japanese Uniqueness*, London: Routledge.

Ellwood, Robert S. 1982 *Tenrikyo: A Pilgrimage of Faith: The Structure and Meaning of a Modern Japanese Religion*, Tenri: Oyasato Research Institute, Tenri University.

Friedman, Maurice 1992 *Religion and Psychology: A Dialogical Approach*, New York: Paragon House Publishers.

Hamrin, Tina 1996 *Dansreligionen i japansk immigrantmiljo pa Hawai'i. Via helbragdagorare och Jodo shinshu-praster till nationalistik millennarism*, Stockholm: Almqvist and Wilsell International.

Hashimoto, Taketo 1979 "The teaching of *innen* in Tenrikyo," *Tenri Journal of Religion* 13, pp. 29–47.

Kisala, Robert 1994 "Contemporary Karma: Interpretations of Karma in Tenrikyo and Rissho Koseikai," *Japanese Journal of Religious Studies*, 21,1, pp. 73–91.

Kuo, Eddie C.Y., Jon S.T. Quah and C.K. Tong 1988 *Religion and Religious Revival in Singapore*, Singapore: Ministry of Community Development.

Lim Hua Sing 1995 *Japan's Role in Asia: Issues and Prospects*, Singapore: Times Academic Press.

Low, N.I. 1995 *When Singapore Was Syonan-to*, Singapore: Times Books International.

Matsumoto, Shigeru 1996 "On the Truth of *Innen*" *Tenri Journal of Religion*, 24 pp. 1–18.

Murray, Geoffrey and Perera, Audrey 1996 *Singapore: The Global City-State*, Sandgate: China Library.

Nakamura, Hajime 1997 "The Bodhisattva Path," in Mircea Eliade (ed.) *Encyclopedia of Religion*, pp. 265–269, New York: Macmillan.

Offner, C.B. and H. van Straelen 1963 *Modern Japanese Religions*, New York: Twayne Publishers.

Okubo, Akinori 1982 "Social Welfare and Practicality of *Hinokishin* in Tenrikyo: A Proposal to the International Year of Diabled Persons." *Tenrikyo* 16, pp. 1–30.

Robison, Richard and David S.G. Goodman (eds) 1996 *The New Rich in Asia: Mobile Phones, McDonalds and Middle Class Revolution*, London: Routledge.

Shimazono, Susumu 1991 "The development of milleniastic thought in Japan's new religions: from Tenrikyo to Honmichi," in James A. Beckford (ed.) *New Religious Movements and Rapid Social Change*, London: Sage/UNESCO, pp. 58–86.

Streng, Frederick J. 1991 *Understanding Religious Life*, Belmont: Wadsworth.

Tanaka, Shiro 1976 "Volunteer Activities in a *Hinokishin* Spirit," *Tenrikyo*, Tenri: Tenrikyo Overseas Mission Department.

Tenrikyo 1981 *Tenrikyo Yearbook*, Tenri: Tenrikyo Church Headquarters.

Tenrikyo 1990 "Tenrikyo *Hinokishin* Day Observed in 2000 Locations," *Tenrikyo*, June, Tenri: Tenrikyo Overseas Mission Department.

Tenrikyo 1993a "Tenrikyo *Hinokishin* Day: Joy of Faith Expressed Throughout the World," *Tenrikyo*. Tenri: Tenrikyo Overseas Mission Department.

Tenrikyo 1993b *The Doctrine of Tenrikyo*, Tenri: Tenrikyo Church Headquarters.

Toynbee, A. and Ikeda, D. 1989 *Choose Life: A Dialogue*, Oxford: Oxford University Press.

Williams, Paul 1989 *Mahayana Buddhism: The Doctrinal Foundations*, London: Routledge.

Index

46–8; lack of interaction with locals 169–73; leisure activities 127, 150–3; and life-long learning 44; and need to be rehabilitated/reeducated on return to Japan 48; patterns of drinking, eating, singing 156–9; potentials/hazards of being 44; reading habits 128; services for 84–5; size of communities 40; and terminology of centers/ peripheries 42–4; understanding of internationalization 58; wives of 84, 85; *see also* female expatriates

Fardon, R. 33
fashion: ethnicization of 137–8; formal wear 137; insignificance of Japanese influence on 136–8, 147; internationalization of 139; Japanese dress code 138; youth market 136–7, 147
female expatriates 31; advantages/ disadvantages of 110–11; clothing 94; conditions/benefits for 90–2; as cultural mediators 98–9; described 86–8; and entertainment 96–7; estrangement from male colleagues and wives 100–1, 106, 110; growing number of 85; as in-betweeners 98–100; and Japanese community 83–8; and local interaction 99–100, 101–2; male attitudes/sexual harassment towards 96–7, 100–1; male perceptions/expectations of 93–5; and membership of clubs/ associations 105–9; reasons for becoming 88–90; residential choice/neighboring 102–5, 109–10; and taking up work in Singapore 88–92; ties outside work 100–2, 109; as twice marginalized 82, 110; work interactions 92–3; working hours 92; workplace mores 92–7, 109; and youth

organization membership 108–9; *see also* expatriates
females, encouragement to marry/ have children 73–4
firm-as-family 115–117, 166
folk model 27
food 17; Japanese influence on 142–3, 144, 147
Friedman, M. 210–11
Fruin, W.M. 115, 116, 166
Fuji Television-TCS 142
Fujimoto, T. 150
Fungtammasan, A. 28

Geertz, C. 4
global cities 37
global talk 51–3, 61–2; corporate culture 53; cultural nationalism 53–4; international standards 54–5
globalization 24–6, 29–30, 37, 58, 151; effect on Japan 12; expatriates as aspect of 38–9
golf 150; and business transactions 163; corporate membership 154–5; development of 153; frequency in playing 155; with graduates of universities 170; hierarchy of 153–4; with Japan Chamber of Commerce/Japanese Association 170; local/foreigner differences 153; as part of entertaining 156; with partners/ friends from "families" of corporations 169; patterns of play/participation 154–6, 169–70; popularity of 154
Gong, G.W. 27, 49, 50
Goodman, R. 32, 39, 48, 62, 82
Greater East Asian Co-Prosperity Sphere 6, 27
Griffin, R.W. 123
Gupta, A. and Ferguson, J. 58

Hall, I.P. 73
Hamabata, M.M. 117
Hamada, T. 39, 41, 42, 44, 101, 127, 150
Hamrin, T. 202